Cultural Representations of
Feminicidio at the US-Mexico Border

Since the early 1990s, the repeated murders of women from Ciudad Juárez, Mexico have become something of a global cause célèbre. *Cultural Representations of* Feminicidio *at the US-Mexico Border* examines creative responses to these acts of violence. It reveals how theatre, art, film, fiction and other popular cultural forms seek to remember and mourn the female victims of violent death in the city at the same time as they interrogate the political, legal and societal structures that produce the crimes.

Different chapters examine the varying art forms to engage with Ciudad Juárez's feminicidal wave. Finnegan discusses Àlex Rigola's theatrical adaptation of Roberto Bolaño's novel 2666 by Teatre Lliure in Barcelona as well as painting about the victims of *feminicidio* by Irish painter Brian Maguire. There is analysis of documentary film about Ciudad Juárez, including Lourdes Portillo's acclaimed *Señorita Extraviada* (2001). The final chapter turns its attention to writing about feminicide and examines testimonial and crime fiction narratives like the mystery novel *Desert Blood: The Juárez Murders* by Alicia Gaspar de Alba, among other examples.

By drawing on a range of artistic responses to the murders in Ciudad Juárez, *Cultural Representations of* Feminicidio *at the US-Mexico Border* shows how art, film, theatre and fiction can unsettle official narratives about the crimes and undo the static paradigms that are frequently used to interpret them.

Nuala Finnegan is Professor in the Department of Spanish, Portuguese and Latin American Studies at University College Cork, Ireland, and the Director of the Centre for Mexican Studies. Her research interests lie in Mexican cultural studies with a particular focus on gender.

Global Gender

The *Global Gender* series provides original research from across the humanities and social sciences, casting light on a range of topics from international authors examining the diverse and shifting issues of gender and sexuality on the world stage. Utilising a range of approaches and interventions, these texts are a lively and accessible resource for both scholars and upper level students from a wide array of fields including Gender and Women's Studies, Sociology, Politics, Communication, Cultural Studies and Literature.

Gender, Heteronormativity and the American Presidency
Aidan Smith

Cultural Representations of *Feminicidio* at the US-Mexico Border
Nuala Finnegan

www.routledge.com/Global-Gender/book-series/RGG

Cultural Representations of *Feminicidio* at the US-Mexico Border

Nuala Finnegan

LONDON AND NEW YORK

First published 2019
by Routledge
2 Park Square, Milton Park, Abingdon, Oxon OX14 4RN

and by Routledge
711 Third Avenue, New York, NY 10017

Routledge is an imprint of the Taylor & Francis Group, an informa business

First issued in paperback 2021

© 2019 Nuala Finnegan

The right of Nuala Finnegan to be identified as author of this work has been asserted by her in accordance with sections 77 and 78 of the Copyright, Designs and Patents Act 1988.

All rights reserved. No part of this book may be reprinted or reproduced or utilised in any form or by any electronic, mechanical, or other means, now known or hereafter invented, including photocopying and recording, or in any information storage or retrieval system, without permission in writing from the publishers.

Trademark notice: Product or corporate names may be trademarks or registered trademarks, and are used only for identification and explanation without intent to infringe.

British Library Cataloguing-in-Publication Data
A catalogue record for this book is available from the British Library

Library of Congress Cataloging-in-Publication Data
A catalog record for this book has been requested

ISBN: 978-1-138-48217-3 (hbk)
ISBN: 978-0-367-90364-0 (pbk)
ISBN: 978-1-351-05883-4 (ebk)

Typeset in Goudy
by Apex CoVantage, LLC

This book is dedicated to the memory of the victims of *feminicidio* in Ciudad Juárez since 1993, and to all those in the city who challenge the patterns of structural violence that continue to affect the lives of its citizens.

Contents

List of figures		viii
Acknowledgements		ix
	Introduction: *no nos cabe tanta muerte* [unbearable deaths]	1
1	Framing *feminicidio*: the spectral politics of death in Ciudad Juárez	22
2	Sacrificial screams: excess in Àlex Rigola's stage adaptation of *2666*	53
3	Remember them: ethics and witnessing in artistic responses to feminicide	83
4	Resilience and renewal in documentary film about *feminicidio* in Ciudad Juárez	114
5	Toward an activist poetics: fiction responds to *feminicidio* in Ciudad Juárez	149
	Conclusion: notes towards the possible	181
	Appendix	188
	Index	193

Figures

2.1	Photographic image from Part IV of the stage version of Roberto Bolaño's 2666 performed at Teatre Lliure in Barcelona in 2007	60
3.1	Portrait of Brenda Berenice Castillo García, Brian Maguire 2011. Acrylic on canvas. 71 × 55 cm.	88
3.2	Portrait of Airis Estrella Enríquez Pando, Brian Maguire 2005, 2010. Acrylic on canvas. 145 × 120 cm.	93
3.3	Portrait of Erika Pérez Escobedo, Brian Maguire 2012. Acrylic on linen. 81.5 × 73 cm.	95
4.1	Woman stepping out of white shoes. *Señorita Extraviada*, directed by Lourdes Portillo, 2001	123
4.2	Woman stepping back into white shoes. *Señorita Extraviada*, directed by Lourdes Portillo, 2001	123
4.3	Paula Flores, from *La carta*, directed by Rafael Bonilla, 2010	131

Acknowledgements

I wish to thank a large number of people who made the project possible and who have helped see it to completion. This book emerged from a series of dialogues generated during presentations given in various locations including London (September 2014); Nantes (April 2013); Dublin (June 2014); Miami (February 2017); Ciudad Juárez (February–March 2017); Cork on the occasion of the WISPS annual conference (November 2014); at a workshop on Trauma in the Hispanic World (May 2014) and again at the BodyStories conference in June 2016. I also received valuable feedback from invited seminars delivered in St. Andrews (February 2015) and in Queen's University Belfast (November 2011). The book began in NUI Galway in May 2011 at a symposium on Gender, Nation and Text and I am grateful to the organizers there, particularly Lorraine Kelly, for inviting me to be a part and for kick-starting those preliminary enquiries into a full-length book project. I have benefited immensely from interventions at all of these fora and also from careful readers and listeners including Catherine Grant, Andrea Noble, Patricia Torres, Ignacio Sánchez Prado, Chris Harris, Róisín O'Gorman, Claire Lindsay and Cara Levey. Special thanks are reserved for Helena Buffery for her friendship as well as her words of encouragement at exactly the right moments. To my friends and colleagues in the Department of Spanish, Portuguese and Latin American Studies, Terry, Martín, Stephen, Cara, Elisa, Laura, Eugenia, Pedro, Ana, Sofia, Aisling, Seana, Rafa and all those visiting researchers and tutors who make the place so special, I say thank you. Sincere gratitude is also due to doctoral and former doctoral students, Emer Clifford, Donna Alexander, Eva Cabrejas, Cian Warfield, Dylan Brennan, Pat Aylward, Rhys Davies, Nadia Albaladejo, Yairen Jérez and others from whom I have learned a great deal during this writing project; I particularly wish to recognize the insights of Sorcha, David, Maayan and Trevor in my US-Mexico border class, 2015–2016. I acknowledge the generosity of artists, academics and campaigners Brian Maguire and Mark McLoughlin, Kama Gutier (Josebe Martínez), Alicia Gaspar de Alba, Rafael Bonilla, Kathleen Staudt, Ed Vulliamy, and others in sharing their insights on the blurred boundaries between activism and artistic production and their encounters with the horrors of feminicide in Ciudad Juárez. Thanks to Begoña Barrena at the Teatre Lliure for always complying with requests and for generously granting permission to use footage of 2666. I am grateful to Beatriz Adelina Hernández

Zamora at the Centro Universidad Autónoma de la Ciudad de Mexico for allowing me to reproduce the lyrics to the song 'Paula' from the film *La carta* and for explaining the project of the film to me. Peadar King offered a valuable opportunity to me to clarify the ideas underpinning feminicide; I thank him for the opportunity to participate in making a documentary on violence in Ciudad Juárez for RTE television (*Mass Murder in Mexico*, shown in December 2013). Elia Escobedo Garcia was gracious and patient during our interview in Galway in February 2013. More than anything, I am grateful to Patricia Torres for inviting me to participate in the Cátedra Marcela Lagarde in November 2016 at the Centro de Investigación y Estudios Superiores en Antropología social (CIESAS) in Mexico City in 2016 where I had the pleasure of interacting with an extraordinary group of committed scholars including, in no particular order, Alfredo Limas Hernández, Patricia Ravelo Blancas, Patricia Beltrán, Margarita D'Alton, Susana Báez Ayala, Marcela Lagarde y de los Ríos, among many others. Patricia also offered balanced and helpful criticism of my work and invited me to stay in her home. Above all, I salute Paula Flores, tireless activist and long-term campaigner whose work to uncover the truth about the murder of her daughter Sagrario is never finished. I thank her for her hospitality and kindness during my stay in Ciudad Juárez in 2017 and to all the students on the *maestría de género* at the Universidad Autónoma de Ciudad Juárez (UACJ) who took the time to respond to my ideas and generate thoughtful and engaged discussion. Grateful thanks are due to Susana Báez and Pati Beltrán for all the laughs during my 'visita etnográfica' in Ciudad Juárez in 2017 and to Ana Laura Ramírez Vásquez for being such an honest and intelligent respondent. I am intensely appreciative of the friendship from colleagues in the School of Languages, Literatures and Cultures, particularly Pat Crowley and Silvia Ross, and a heartfelt thank you is due to the Professors Connolly – Linda and Claire – who are rocks of support always. The meetings of the Gender, Violence, Conflict cluster in the Centre for the Advanced Study of Languages and Cultures have been immensely useful in widening the various frames of reading and enabling discussion with other colleagues. Myrtle McCarthy let me use her haven on the beautiful Sheep's Head peninsula in West Cork in July 2015 in order to write: I am deeply grateful. Similarly, Vanessa and Rich made me welcome in their home in El Paso, Texas, and generously shared their extensive knowledge with me. Superlatives are insufficient when it comes to Fiona Clancy who remained unflappable throughout the final stages and Silvia Martinelli who helped out with research in the early stages with great enthusiasm. To Debbie O'Shea I would like to say thank you for her friendship. The same goes for many other friends, too numerous to mention, but most especially Kathryn and all the Galway girls.

There has been sadness during the writing of this project. Patrick Aylward, a former Ph.D student, passed away, aged 83, during the summer of 2017. His indefatigable optimism remains a source of constant motivation and his wife, Phil, keeps his spirit alive. Another loss in 2017 was Andrea Noble: a towering presence in the field of Mexican visual culture, she was a frequent visitor to the Centre for Mexican Studies in Cork and was always ready to advise over a glass of wine or two. At Routledge, it has been a pleasure to work with Kitty Imbert and Alexandra McGregor who have been professional and helpful throughout the whole process.

A word of gratitude to my family: my children Cian, Conor, Eoghan and Liadan, who have put up with the takeover of many different spaces of the house with great tolerance. To my Dad who is an inspiration to all of us. Through his dedicated scholarship on local history in East Galway, he has unearthed the buried history of our family, now the subject of two (soon to be three) books. Emer and Niall are great siblings and friends. Writing relies on the presence of loved ones to coax it into being; to John, therefore, go my deepest thanks and love.

My first memory of being conscious of violence against women is associated with my Mum, who worked voluntarily at a women's refuge in Galway, Ireland in the late 1970s. Sadly my Mum is no longer with us, but in these final words I would like to pay tribute to her energy and vitality. Through our memories, she lives on.

Introduction

No nos cabe tanta muerte [unbearable deaths][1]

> *Algo bueno va a salir de esto.*
> Something good will come of this.[2]
>
> —Elia Escobedo García

Speaking about the murder of her daughter, Elia Escobedo García declares her belief that despite the widespread indifference shown towards her family following the crime, something positive might emerge from their tale of destruction and despair. It is to the death of Elia's daughter Erika and the many other women brutally murdered in Ciudad Juárez since the early 1990s that this book turns its attention to examine the ways in which the representation of violent death on the US-Mexico border matters. In *Cultural Representations of Feminicidio at the US-Mexico Border* I scrutinize the outpouring of cultural texts about Ciudad Juárez's feminicidal wave to explore the ways in which art and sculpture, theatre and performance, poetry, documentary and commercial film, dance, detective fiction, opera, popular music as well as myriad other expressions seek to remember and to mourn the victims of violent death in the city at the same time as they interrogate the political, legal and societal structures that produce the crimes. The book argues that the art, performance, poetry, detective fiction, film and other cultural forms that have surfaced in response to the criminal acts breathe life into the bodies of their marginalized, lifeless subjects. These subjects are rendered invisible in a public sphere in which the police, the judiciary and the local and national political system denigrate and degrade them. In this regard, their visibility (and some would argue their hypervisibility) in the cultural sphere is in stark contrast to their erasure from public consciousness. This hypervisibility is paradoxical: their faces haunt the cityscape from the *pesquisas* or missing person advertisements that drape the lampposts of the city and local environs to the multiple songs, films, TV shows and posters that circulate in a global mediasphere. And yet they struggle for recognition from the wider society that ignores them and a justice system that mocks them through legal cases that are either delayed, dismissed or hopelessly compromised. In the texts that the brutalized corpses of Juárez engender, these women are figured, disfigured, fractured, fragmented, remoulded, reimagined, reinvented, revictimized and revitalized, sometimes all at the same time. We could perhaps interpret this as their call to us to remember them. This book forms part of the response to that call.

The *feminicidios*, or murders of women in the US-Mexican border town of Ciudad Juárez, have become something of a global cause célèbre since the early 1990s. More than twenty-five years later, there have been numerous human rights' reports,[3] a well-documented media frenzy and an outpouring of cultural responses, the subject of this particular study. Out of all of this, the Ciudad Juárez feminicidal violence has become something of a curious phenomenon, a story on the periphery of many other stories. On the one hand, despite still going on and amid continuing public disquiet about the embedded nature of misogyny and the prevalence of violence against women in Mexican society, they have become a part of history,[4] a quaint morality tale associated with the early days of the North American Free Trade Agreement (NAFTA). This narrative posits a direct link between NAFTA and the appearance of the disposable bodies of the new urban poor – often workers in the assembly plants or *maquiladoras* so much a part of the US-Mexico border landscape – raped, mutilated, tortured and discarded. In this context, they are the almost forgotten collateral damage of a wider set of systemic cultural and economic change. On the other hand, in the face of the unprecedented violence unleashed by the so-called war on drugs started by Mexican President Felipe Calderón in 2006, they linger on the margin of a much greater escalation of murderous violence and of which they represent a small and almost insignificant part. In the context of at least 234,000 dead (mostly male) and approximately 29,000 disappeared (mostly male) since 2006, the murders of a few hundred women – and of course the figures remain hotly disputed – risk being dismissed as irrelevant.[5] This is particularly the case when it is known that many of the victims were killed by intimate partners or other family members and are therefore just classified as 'ordinary' victims of domestic violence. According to this logic and in the face of the extreme violence that has seen Mexico projected onto the world stage with speculation about the threat to its existence as a viable state,[6] it is almost considered inappropriate to continue to direct scholarly and public focus towards a statistically insignificant number of women's deaths. In this respect, goes the argument, perhaps it is time to divert attention from the murders of the young women to a more sustained approach to tackling violence more generally in the border region.[7] As this book will set out to demonstrate, however, it is an ethical imperative that the feminicidal violence ongoing in Ciudad Juárez continues to demand the attention of scholars, activists, legislators, state and federal authorities, and while there has been substantial progress in forcing recognition of the gendered dimensions of violent crime more generally, there is much work left to be done.

Femicide versus *feminicidio*

The debate about nomenclature, labelling and description of the crimes has been far-reaching and it is not my intention to rehearse it here in its entirety. Instead, a brief discussion should suffice to demonstrate the ever-shifting dynamics around terms and terminology. Frustrated with the gender-neutral discourse commonly employed in discussions of murderous violence more generally, feminist legal scholars advanced arguments in favour of using the term 'femicide'. The terms of this argument involve the contention that the last decade of the twentieth century witnessed a rise in the degradation and violation of women's bodies including their murder and rape in war-torn contexts but also in so-called peacetime. Such was the extreme nature of the crimes – often understood as excessive in nature and involving high levels of sadism and cruelty – that scholars and activists argued for an explicit recognition of this dimension (Fregoso and Bejarano 2010: 3; Ravelo Blancas 2006: 23). As might be expected, there has been a wide-ranging debate about the definition of femicide/feminicide and its usefulness as a category in criminology, human rights and legal spheres with differing opinions. Broadly speaking this scholarship concurs in arguing for the gender bias inherent in femicide to be recognized legally in the same way as homophobic and racist bias is. Furthermore, it argues against the erasure of gendered terminology from reporting on killing, like, for example, the widespread practice of referring to perpetrators as individuals or people when they are almost exclusively male (Russell and Harmes 2001: 5). The understanding of femicide most widely used is based on the work of sociologist Diana Russell who defines it as the killing of women *because* they are women, a label that has been in circulation for over two centuries. According to Russell,

> Femicide is on the extreme end of a continuum of the sexist terrorization of women and girls. Rape, torture, mutilation, sexual slavery, incestuous and extra-familial child sexual abuse, physical and emotional battery, serious cases of sexual harassment are also on this continuum.
>
> (2001: 4)

Insisting on moving beyond the consideration of women-killing as either a private (i.e. domestic) matter or a pathological one (i.e. the result of actions of a murderous individual), Russell insists on the political dimension to the killing of women and in this way, she charts an important pathway for the understanding of the crime worldwide.

When the crimes first began to be reported in Mexico, the term *femicidio* began to appear with increasing frequency as a direct and literal translation of its counterpart in English. Marcela Lagarde y de los Ríos, a feminist anthropologist as well as activist and politician, has been at the forefront of rethinking the concept in its local context. The result of this has been the coining of a term, *feminicidio*, which she argues is a more appropriate cultural translation for the nature of the phenomenon in Ciudad Juárez and elsewhere in the Americas.[8] As has been well documented, the term follows the linguistic conventions for compound nouns in Spanish but crucially allows for a more expanded definition of the term including its systematic nature on the one hand and the involvement of the state on the other.[9] In an interview in *El Universal*, Lagarde y de los Ríos speaks candidly about its emergence as a category to describe crimes that were 'incubated in misogyny;

4   Introduction

in machismo in the disrespect for women's lives, in brutal inequality, in low salaries, in exclusion. All of that is a theory, a theory of feminicide. Feminicide is not a word, it is an entire theory' (2014: n.p.). Following Lagarde y de los Ríos's lead, many other feminist scholars have insisted on using this term as a political gesture. As Fregoso and Bejarano explain:

> In preferring the concept feminicide over femicide, we aim to register the shift in meanings as the concept travelled from its usage in the English-language (North) to a Spanish-speaking (South) context. In other words, we are using feminicide to mark our discursive and material contributions and perspectives as transborder feminist thinkers from the global South (the Americas) in its redefinition – one that exceeds the merely derivative.
>
> (2010: 4)

They define feminicide as

> the murders of women and girls founded on a gender power structure. Second, feminicide is gender-based violence that is both public and private, implicating both the state (directly or indirectly) and individual perpetrators (private or state actors); it thus encompasses systematic, widespread and everyday interpersonal violence. Third, feminicide is systemic violence rooted in social, political, economic, and cultural inequalities.
>
> (Fregoso and Bejarano 2010: 5)

It can be seen, therefore, the extent to which the systematic nature of the crime is emphasized in such definitions as well as the idea of state involvement.[10] For the purposes of this study, I follow the lead shown by Lagarde y de los Ríos, Fregoso and Bejarano, Monárrez Fragoso and many other scholars in naming the crime as feminicide. From my perspective, it is necessary as a feminist critic working in the privileged context of European academia to register the theoretical contribution made by Lagarde and others in relation to understanding the crime and its contexts. In forcing a culturally and linguistically 'awkward' English translation of the Spanish term used to name the crime in the Americas, its use intervenes in the reversal (ongoing for some time now) of the academic perspective of Latin America as object of study, not as creator of knowledge or theory. Finally, using the term, feminicide, given its absence from official, intellectually sanctioned records of English language usage including dictionaries, while incurring the risk of not being understood appropriately, ensures that the term must be rigorously unpicked at every juncture and is therefore properly attentive to its status as a concept under construction, not yet fully finished. In this regard, given the ongoing and increasing rates of feminicide in the Americas as well as the wider global context, an open and evolving concept of gender-based hate crimes is both politically and legally important. In a final word on the subject, Lagarde y de los Ríos reacts with vigour to a question regarding the normalization of the use of the term, *feminicidio*, in Mexico, attesting to its potent force as a category for change:

'We influenced and managed to name feminicide in Mexico. The concept is here to stay' (2014: n.p.).

Cultural entanglements

Sergio González Rodríguez contends that there are multiple narrative strands woven into the discourses that circulate on *feminicidio*, including what he terms the cultural narrative which involves 'reportage, first-person stories, fiction, or beliefs held by the community; word of mouth information and emerging expressions that offer a wealth of content' (2012: 82–83). These strands, he argues, are mobilized in the defence of historical truth and in this way they function as counter-narratives to hegemonic versions of the crimes. The cultural narratives position themselves within the cacophony of competing official voices that seek to name and define *feminicidio* in Juárez and as such, they can be interpreted as writing, painting, singing and performing back to those sanctioned (hi)stories. In common with Theodor Adorno's ideas about the 'truth-content' (*Wahrheitsgehalt*) that resides within cultural narratives, these tousled narrative strands might signal art's critical capacity within the structures of advanced capitalism, a capacity that remains unparalleled both ethically and politically (1970). Adorno famously expounded the idea of the 'shock' as the mode through which art could enable access to the truth,

> The shock aroused by important works is not employed to trigger personal, otherwise repressed emotions. Rather, this shock is the moment in which the recipients forget themselves and disappear into the work; it is the moment of being shaken. The recipients lose their footing, the possibility of truth; embodied in the aesthetic image, becomes tangible.
>
> (1997: 244)

Whatever the critiques of Adorno's position,[11] the central idea that truth may acquire form through its aesthetic embodiment presents us with a political, ethical and intellectual challenge. Writing specifically about this challenge in relation to Ciudad Juárez, scholars like Driver (2015), Mata (2011), González Rodríguez (2012) and others insist on the potential power of cultural responses to offer new ways of seeing and thinking about the murders, a hypothesis advanced also by Volk and Schlotterbeck (2010) and one that the investigations in this book might test. Indeed, Volk and Schlotterbeck argue that 'it is precisely because the state has failed so abjectly in stopping these murders that "fictional" narratives have become both the site where victims are mourned and the means by which justice can be restored' (2010: 121–122). They underscore the profound role played by artists and cultural practitioners in this process and gesture towards the potentially transformative role of culture that to date has received comparatively little critical attention in respect of the atrocities committed in Ciudad Juárez.

This emphasis on the transformative potential of art, hinted at by Volk and Schlotterbeck and indeed the interplay between art and activism more generally is of paramount importance in understanding how political art is mediated and consumed in different contexts. The relationship between art and transformation and indeed how cultural texts 'mean' illuminates the time-honoured tensions between aesthetics and politics rehearsed at length in the work of scholars within cultural studies including key figures such as Walter Benjamin and Theodor Adorno, already mentioned.[12] This tension lies at the heart of many of the artistic interventions about *feminicidio* in Ciudad Juárez and with this in mind, it is not surprising to note that fluid boundaries between activism, art and scholarship are commonplace in many of the cultural responses to the crimes. Furthermore, there is increased emphasis globally on the role of creativity in activism and in the political and transformative potential of creative projects. We can see this in the 'One Billion Rising' project, a mass action designed to protest violence against women and children globally and which explicitly invites its members to *drum and dance* drawing attention to their 'creativity and energy'. It states its belief in art as a vehicle for revolution in explicit terms:

> *We will keep highlighting, creating and envisioning new, brave and radical artistic initiatives to bring in the new revolutionary world of equality, dignity and freedom for all women and girls.* THERE IS NOTHING MORE POWERFUL THAN ART AS A TOOL FOR TRANSFORMATION.[13]

The relationship between radical art and revolutionary politics is laid bare here in rather clichéd terms; however, it reinforces the work of vision-creation that is at the core of both politics and art but identifies art's particular capacity to energize and envision political transformation. 'Art', as Christina B. Arce perceptively writes, 'while not a political antidote to inequality and oppression, is also not just a product of it, or against it; it is a way' (2015: 21).

The book explores those shifting boundaries between artistic production, academic work and what might traditionally be understood as activist activity including marching, political lobbying and the work of information dissemination that is so critical to politically inflected cultural forms. Furthermore, it explores culture's crucial contribution to the work of dissemination and raising awareness, that is to say its relevance to what Swanson Goldberg and Schultheis Moore denominate the 'rhetoric of exposure' (2011: 233). Exposure should not be under-estimated either; it is both powerful and persuasive and culture's frequently superior role in forging emotional and affective responses ensures that for many spectators/publics, the artistic responses endure in ways that other interventions cannot. In this regard it should be noted that in 2004, Eve Ensler's celebrated play, *The Vagina Monologues: Until the Violence Stops*, conceived as a tool to draw global attention to violence against women, was performed 2,300 times worldwide in 1,100 cities (Staudt 2008: 18). Considering this phenomenon, Baumgardner and Richards in their book on grassroots feminist activism contend that those plays and accompanying activism 'have exposed more people to feminism than any other entity in the last decade' (2005: 177). Linked to this function of exposure is culture's relevance to pedagogy: its didactic dimension or usefulness as part of a 'press play' mode of activism; the showing of a film, for example, as a way of illustrating a given reality. In this envisioning of culture's role, it serves a utilitarian function – denoting and sometimes connoting – but always pointing to a political truth beyond the text.[14]

Jacques Rancière's work is especially helpful in thinking through the place of art and aesthetics within the contemporary moment. In particular his words resonate in respect of the dilemmas provoked by cultural narratives about Juárez when he says,

> the 'logic of stories' and the ability to act as historical agents go together. Politics and art, like forms of knowledge, construct 'fictions', that is to say, *material* rearrangements of signs and images, relationships between what is seen and what is said, between what is done and what can be done.
>
> (2013: 35)

On one level, any discussion about the efficacy or indeed the impotence of art[15] in the context of raising consciousness around the subject of feminicidal violence in Juárez takes us to this point of contemplation, to the gap between what is said or seen and what can be done. Or put another way, they direct us to the multiple gaps between empathy, analysis and political agency. Rancière's work also has important ramifications for the way in which it helps us to understand how artworks can actually forge communities and therefore new modes of communication.[16] Particularly important here is the pivotal concept of 'emotional communities', so important in the context of Ciudad Juárez and through which communities rooted in relations of solidarity can be sustained by their shared responses to artwork and other cultural narratives.[17] As Arce points out, the value of Rancière's input can be seen in the way in which he insists on ascribing a radical potential to the aesthetic realm to not only intervene in the telling of history but also to make it (2016: 17). The participation of the community in the making, the sharing and the dissemination of (hi)stories about their experience inscribes their value as historical agents. Deleuze and Guattari's insights are also of interest in this regard. Maintaining that art has the potential to become political, not in the least because of its ability to name and give shape to the order of our world rather than its representation (Porter 2009), they register the politically charged contours of the artistic project. In this regard, the cultural texts are not just about representation (though, of course, they are about that too).

Much has been written already about the artistic responses to these atrocities; with excellent examples of scholarship on film (particularly Lourdes Portillo's documentary film, *Señorita Extraviada*); fiction (Roberto Bolaño's novel, *2666*, remains the most visible text in this regard); but also art, photography, music, theatre and poetry.[18] What is more, it is clear that for the majority of citizens outside of the immediate environment of Ciudad Juárez, the primary mode of access to the crimes is through the cultural texts that proliferate – through songs by Lila Downes, films such as *Bordertown* (2006) or *Traspatio* (2009), detective fiction from both sides of the border, theatre performances, dance, poetry readings and the numerous art exhibits. Questions of ethics, of positionality, of representation and of the affective power of such texts to transform and transfix their audiences, therefore, acquire political importance as the murders remain largely unsolved and forgotten. In this regard, it is imperative to scrutinize this body of work in order to uncover the ways in which it participates in the work of mourning, re-humanization and commemoration. We must also be attentive to the ways in which the cultural texts actively intervene in a politics of *denuncia* or condemnation so deeply rooted in discourses of Latin American activism since the wave of military dictatorships in the continent from the 1960s onwards. Arce strikingly asserts that 'history can be narrated differently' through 'The insistent will to reproduce these figures in the aesthetic realm and the concomitant desire by members of diverse classes to consume these products' (2016: 10). While she is speaking in a different context about other kinds of forgotten women from Mexican cultural history, her words are apposite here. Ultimately, perhaps the aesthetic works produced in response to the horrors of *feminicidio* in Ciudad Juárez signal possibility, an opening, a refusal to fix meaning. But they also trouble the official narratives or beliefs and have the power to unsettle deadening paradigms that lock the victims of *feminicidio* within a political and cultural battleground where they have no control and are utterly silenced. It is not expected that this book will answer all of these questions, but it does hope to unravel some of the complexities inherent in the many and varied cultural responses to the feminicidal violence in Ciudad Juárez.

The 'perilous aesthetics of murder'[19]

While it may be problematic to assert that these brutal murders have 'inspired' countless artistic responses, it is certainly true to state that they have triggered a dynamic cultural response in the form of films, documentaries, songs and art expressions around the world. Indeed, one of the more interesting aspects to consider in this regard is that in spite of the move in focus on gender violence away from Ciudad Juárez to other parts of Mexico and the Americas, the cultural responses to *feminicidio* in the city continue to proliferate. This might in turn have to do with the way, already mentioned, in which the *feminicidios* manage to be about Mexico's past and present at the same time. The book draws from a vast range of existing cultural texts on the subject of the feminicide in Juárez. These include songs, poetry, dance, detective fiction, essay-writing, blogs, documentary and feature films, short films, photography, performance art and more traditionally understood theatre performances, and art exhibitions including video installations. It cannot hope to map exhaustively the range of cultural responses that exists but it does attempt to be comprehensive in its approach and a list of the main texts in each area is included in the Appendix. From this corpus of texts, a selection has been made to isolate certain key interventions in the arenas of writing, theatre, documentary film and visual culture.[20] Given the scope of the project, many fascinating texts remain beyond enquiry and there is much work needed to properly evaluate the impact, meaning and reach of these cultural interventions.

In her diary entry, Perla Bonilla states, '*lo que sucede en el norte de México* [. . .] *suena como una película y hay veces que no lo creo*' (*An Oasis of Horror* Exhibition Catalogue 2012: 148) [what's happening in the north of Mexico seems like a movie and sometimes I just can't believe it].[21] Contentions like this one permeate discourse on violence more generally in Mexico, alluding on the one hand to that hoary cliché, that you really couldn't make it up, and on the other to the fact that the horrors of the Ciudad Juárez feminicides have lent themselves time and again to being imagined and re-created in imagistic form, and of which the many artistic, photographic and filmic responses to the phenomenon constitute compelling examples. In this way, the power of the photographic, artistic and moving image to dictate, shape and change discourses and influence debates on the murders is amply demonstrated. Similarly, public narratives about *feminicidio* and in particular the proliferation of theories about serial killers, snuff movies and drug lords also fuelled the 'fictional' end of the Juárez industry with numerous books of detective fiction and other forms using the thriller genre as a basis for fictional explorations, often with glamorous women at the centre: Jennifer Lopez in *Bordertown* (Gregory Nava 2006); Ana de la Reguera in *El traspatio* (Carlos Carrera 2009); Minnie Driver in *The Virgin of Juárez* (Kevin James Dobson 2006), among others. In fact, it is probably true to state that in many of the responses to Juárez – journalistic, legal, public and popular – there has been a rather pronounced and problematic commodification, eroticization and in some cases sexualization of the women involved. This trend is exemplified by some of the posters that featured as part of a campaign *Las mujeres de Juárez demandan justicia* shown in the metro in Mexico City in 2002 and which featured female bodies in various eroticized poses.[22]

In the international arena, the MAC makeup campaign of 2010 in which a line of Juárez makeup was devised serves as a good example of commodification[23] and indeed, there has been much attack and counter-attack around who profits or not from *feminicidio* with certain organizations facing precisely these accusations.[24] In examples like these, while it is undeniable that as artistic responses they render the disappeared and mutilated women visible, they also raise important questions about the art world's complicity in sustaining multiple forms of raced and gendered erasure as well as the commodification of the women's deaths. Moreover, as Avila reminds us, 'necropower as it relates specifically to feminicide and anti-female terror, operates on the principle of hypervisibility' (2012: 14), a concept amply illustrated by the examples just cited.[25] If we accept Avila's contention about the principle of hypervisibility, we must therefore be attentive to the challenge the murders pose to artists and cultural practitioners in terms of the ethics of representation. Alicia Schmidt Camacho discusses the rather controversial work of US writer Charles Bowden and warns against work like his in which there is a 'deliberate conversion of the dead body into an aesthetic object' arguing that it can in turn repeat 'the violence of the murder itself' (2004: 39).[26] Adriana Martínez (2009) evinces similar concerns that well-intentioned representations of the *feminicidios* become trapped within narratives of victimhood, disempowerment and denial of agency. Added to this representational dilemma is the bigger question around the industry of violence itself. As Ileana Rodríguez acerbically points out, 'the stylistics of death' is

> a very lucrative business, one that accounts for feminicidio. [. . .] Things being the way they are, I must conclude that the production, processing and representation of death – criminal, artistic, or forensic – is an organic part of the new state of capitalism, yet another example of necropolitics.
>
> (2009: 196)

In this way the cultural representations of death become part of the business of death and presumably, so too do the scholarly studies of such phenomena. Acutely aware of the dangers involved in theorizing and interpreting the structures of violence and the cultural products they generate, Ignacio Sánchez Prado cautions us that

> cultural technologies institutionalized to make sense of death and violence in Mexico gradually become more effective in sustaining the cultural capital of the intellectual class than in contributing to the symbolic reorganization of the order of violence that structurally generates mass killings.
>
> (2016: 4).[27]

These concerns must remain central to the scholarship of violence in Mexico. Currently those involved in initiatives that reveal and denounce violent practice, including creative practitioners, activists and researchers, hover uneasily between their ethical commitment to unlocking those structures that sustain patterns of violent behaviour and the concern that their very insertion into the struggle against violence risks nurturing further the industry of violence and all it represents. There are no easy answers to this dilemma; my role as educator in a public university in a post-colonial site on the periphery of Europe means that my interventions inevitably fall mostly into the realm of the mundane – that of exposure and the creation of awareness and consciousness. It is difficult to argue that any such intervention contributes to the symbolic re-organization of the order of violence called for by Sánchez Prado and yet, it is probably through the very ordinary (not to say simple) tactics of education and awareness creation that (in the short term), transitional justice objectives might be achieved.

It is important too not to underestimate the impact of cultural production on the relatives and family members of victims. In this regard, there is much to be gained from an understanding of the concept of 'emotional climate' in the sense that the cultural responses and other initiatives that generate solidarity between activists and victims contribute towards healing and the creation of resilience. Indeed, 'emotional climate', a concept anchored in psychology, is a useful lens to think through the multiple ways in which the trauma of *feminicidio* is dispersed in Ciudad Juárez across lines of ethnicity, social class, generation and political ideology (Ravelo Blancas and Sánchez Díaz 2015). In work on emotional climate in Maya communities in Guatemala, feelings of sadness, despair and melancholy emerge as deeply rooted – not just at the level of individuals – but shaping also collective activities.[28] Paula Flores, one of the best known of the many mother activists in Ciudad Juárez, speaks eloquently to this dimension when she says of the many documentary films, art exhibitions and other cultural expressions: '*a mi me ayuda a seguir luchando, me da fuerzas para seguir*' [they help me to continue the battle, they give me the strength to go on].[29] For this reason alone, perhaps, while recognizing that the ideal of symbolic re-organization should remain paramount, this approach would also recognize that the simple acts of creating awareness and the generation of solidarity through artistic gestures matter.

Cultural Representations of Feminicidio at the US-Mexico Border has five chapters, four of which look at different generic responses to the feminicidal violence, and each of those chapters isolates one dominant trope of feminicidal discourse as an overarching framework through which the selected text(s) can be interpreted. Chapter 1, 'Framing *Feminicidio*: The Spectral Politics of Death in Ciudad Juárez' provides a comprehensive, historical overview of *feminicidio* in Ciudad Juárez since 1993, and I argue that the horrors of the crimes are best communicated when viewed through distinct conceptual and thematic frameworks. These include ideas rehearsed extensively in the media, academy and public sphere around the corrosive impact of globalized labour practices and the notion of Ciudad Juárez itself as a monstrous, grotesque entity that, in the words of its critics, is devouring its children (Cordero and Sánchez 2006; Bellatin 2012). I also consider necropolitics, frequently isolated as a framework through which the crimes against women might be evaluated. In alignment with these strands of thinking is the constant mediatic, legal and societal reframing of women through narratives of contaminated femininity interlaced with anxiety about the enhanced presence of women in the local workforces, symbolized by the *maquila*, or the assembly plants that span the length of the US-Mexico border. The chapter concludes by evaluating perspectives on masculinity from within scholarship on *feminicidio*, arguing that it is central to any understanding of the levels of violence against women in this northern border city.

Chapter 2, 'Sacrificial Screams: Excess in Àlex Rigola's Stage Adaptation of 2666' looks at Roberto Bolaño's celebrated novel, *2666*, and its transposition to dramatic mode in the form of Àlex Rigola's theatrical interpretation with Teatre Lliure, first performed in Barcelona in 2007. Taking sacrifice as a central trope, the chapter is interested in the ways in which the representation of pain and death receives such a radically different treatment in Rigola's stage version. Arguing that this is part of a continuum of representations of *feminicidio* as sacrificial victims, it examines the implications of such treatment in the context of audiences in Catalunya in 2007 in the aftermath of the passing of the Ley de Memoria Histórica or the Law of Historical Memory relating to the victims of Spain's civil war past. While the writhing, screaming body of the principal actor (Alba Pujol) raises troubling questions about the way in which portrayals of 'other' women are frequently locked into discourses of hysteria, I also argue that Rigola's reliance on a theatrical repertoire based on excess in the representation of rape and murder opens up a space in which the possibility of agency is enabled and indeed, energized.

12   Introduction

Chapter 3, 'Remember Them: Ethics and Witnessing in Artistic Responses to Feminicide' considers the ethics and politics of transnational witnessing in Ciudad Juárez art, paying particular attention to the project by Irish artist Brian Maguire, *An Oasis of Horror in a Desert of Boredom*, exhibited in various locations including Carlow, Ireland (2012); Cork, Ireland (2013); Liverpool, UK (2014); and the European Parliament in Brussels (2013). Using the work of Emmanuel Levinas and Judith Butler as a lens through which to frame Western audiences' responses to atrocities in the 'elsewheres of the World' (Butler 2011), it argues for the possibility of 'empathic encounters' while remaining attentive to the tensions posed by the creation of such networks of global solidarity. In this regard, it scrutinizes the limitations of empathy and the risks always inherent in any 'aesthetics of immediacy' that posits systemic gender violence as some kind of emergency requiring immediate rectification on the part of its first world witnesses.

Chapter 4, 'Resilience and Renewal in Documentary Film about *Feminicidio* in Ciudad Juárez', examines documentary film about Juárez, focusing in particular on Lourdes Portillo's acclaimed *Señorita Extraviada* (2001) and Rafael Bonilla's *La carta* (2010). Arguing that the films are released at particularly pivotal moments in the recent history of feminicidal violence, I contend that distinct sets of tactics or representational modes are mobilized in response to those moments. The first documentary references the year 2001, the high point of the public focus on the association between the violence against women and the *maquila*. This connection was intensified by the discovery of the bodies of eight women in the Campo Algodonero (Cotton Fields) and the ensuing media frenzy. In this regard, the film speaks back to dominant scripts about the crimes and the exceptionality of Ciudad Juárez and performs moments of wholeness, everyday life, and renewal, signified most poignantly by the frequent shots of shoes threaded throughout. The second documentary studied here, *La carta*, captures the atmosphere of 2010 when Ciudad Juárez might properly be denominated an 'emergency zone' given the extreme levels of violence registered in the city with over 3,000 deaths recorded in 2010 alone. It looks at the use of the pre-modern communicative form of letter-writing as part of a project to build alliances between the citizens in Ciudad Juárez and a community project in Mexico city. Its portrayal of the primary protagonist, Paula Flores, long-term activist and mother of *feminicidio* victim Sagrario González, charts new territory about mother-activism and it presents the processes of reading and writing as possible vehicles for healing and regeneration from the wounds caused by *feminicidio*. Noting the different strategies deployed by each documentary, I explore the 'working through' (LaCapra 2000) of unspeakable trauma portrayed in *Señorita Extraviada* and the project of solidarity between centre and periphery depicted in *La carta*. Following this analysis, I examine the cinephiliac moments (Keathley 2006) experienced by this viewer in relation to both documentary films and explore the transformative potential of these moments for forging solidarity and resistance. These documentary films thus, both provide innovative visual treatments of the pain of *feminicidio* and are a fitting showcase of the potential of documentary film to respond to its multiple complexities.

Chapter 5 turns its attention to writing, selecting three case studies from the corpus of written texts available: the mystery novel, *Desert Blood: The Juárez Murders* by Chicana writer Alicia Gaspar de Alba which is examined alongside the much less known, but equally intriguing, *Ciudad final* [Final City] by Spanish author and academic Kama Gutier. I bookend the discussion of these two texts with an appraisal of the collaboratively assembled text, *El silencio que la voz de todas quiebra* [The silence that breaks the voice of all women], and one of the first written texts about the femicidal crime wave that erupted in Ciudad Juárez in the early 1990s. All of the writers considered in the chapter are activists in the sense that they seek out social and political change at the same time as they craft their creative responses to the crimes. Indeed, their texts shed light on the blurred boundaries between art and activism, exposing the limits of writing as well as its power. I will explore the texts' function of 'making visible' [*visibilizar*], not just in terms of naming and re-humanizing the victims of the crimes but also in terms of their revelation of those structural layers that make the violence possible. The reliance on hybridity in the texts further showcases the need to go beyond traditional generic boundaries to identify more fluid ways of moving between these structural layers. In the texts' symbolic investment in making the crimes visible, they are located within a wider panorama of much current writing in Mexico about violence including that of Cristina Rivera Garza. In the final section, reading through Rivera Garza's reflections on writing as a response to pain and her innovative rethinking of the role of the Mexican writer working from a 'wounded place' (Rivera Garza 2015), the chapter considers the writerly interventions as an urgent call for societal change.

Through close readings of a necessarily limited selection of art, film, theatre and literary works, the study has obviously occluded many of the numerous cultural products that exist, as already mentioned. However, it does attempt a balance in terms of selection through including both male and female artists, writers and creative practitioners; texts that are the focus of sustained study (Portillo); and texts that have escaped attention completely (Gutier). It includes work from Mexican writers and filmmakers (Bonilla; Benítez et al.) as well as cultural expressions from Europe including those of Irish artist Brian Maguire, Catalan theatre director Àlex Rigola, and Basque academic and activist, Kama Gutier. It also invokes the perspective of Chicano artists and writers, most particularly Alicia Gaspar de Alba and Lourdes Portillo. Furthermore, it intersperses insights from conversations held with practitioners, activists and those multiple interlocutors who made up the audiences for the many different presentations, seminars, conferences where the material in the book was rehearsed and which included audiences in Mexico, Ireland, France, the UK, and the US. In this way, I have integrated multiple and variegated perspectives articulated from different artistic, ideological and socio-political points of view.[30]

Critical to the process through which Juárez became known for a short time as the murder capital of the world[31] has been an ambivalence characterizing the responses of the Mexican state to activities on its northern frontier. On the one hand, the border region was anticipated as the harbinger of development that would spread capitalist modernization not just to the border but to the whole country. At the other end of the scale, it was to plaster over the cracks of border life (violence, crime) that made Juárez an embarrassment to metropolitan Mexico. This paradox is reproduced in a series of binary oppositions that characterize discourses about *feminicidio* in Ciudad Juárez more generally: public versus private; virgin versus whore; centre versus periphery; tradition versus modernity. It is reproduced further in a dynamic that sees Ciudad Juárez set against central Mexico involving traditional suppositions about savagery and otherness on the periphery. These interlinking discourses about class (the poor girls of Juárez); about ethnicity (the poor indigenous girls of Juárez); about gender (the loose women of Juárez); and about globalization (the poor exploited workers of Juárez) coalesce around a grotesque parade of maimed, tortured and brutalized female bodies. Examining the power of art and culture to dismantle – or at the very least unsettle – these static interpretative frameworks shows how cultural texts can intervene in human rights discourses in ways that can expand, enhance and reconfigure, charting a way out of stasis and paving the way for new understandings. With projects of this kind, the role of culture might be more properly exhumed not only in the interests of exposure and education but as a mechanism for political and cultural change.

This book, then, is an attempt to evaluate the role played by these cultural texts in the shaping of national and international perceptions of the crime but also in terms of framing and constructing a response to the crimes that differs fundamentally from interventions derived from the worlds of media, academia and human rights, to name but a few. This is partly due to the popular investment in forms of culture that is in turn linked to ideas around affect but also pleasure.[32] Also perhaps, because the nature of the crimes themselves is aligned so deeply to the concept of excess, it showcases the power of representation as a way of illuminating to be sure, but also as a way of framing the murders in a different way. Much of the work produced in response to the Juárez killings therefore, represents an attempt to disinter the cultural logic that informs the intersections of economics, culture and politics which collide in the systematic obliteration of women in the town from the early 1990s onwards. The extent to which the killing of these women and the multiple responses they have generated, become a contested terrain of competing discourses about globalization, disposable life, corporate culpability and the place of women in this new globalized world will be amply demonstrated. In addition to the usual role of exposure and awareness creation, therefore, the responses to the Juárez murders radically interrogate ideas about the gendered nature of death on the border in ways that shock, dazzle and awe their audiences eliciting a wide range of bodily, affective and intellectual reactions. The cultural responses studied in the book show the ways in which multiple forms of art function to re-humanize, commemorate, mourn and pay homage to the victims in powerfully compelling, if very diverse ways. They also operate as forceful weapons of denunciation and condemnation. In the highly charged atmosphere that prevails in Mexico in 2018, art arguably remains the sphere in which the emotional impact of violence can be most vividly felt. To continue to explore that emotional impact and to raise awareness about the lived experiences of the thousands of Mexican citizens suffering from the threat of violence that continues to assault their daily life is both politically necessary and artistically important.

There are no survivors of feminicide: these cultural responses therefore have been forged from the bodies of the deceased women and from the stories those bodies convey of fragmentation, destruction and death. At this stage, twenty-five-odd years after the commencement of this particularly violent wave, with only a tiny percentage of the crimes prosecuted appropriately, the cultural texts that have emerged from these discarded bodies will resonate and endure as ultimate testimony to the inhumanity of the crimes. I opened this introduction with a quotation from the mother of *feminicidio* victim Elia Escobedo García. Her statement is reproduced here again as she affirms that '*algo bueno va a salir de esto*' [something good will come of this], because it is from the resolute certainty with which she pronounces those words that we must take hope.

Notes

1 The phrase '*No nos cabe tanta muerte*' is the title of an art exhibition, *No nos cabe tanta muerte: Memorial a Ciudad Juárez, Mexico*, a collective project led by Mexican artist Paula Laverde involving painting, audiovisual, installation and performance pieces from a range of artists from Europe, Latin America and Japan and shown in Barcelona in 2014. The loose translation of this phrase – 'unbearable deaths' – is mine. All translations in the text are mine unless otherwise stated.

2 Public interview with Elia Escobedo García conducted by me as part of a screening and Q&A of the documentary film, *Blood Rising* (2013) with the director Mark McLoughlin and the artist Brian Maguire. Funded by Front Line Defenders and hosted by the Centre for Human Rights, National University Ireland, Galway, 12 February 2013.

3 It is estimated that there are over fifty such reports. Notable examples include Mexico's Comisión Nacional de los Derechos Humanos (National Commission on Human Rights) which issued Recommendation 44/98 in 1998, demanding that police and authorities be investigated for the murders of women in Ciudad Juárez. In 2003, the Commission issued a report condemning the federal government's oversight of the investigations. The Report from the UN International Commission of Experts, Office of Drugs and Crime, regarding their Mission in Ciudad Juárez, Chihuahua, Mexico, November 2003 also condemned the Mexican authorities for their inefficient action in the case of the murders of women in Juárez (Sergio González Rodríguez 2012: 77). In 2009, the Corte Interamericana de Derechos Humanos (Interamerican Court of Human Rights) issued a landmark judgement against the Mexican state for its culpability in the cases of three bodies found at the Campo Algodonero (Cotton Fields) in 2001. Available at: www.corteidh.or.cr/docs/casos/articulos/seriec_205_esp.pdf [Accessed 14 February 2018].

4 Javier Juárez highlights the extent to which both murder and disappearance increased substantially after 2008 when public perception would have judged otherwise: 'In five years, between 2008 and 2013, while the local, state and federal forces were in Ciudad Juárez, more women disappeared and were murdered than between 1993 and 2007' (cited in Chaparro 2015). Available at: https://news.vice.com/article/cartel-gangsters-face-697-years-behind-bars-in-historic-femicide-case-in-Juárez-mexico [Accessed 7 February 2018].

5 The Commission for the Defence and Promotion of Human Rights [Comisión Mexicana de Defensa y Promoción de los Derechos Humanos (CMDPDI I)] estimated the number of disappeared at 28,161 in 2016. The year 2017 ended as the most violent on

recent record for Mexico with 25,339 homicides registered in that year alone according to official statistics (Secretariado Ejecutivo del Sistema Nacional de Seguridad Pública (SESNSP).

6 Uruguayan President José Mujica controversially labelled Mexico '*un estado fallido*' or a failed state following the international outcry over the disappearance of the 43 students from Ayotzinapa in September 2014. See www.lanacion.com.ar/1746539-pepe-mujica-dijo-que-mexico-parece-un-estado-fallido-y-debio-rectificarse [Accessed 7 February 2018]. There is little consensus over the definition of 'failure' in this context; however it is clear that soon after the launch of President Felipe Calderón's offensive against the cartels in 2006, the idea of Mexico as a failed state began to gain traction in literature in security studies. For an excellent overview, see José Fernando Flórez Ruiz's article '*¿Estado o concepto fallido? Problemas que plantea la noción de falla estatal y los índices que intentan medirla*' (2011). For an important historical perspective, see Astorga (1996).

7 A backlash against the gendered focus on the crimes was discernible among the authorities from the beginning. Cristina Delgado cites Javier Benavides, the former commissioner of the Municipal Police, who 'claimed that NGOs were magnifying the cases of murdered women and were neglecting incidences of murdered men, whose cases were also very lamentable' (cited in Tabuenca Córdoba 2010: 109). This tension between acknowledging the wider wave of violence predominantly affecting men and the attention paid to crimes of violence against women is noticeable in much academic and media discourse on feminicide.

8 It is worth noting that Patricia Ravelo Blancas and Alfredo Limas Hernández proposed the term 'femenicidio' in an article published in 2002 titled '*Femenicidio en Ciudad Juárez: una civilización sacrificial*'. In later work, Ravelo Blancas explains that their proposal allows for the description of the specific social form and character of the murder of women (2006: 23).

9 Fregoso and Bejarano elaborate on this saying that, 'from a linguistic angle *feminicidio* (rather than *femicidio*) is a more accurate translation for femicide, given the particularities of the Spanish language, which requires the use of "I" to create compound words from two terms with etymological roots in Latin (femina for 'female; caedo, caesum for 'to kill')' (2010: 4). For a fuller explanation, see Monárrez Fragoso (2009).

10 Alice Driver's work on cultural responses to the atrocities against women in Ciudad Juárez provides an interesting snapshot of the complexities of terminology. Her detailed study (2015) relies on the use of the term '*feminicidio*' but she writes subsequently, 'on a practical level, nobody outside of academia uses the term "feminicide", and people find it confusing. [. . .] I think it's great to have these kind of intellectual debates, but if no one uses the term in real life, then I don't know that it makes sense to continue to champion the term' (cited in Wick 2016). Molly Molloy is similarly opposed to the use of the term. For her, a focus on gender places too much emphasis on the killing of women, not merited in a strictly statistical sense (Hooks 2014). This reticence comes from scholars working in the English-language context; understandable given that the term 'feminicide' sits rather awkwardly on the tongue and on the page. Perhaps, however, its awkwardness is the point.

11 In the Latin American context, see Neil Larsen (1990). Renée Heberle's edited collection, *Feminist Interpretations of Adorno* (2006), considers those aspects of Adorno's work that can be harnessed for the advancement of feminist thinking.

12 The debate between major German Marxist thinkers between the 1930s and 1950s, the so-called Frankfurt School, includes work by Bertolt Brecht, Georg Lukács, Theodor Adorno, Walter Benjamin and others. See *Aesthetics and Politics* (2006).

13 From the One Billion Rising 2015 call for projects. Available at: https://modemworld.me/tag/one-billion-rising/ [Accessed 7 February 2018]. For further information, consult www.onebillionrising.org/ [Accessed 7 February 2018].

14 For an interesting discussion of the didactic dimension in relation to Ciudad Juárez cultural production, see Irene Mata (2011).

15 See Hector Villareal's article, '*El feminicidio en Juárez y la impotencia del arte*' (2016). Available at: https://hectorvillarreal.wordpress.com/2016/05/10/femi/ [Accessed 7 February 2018].
16 Much has been written about the appropriation of Rancière's ideas in a Latin American context. Particularly useful in this regard is Ignacio Sánchez Prado's article, 'The Limitations of the Sensible' (2014) as well as work by Gareth Williams (2011), *The Mexican Exception*. As Christina B. Arce notes in relation to the sometimes fraught transposition of Rancière's ideas to Mexico, 'Rancière's insights cannot speak to the point [. . .] regarding the multilayered processes of subalternization in a country marked by violent coloniality' (2016: 19).
17 The term *comunidad emocional* or emotional community is defined by Michael Maffesoli (1990) as an emergence of commonality in terms of sensibility and affect among community groups. Within the field of anthropology in Colombia, there has been a particular emphasis on the notion of emotional community construction with reference to personal testimonies of violence and trauma that have political ramifications through their creation of a shared narrative forcing recognition and reparation on the part of the State. See Myriam Jimeno (2009).
18 Marco Kunz (2016: 146) goes as far as to affirm that there is a canon of cultural texts about *feminicidio* in Ciudad Juárez in which he includes Roberto Bolaño's novel, *2666*, Portillo's film, *Señorita Extraviada* and Sergio González Rodríguez's *Huesos en el desierto*. All of these texts receive consideration in the book.
19 This phrase is from Edward E. Avila's far-reaching study of Chicano/a film and literary responses to *feminicidio* in Juárez (2012: 118).
20 The website of activist organization Nuestras Hijas de Regreso a Casa maintains a list of cultural texts produced in response to feminicidal violence in Ciudad Juárez. Other lists of films and cultural products can be found in Driver (2015) and Gaspar de Alba and Guzmán (2010).
21 Extract from Perla Bonilla's diary, included in the catalogue to accompany the exhibition, *An Oasis of Horror in a Desert of Boredom* with artists, Brian Maguire, Teresa Margolles, Lise Bjørne Linnert, Mark McLoughlin, Lanka Haouche Perren. Visual, Carlow, Ireland. This project is the subject of Chapter 3.
22 This poster campaign in which sixty-four different designers participated had the explicit aim of promoting the cause of the victims of *feminicidio* in Ciudad Juárez throughout the capital. It is further explored in Chapter 3.
23 The MAC-Rodarte campaign involved a line of cosmetics with names such as, 'Ghost Town', 'Juarez', 'Badlands', 'Factory', and 'Sleepwalker'. In response to the furore generated, they apologised, withdrew the collection and stated that they were, 'committed to donating $100,000 to a non-profit organization that has a proven, successful track-record helping women in need and that can directly improve the lives of women in Juárez in a meaningful way'. See Barry (2010), available at: https://theantiroom.wordpress.com/2010/07/20/wheres-the-beauty-in-the-femicides-of-ciudad-juarez/ [Accessed 7 February 2018]. The most widely circulated image can be seen at the following location: https://i1.wp.com/www.hispanicla.com/wp-content/uploads/2010/08/MAC.jpg?fit=640%2C335 [Accessed 16 February 2018].
24 Melissa W. Wright elucidates this aspect (2009, 2010).
25 Schmidt Camacho writes, 'The hyper-visibility of the *feminicidio* in the international arena thus points to a paradox in the politics of human rights. The recognition that many thousands of Mexican nationals live outside the boundaries of the most minimal legal protections unsettles the very concepts of justice and rights that animate the campaign against the murders. Before these violations, state institutions of civil rights and international conventions devoted to human rights show their debility in permitting cases of *feminicidio* to arise and persist' (2006: n.p.).
26 Tobias Jochum (2015) is among a number of critics to take Bowden to task in a list that includes Rosa Linda Fregoso (2003), Alicia Schmidt Camacho (2004) and Alice Driver (2015).

18 *Introduction*

27 I am indebted to Ignacio Sánchez Prado for generously providing me with a copy of this invited presentation at the University of Florida, 2016.
28 Brinton Lykes et al. (2007) evaluate this concept in the context of post-conflict Maya communities in Guatemala.
29 Personal communication, 25 November 2016.
30 I have also integrated many of the other cultural products into my teaching and different community engagement initiatives. There are articles written and in preparation on other examples of theatre and documentary film.
31 This widely reported statistic makes reference to the extreme violence between 2008–2012 with 2010 registering as the most extreme year with 3,622 deaths. Statistics are taken from *Frontera list*, an invaluable resource for researchers and activists which is compiled by Molly Molloy. This source in turn utilizes data from the Chihuahua prosecutor's office as reported in *El Diario de Juárez*. Available at: https://fronteralist.org/ [Accessed 7 February 2018].
32 Ileana Rodríguez, in her long discussion about pleasure, eroticism and the tension between ethics and aesthetics around *feminicidio* in Ciudad Juárez ends her deliberation with the provocative, 'So, the question is: why are representations of killed women pleasurable?' (2009: 191).

Works cited

Adorno, Theodor, 1997 [1970]. *Aesthetic Theory*. Trans. by Robert Hullot-Kentor. Gretel Adorno and Rolf Tiedemann, eds. London, New York: Continuum.

———, et al., 2006. *Aesthetics and Politics*. London: Verso.

Arce, Christina B., 2016. *Mexico's Nobodies: The Cultural Legacy of the Soldadera and Afro-Mexican Women*. New York: SUNY Press.

Astorga, Luis, 1996. *El siglo de las drogas: El narco tráfico, del Porfiriato al nuevo milenio*. Mexico: Espasa.

Avila, Edward A., 2012. *Conditions of (Im)possibility: Necropolitics, Neoliberalism and the Cultural Politics of Death in Contemporary Chicano/a Film and Literature*. Thesis (Ph.D). University of San Diego. [online]. Available at: https://cloudfront.escholarship.org/dist/prd/content/qt7sh1f55b/qt7sh1f55b.pdf?t=ml5m0g [Accessed 15 February 2018].

Avila, José Juan de, 2014. Interview with Marcela Lagarde y de los Rios. El feminicidio no es una palabra, es toda una teoría. [online]. *El universal*, 15 November [online]. Available at: http://archivo.eluniversal.com.mx/cultura/2014/impreso/-8220el-feminicidio-no-es-una-palabra-es-toda-una-teoria-8221–75555.html [Accessed 4 February 2018].

Bajo Juárez: la ciudad devorando a sus hijas, 2006. [Film]. Directed by Antonio Cordero and Alejandra Sánchez.

Barry, Aoife, 2010. Where's the Beauty in the Femicides of Ciudad Juárez? *Anti-Room*, 20 July [online]. Available at: https://theantiroom.wordpress.com/2010/07/20/wheres-the-beauty-in-the-femicides-of-ciudad-juarez/ [Accessed 14 February 2018].

Baumgardner, Jennifer, and Richards, Amy, 2005. *Grassroots: A Field Guide for Feminist Activism*. New York: Farrar, Strauss and Giroux.

Blood Rising, 2013. [Film]. Directed by Mark McLoughlin. Bang Bang Teo.

Bola negra: El musical de Ciudad Juárez, 2012. [Film]. Directed by Mario Bellatin with composer Marcela Rodríguez.

Bordertown, 2006. [Film]. Directed by Gregory Nava. Mobius Entertainment/El Norte Productions.

Butler, Judith, 2011. *Precarious Life: The Obligations of Proximity*. The Neale Wheeler Watson Lecture 2011. Location: Nobel Museum, Svenska Akademiens Börssal, 24 May.

[online]. Available at: www.youtube.com/user/NobelMuseum/videos. [Accessed 17 January 2018].

Chaparro, Luis, 2015. Cartel Gangsters Face 697 Years Behind Bars in Historic Femicide Case in Juárez, Mexico. *Vice News*, 28 July. [online]. Available at: https://news.vice.com/article/cartel-gangsters-face-697-years-behind-bars-in-historic-femicide-case-in-Juárez-mexico [Accessed 7 Feb 2018].

Driver, Alice, 2015. *More or Less Dead: Feminicide, Haunting and the Ethics of Representation in Mexico*. Tucson: University of Arizona Press.

El traspatio [Backyard], 2009. [Film]. Directed by Carlos Carrera.

Flórez Ruiz, José Fernando, 2011. ¿Estado o concepto fallido? Problemas que plantea la noción de falla estatal y los índices que intentan medirla. *Revista Derecho del Estado*, 27 (julio–diciembre), 193–234.

Fregoso, Rosa Linda, 2003. *MeXicana Encounters: The Making of Social Identities on the Borderlands*. Berkeley, Los Angeles, London: University of California Press.

———, and Bejarano, Cynthia, 2010. Introduction: A Cartography of Feminicide in the Américas. In Rosa Linda Fregoso and Cynthia Bejarano, eds., *Terrorizing Women: Feminicide in the Américas*. Durham, NC: Duke University Press, 1–44.

Gaspar de Alba, Alicia and Guzman, Georgina eds., 2010. *Making a Killing: Femicide, Free Trade and La Frontera*. Austin: University of Texas Press.

González Rodríguez, Sergio, 2002. *Huesos en el desierto*. Barcelona: Anagrama.

———, 2012. *The Femicide Machine*. Los Angeles: Semiotext(e).

Hooks, Christopher, 2014. Q & A with Molly Molloy: The Story of the Juárez Femicides Is a 'Myth'. *Texas Observer*, 9 Jan. [online]. Available at: www.texasobserver.org/qa-molly-molloy-story-Juárez-femicides-myth [Accessed 12 February 2018].

Heberle, Renée, ed., 2006. *Feminist Interpretations of Adorno*. Philadelphia: Penn State University Press.

Jimeno, Myriam R., 2009. *¿Hay progreso en Colombia?: La "víctima" y la construcción de comunidades emocionales*. [online]. Available at: www.colombianistas.org/Portals/0/Revista/REC36/5.REC_36_MyriamJimeno.pdf [Accessed 7 Feb 2018].

Jochum, Tobias, 2015. "The Weight of Words, the Shock of Photos": Poetic Testimony and Elliptical Imagery in Sergio González Rodríguez. *The Femicide Machine: FIAR – Forum for Interamerican Research*, 8 (2) (Sep), 92–119. [online]. Available at: http://interamerica.de/volume-8-2/jochum/ [Accessed 24 January 2018].

Keathley, Christian, 2006. *Cinephilia and History, or The Wind in the Trees*. Bloomington, IN: Indiana University Press.

Kunz, Marco et al., 2016. *Acontecimientos históricos y su productividad cultural en el mundo hispánico*. Germany: Lit-Verlag.

LaCapra, Dominick, 2000. *Writing History, Writing Trauma*. Baltimore: Johns Hopkins University Press.

La carta [The Letter], 2010. [Film]. Directed by Rafael Bonilla.

Larsen, Neil, 1990. *Modernism and Hegemony: A Materialist Critique of Aesthetic Agencies*. Minneapolis: University of Minnesota Press.

Limas Hernández, Alfredo, and Limas Hernández, Myrna, 2016. *Trata de Personas y Violencia Feminicida: Factores de vulnerabilidad ante la desaparición de niñas y mujeres jóvenes en Juárez*. [Presentation]. Globalización, violencias y feminismos: Desafíos actuales, Reunión Binacional sobre Violencia de Género "*Cátedra Internacional Marcela Lagarde y de los Ríos*" y Seminario Binacional "*Diversidad sin Violencia*", 24–25 November Centro de Investigación y Estudios Superiores en Antropología social (CIESAS), Mexico. (Unpublished).

Lykes, Brinton et al., 2007. Political Violence, Impunity, and Emotional Climate in Maya Communities. *Journal of Social Issues*, 63 (2), 369–385.

Maguire, Brian, 2012. *An Oasis of Horror in a Desert of Boredom* [Exhibition]. VISUAL Centre for Contemporary Art, Carlow. 6 Oct 2012–6 Jan 2013.

Maffesoli, Michael, 1990. *El tiempo de las tribus: el declive del individualismo en la sociedad de masas*. Barcelona: Icaria.

Martínez, Adriana, 2009. 'Mujer constante más allá de la muerte', or the Overpowering Constructions of Feminicide in Ciudad Juárez. *Tiresías: Culture, Politics and Critical Theory*, 3 (Apr), 91–113.

Mata, Irene, 2011. Documenting Feminicide: The Importance of Teaching Lourdes Portillo's *Señorita Extraviada*. *Chicana/Latina Studies*, 10 (2 Spring), 92–127.

Monárrez Fragoso, Julia Estela, 2009. *Trama de una injusticia: Feminicidio sexual sistémico en Ciudad Juárez*. Mexico: El Colegio de la Frontera Norte y Miguel Ángel Porrúa.

An Oasis of Horror in a Desert of Boredom, 2012. [Exhibition Catalogue]. Carlow, Ireland. Visual Centre for Contemporary Art and the George Bernard Shaw Theatre.

One Billion Rising, 2018. *Revolution 2018 Solidarity Campaign*. [online]. Available at: www.onebillionrising.org/ [Accessed 14 February 2018].

Porter, Robert, 2009. *Deleuze and Guattari: Aesthetics and Politics*. Chicago: University of Chicago Press.

Rancière, Jacques, 2013 [2004]. *The Politics of Aesthetics: The Distribution of the Sensible*. Trans. by Gabriel Rockhill. New York: Bloomsbury.

Ravelo Blancas, Patricia, 2006. Violencia sexual en Ciudad Juárez: Percepción de trabajadoras y trabajadores de la maquila sobre el sistema de gobierno. In Patricia Ravelo Blancas and Héctor Domínguez-Ruvalcaba, eds., *Entre las duras aristas de las armas: Violencia y Victimización en Ciudad Juárez*. Mexico: CIESAS, Publicaciones de la Casa Chata, 21–54.

———, and Limas Hernández, Alfredo, 2002. Femenicidio en Ciudad Juárez: Una civilización sacrificial. *El cotidiano*, 111, 47–57.

———, and Sánchez Díaz, Sergio G., 2015. *Tácticas y Estrategias contra la Violencia de Género*. Mexico: Ediciones Eón.

Rivera Garza, Cristina, 2015. *Dolerse: Textos desde un país herido*. Mexico: Tusquets Editores.

Rodríguez, Ileana, 2009. *Liberalism at Its Limits: Crime and Terror in the Latin American Cultural Text*. Pittsburgh: University of Pittsburgh Press.

Russell, Diana E.H., and Harmes, Roberta H., 2001. *Femicide in Global Perspective*. Columbia Unitersity New York and London: Teachers College Press.

Sánchez Prado, Ignacio, M., 2014. The Limitations of the Sensible: Reading Rancière in Mexico's Failed Transition. *Parallax*, 20 (4), 372–383.

———., 2016. *War and the Neo-Liberal Condition: Death and Vulnerability in Contemporary Mexico*. [Presentation]. University of Florida, 15 September (Unpublished).

Schmidt Camacho, Alicia, 2004. Body Counts on the Mexico-U.S. Border: Feminicidio, Reification, and the Theft of Mexicana Subjectivity. *Chicana/Latina Studies*, 4 (1) (Fall), 22–60.

———, 2006. *Integral Bodies, Cuerpos íntegros: Impunity and the Pursuit of Justice in the Chihuahuan Feminicidio'*. [online]. Available at: http://hemisphericinstitute.org/journal/3.1/eng/en31_pg_camacho.html [Accessed 7 Feb 2018].

Señorita Extraviada, 2001. [Film]. Directed by Lourdes Portillo.

Staudt, Kathleen, 2008. *Violence and Activism at the Border: Gender, Fear and Everyday Life in Ciudad Juárez*. Austin: University of Texas Press.

Swanson Goldberg, Elizabeth and Schultheis Moore, Alexandra, 2011. Old Questions in New Boxes: Mia Kirshner's *I Live Here* and the Problematics of Transnational Witnessing. *Humanity: An International Journal of Human Rights, Humanitarianism, and Development*, 2 (2), 233–253.

Tabuenca Córdoba, María Socorro, 2010. Ghost Dance in Ciudad Juárez at the End/Beginning of the Millenium. In Alicia Gaspar de Alba and Georgina Guzmán, eds., *Making a Killing: Femicide, Free Trade and La Frontera*. Austin: University of Texas Press, 95–119.

Villareal, Héctor, 2016. *El feminicidio* en Juárez y la impotencia del arte. *Dystopia*, 10 February [online]. Available at: https://hectorvillarreal.wordpress.com/2016/05/10/femi/ [Accessed 12 February 2018].

The Virgin of Juárez, 2006. [Film]. Directed by Kevin James Dobson.

Volk, Steven S., and Schlotterbeck, Marian E., 2010. Gender, Order, and Femicide: Reading the Popular Culture of Murder in Ciudad Juárez. In Alicia Gaspar de Alba and Georgina Guzmán, eds., *Making a Killing: Femicide, Free Trade, and La Frontera*. Austin: University of Texas Press, 121–153.

Wick, Julia, 2016. *Talking to Alice Driver About Violence Against Women in Juárez*. [online]. Available at: https://longreads.com/2016/02/03/talking-to-alice-driver-about-violence-against-women-in-juarez/ [Accessed 13 February 2018].

Williams, Gareth, 2011. *The Mexican Exception: Sovereignty, Police and Democracy*. London: Palgrave Macmillan.

Wright, Melissa M., 2009. Justice and the Geographies of Moral Protest. *Environment and Planning D: Society and Space*, 27, 216–233.

———, 2010. Paradoxes, Protests, and the Mujeres de Negro of Northern Mexico. In Rosa Linda Fregoso and Cynthia Bejarano, eds., *Terrorizing Women: Feminicide in the Américas*. Durham, NC: Duke University Press, 312–330.

1 Framing *feminicidio*
The spectral politics of death in Ciudad Juárez

Before commencing the study of a selection of cultural responses, and relying on the vast body of international scholarship available on the subject, this chapter will sketch the backdrop to the gender violence ongoing in Ciudad Juárez with a view to elucidating the conditions and circumstances that have enabled the crimes to continue. Following this outline of what might be termed the narrative arc of feminicidal discourse, I suggest a series of frames or viewing parameters through which the *feminicidios* in the border city have been conceptualized and narrativized since the early 1990s. These include the debate generated around globalization and the economic, political and symbolic association, in particular, between the feminicidal wave and the *maquiladora* industry in the region. Linked to this seam of scholarship is a debate about necropolitics as a framework through which the crimes against women might be evaluated. In concert with these two strands of thinking is the motif of Ciudad Juárez itself as a monstrous, tainted city, a motif sustained in the public imaginary that threads through most discussions of feminicidal violence. Finally, I turn to ideas that have circulated about gender roles and, in particular, about a version of femininity that is contaminated and suspect. Interwoven with societal anxiety about the enhanced presence of women in the local workforces, this construction of women in the public imaginary contributed to the emergence of a pronounced victim-blaming discourse. The section concludes by considering society's social investment in a destructive and toxic model of masculinity. Fuelled by poverty, it is central to any understanding of the levels of violence against women in this northern border city.

The what and the when

Beyond the terrifyingly simple facts of violent death, it has become almost impossible to generalize about the feminicidal wave of violence in Ciudad Juárez from the early 1990s onwards. There is no single explanation for the murders committed in the city and any examination of the deaths must remain attentive to the specificities of the women's stories as well as the diversity of the contexts involved. The date when the murders commence really depends on when you start to count: some studies start in 1992, others in 1993 and 1994, but 1993 is the date most frequently cited by activists and scholars as their starting point

(Monárrez Fragoso 2000, 2002, 2005a, 2005b; Rojas 2005; Staudt 2008). Monárrez Fragoso, however, cautions us against picking a single date, and indeed it is important to signal that while the *feminicidios* are frequently conceptualized as a 'new' phenomenon and Ciudad Juárez as some sort of emergency zone, it can be forcefully argued that the crimes committed in Ciudad Juárez since the 1990s simply represent an intensified acceleration of a line of violence against women that has always existed. Of course, all violence has a history (Young cited in Critchley and Evans 2016),[1] and Nicole M. Guidotti-Hernández's work charts the trajectory of violence in the borderlands region (2011) to show how it is rooted in its history, culture and politics. Indeed, the multi-generational experience of violent death is prominent in many of the cultural responses explored in this book. In this regard then, any examination of the Juárez *feminicidios* must take a longitudinal approach that seeks to locate the violence in the past twenty-five years along a continuum of gender violence that has simply taken a terrifying new turn.

Any consideration of the phenomenon must also grapple with the numbers issue, and in this regard it goes without saying that the numbers of *feminicidios* actually committed in the city are continuously contested. By way of example, this can be seen in three contrasting sets of figures: in April 2009, the *El Paso Times* reported a figure of more than 600 girls and women since 1993, but this figure had risen to 1,000 by the end of 2010; the office of the Mexican Attorney General (Procuraduría General de la República) cites a figure of 379 between 1992 and 2005 (Fregoso and Bejarano 2010) while Amnesty International counted 370 in the decade 1993–2003 (Staudt 2008).[2] There are considerable methodological differences between the multiple studies: some sources include girls and women; some deal only with cases of 'intentional homicide'; some include the numbers of disappeared; among many other variables. Perhaps scholars should heed Gaspar de Alba who reminds us that

> any attempt at deciphering the mechanics of femicide on the U.S.-Mexico border must take the numbers game for what it is: a riddle intended to obfuscate the public as much as the authorities. To this day no one really knows the exact number of victims.
>
> (2014: 148)[3]

Following this logic, it may be counter-productive to try and establish definitive statistics; however, it should also be acknowledged that the painstaking work of scholars in the region such as Julia Estela Monárrez Fragoso in trying to get to the 'truth' of the figures has been critical, particularly given its wider impact in terms of mapping the geography of the crimes.

Critics signal different turning points in the feminicidal narratives and indeed there have been numerous attempts to order the patterns and arc of the crimes since the early 1990s. According to Nancy Piñeda-Madrid, 2001 marked a turning point with the discovery of Lilia Alejandra García Andrade's body wrapped in a blanket in an empty lot next to the Centro Comercial Soriano.[4] She had been strangled to death and her body displayed signs of torture and sexual violence including rape. Following this crime, her mother, Norma Andrade de García, along with the mothers of six other victims, founded the organization, Nuestras Hijas de Regreso a Casa, to demand justice. A few weeks after the discovery of Lilia Alejandra's body, on International Women's Day, 8 March 2001, several women from Ciudad Juárez and El Paso carried wooden crosses and life-size photos of the murdered girls and women with them as they marched to and stormed the office of the Special Prosecutor for the Investigation of the Homicide of Women. The different discoveries of multiple corpses at particular sites in the city including Valle de Juárez (2012),[5] Lomas de Poleo (2005), Campo Algodonero (2001) and Lote Bravo (1995) have become for many the iconic sites of feminicide in Juárez, their cases generating media hysteria, public disquiet and international opprobrium. The discovery of eight bodies in Campo Algodonero in particular prompted an international investigation by the Corte Interamericana de Derechos Humanos (Inter-American Court of Human Rights) and the landmark judgement from this body in 2009 excoriated the negligence of the Mexican state in relation to the crimes.[6] The Campo Algodonero cases also served as a catalyst for human rights groups and indeed the Ni Una Más campaign, the most publicly visible campaign of awareness during the history of the violence, dates from this time (Staudt 2008). Others would isolate as pivotal the heartbreaking murder of seven-year-old Airis Estrella in 2005 which united and mobilized the local community against *feminicidio* in new and effective ways.[7] Several years later, the sentencing of perpetrators in the cases of Hotel Verde victims in 2015 would be seen as another historic turning point even when those cases were under-reported nationally because of the unprecedented focus on the fate of the forty-three missing Ayotzinapa students, disappeared in September 2014.

Alfredo and Myrna Limas Hernández (2016) provide a timeline of feminicidal crimes in Ciudad Juárez that is immensely useful. Their analysis identifies four discrete phases: what they term the emergence of feminicidal violence involving serial or multiple killings (1993–2001); the consolidation of a politics of impunity (2002–2007); an escalation of feminicide in the context of the so-called drug war including the case of the unmarked grave at Valle de Juárez (2008–2012); and the current phase from 2013 onwards during which time the crime of *feminicidio* continues to acquire presence and symbolic power in the community.[8] This overview comprehensively dispels any notion that the violence against women in Ciudad Juárez is somehow over and that the problem has moved elsewhere. Indeed, a more nuanced reading of figures nationally would conclude that there is now a high visibility pertaining to the crime in Mexico.[9] This visibility, while welcome of course, has not led to a cessation of the crime; rather, it has simply directed attention to the many other sites where that violence is being produced.

Besides the 'numbers game', the other element essential to any consideration of the crimes is the sustained construction of myths and stereotypes surrounding the victims, the perpetrators, the methods and indeed the causes. The murders, as the result perhaps of intense media scrutiny, often became portrayed in reductive and simplistic terms and certain myths pertaining to the victims and to the nature of the crime, began to circulate widely. These myths asserted that the victims were young factory workers, poor, of a certain build and colouring and that the crimes were characterized by high levels of sexual torture as well as mutilation. In contrast to these prevailing myths, it is well established in the literature that the profile of victims is wide-ranging and diverse and includes Mexican and non-Mexican citizens from the Netherlands,[10] US and Central America, to name just a few of the locations of origin. Of the Mexican victims, they include Ciudad Juárez natives, as well as women from other states within Mexico and members of indigenous communities. Indeed one of the media tag lines in reporting the crimes was of *las inditas del sur* [the little Indian girls from the South], and the racialized as well as the gendered nature of the crime was clear from an early point. Again, this myth is also dispelled by the evidence which points to the majority of the victims being from Chihuahua (Monárrez Fragoso 2005b: 358);[11] however, this did not prevent images and stories circulating, in which it was inferred that the ethnicity and the 'brownness' of the women's skin became a factor in their demise.

Furthermore, while the crimes became synonymous with the *maquilas* or the multinational assembly plants that proliferate along the border particularly in the first decade (1993–2003), according to some studies as few as 10% of the victims overall worked in these factories (Monárrez Fragoso 2005b). This contrasts starkly with their representation from the outset as directly relating to the *maquilas* and copper-fastened in 2001 with the discovery of eight corpses found in the Campo Algodonero (Cotton Fields) directly opposite the *maquila* headquarters. This discovery underscored – in symbolic terms at least – the association in the public's mind between the *maquilas* and the murders of the young women.[12] Indeed for many years, the feminicides were frequently referred to as the *maquila/maquiladora* murders (Quiñones 1998).[13] The other myth relating to the sexual nature of the feminicidal violence has also not withstood detailed scrutiny and while many of the murder victims did display signs of sexual mutilation, many others did not. Instead, if a single determining factor were to be identified in the cases reported, it is likely that poverty would be the primary contender. According to Staudt, approximately one-third of the murders involved the rape and mutilation of victims who were disproportionately poor and young. Monárrez Fragoso's work (2000, 2002, 2009), has been important too in drawing attention to this aspect. Indeed, the recognition of poverty as a primary shared factor in the profile of the victims is central also to research that links the *maquilas* with the rise in feminicidal violence and, perhaps more critically, the links with impunity. As the following question which appeared in an open letter from the Chihuahua based non-governmental organization (NGO), Justicia para Nuestras Hijas [Justice for our daughters] baldly puts it: '*¿Por qué no hay atención, personal y recursos para investigar la desaparición de nuestras hijas? Lo sabemos muy bien, porque todas las desaparecidas y muertas son pobres*' [Why is there no attention, no staff or no resources to investigate the disappearance of our daughters? We know only too well that it is because the disappeared and the dead are poor] (Justicia para Nuestras Hijas 2003).[14]

Feminicide in Ciudad Juárez: action and resistance

It is no surprise given the scale of the violence against women experienced in Ciudad Juárez from 1993 onwards that there has been a complex, wide-ranging set of responses from the spheres of media, academia, human rights and art. The role of human rights agencies, NGOs and grassroots organizations, working locally, nationally and internationally has been crucial. There have been responses from the communications media including the print media, radio and television as well as national and international news programmes that have covered the issue from various perspectives. Journalists worthy of particular mention in terms of their contribution to the dissemination of information around *feminicidio* in Juárez include Diana Washington Valdez, whose investigative journalism resulted in an award-winning series titled 'Death Stalks the Border', published by the *El Paso Times* in 2002.[15] The work of Sergio González Rodríguez was also critically important in the Mexican and Spanish-speaking world, and his groundbreaking hybrid text, *Huesos en el desierto* (2002), provided the base for Roberto Bolaño's literary approach to the crimes in the novel, *2666*.[16]

The role played by NGOs has also been of critical importance providing 'legal, psychological, and economic services and support to the victims while also constituting a forum for critical discussion, information, lobbying and pressuring the authorities' (Lagarde y de los Ríos in Fregoso and Bejarano 2010: xiii). As many scholars have pointed out (Wright 2009; Gaspar de Alba 2014; Staudt 2008), activists published lists of murder victims, organized rallies and protests, petitions and community events of commemoration. Victims' mothers' groups emerged, each with different discursive strategies and priorities. They included Voces sin Eco, Mujeres de Negro, Nuestra Hijas de Regreso a Casa, Mujeres por Juárez, Madres en Busca de Justicia, and Fundación Sagrario. To this we could add the Ni Una Más campaign already mentioned and the feminist group Ocho de Marzo. In 2004, an academic group of experts in violence against women proposed an alternative plan [*Plan alternativo para solucionar el feminicidio en Ciudad Juárez*] to Mexican authorities in order to confront the problem (González Rodríguez 2012). The plan sought to shed light on the murders by establishing a unique investigative structure that would examine each and every case. There would be justice for the victims and damages suffered by family members would be repaired. In addition, a greater awareness of crimes committed along the border would be fostered. The plan proposed legal reforms, as well as a number of political and administrative measures that would be taken on federal, state and local levels. The initiative was presented to the executive and legislative branches of the government but was never put into practice.

Staudt maintains that by the end of 2002, border activists had made feminicide widely visible and succinctly synthesizes the breadth and scope of the activities ongoing:

> Representatives from international and regional organizations visited the border and criticized it from afar. The Mexico Solidarity Network organized caravans across borders, taking traveling testimonials as far as the

northeastern United States and southern Mexico. The Washington Office on Latin America helped organize U.S. congressional visits to the border. Feminists in the Mexican Congress spoke individually and collectively.

(2008: 90)

She emphasizes the cultural resonance of the staging and restaging of Eve Ensler's *The Vagina Monologues*, to which Ensler devoted an additional monologue on the Juárez feminicides in 2003 (Staudt 2008).[17] Moreover, Amnesty International published a substantive report on the subject, titled *Intolerable Killings* (2003), and a US congressional visit was organized at which the report took centre stage.[18] The part played by Hilda Solis, US Democratic congresswoman from California, who led the congressional delegation meeting with officials and activists has also been well documented (Staudt 2008; Gaspar de Alba and Guzman 2010). Representative Solis introduced a resolution to denounce the murders and inadequate governmental response. Offering symbolic rather than substantive leverage, it nevertheless continued to keep the issue visible in the US political sphere. During this time, however, tensions arose between the various emerging and established grassroots groups. These tensions have been well chronicled elsewhere (Rojas 2005, 2010; Wright 2007, 2009, 2010, 2011) and there is no scope to address them in any depth here. Suffice to say that they primarily centred around discord over compensation arrangements for victims' families, the perceived need for some activists to be more centre stage at media events [*protagonismo*] and the different priorities given to framing gender violence that involved conflicts over social class.

In Mexico, feminicidal violence in Juárez permeated press coverage of the region and occupied a significant space in the national imaginary giving rise to the most varied of political expressions: demonstrations, rallies, concerts, religious rituals, protest encampments, exhibitions and installation. The discovery of the bodies in Campo Algodonero prompted NGOs as well as national and international groups to join forces. In mid-December 2001 a candlelight vigil was organized with approximately 25,000 people in attendance. By early 2002, these groups, some 300 in all, came together under the umbrella Campaña Alto a la Impunidad: Ni Una Muerte Más [Campaign against Impunity: No more Deaths], better known as Ni Una Más. In March 2002, the Ni Una Más coalition along with the Chihuahua City–based Mujeres de Negro organized a march from Chihuahua City to el Paso del Norte International Bridge in Juárez, naming their campaign Éxodo por la Vida. The 230-mile march began on International Women's Day and ended many days later (Washington Valdez 2005). In addition, there have been several serious changes in politico-juridical structures, chief among these the introduction of the Ley General de Acceso de las Mujeres a una Vida Libre de Violencia in Feburary 2007 [General Law of Access for Women to a Life Free from Violence]. This landmark achievement has ushered in a robust legal framework for the protection of women's rights and more than any other intervention speaks to the way in which consciousness of the crime of feminicide is now widespread across Mexican society. This does not mean, of course, that the crimes have stopped or that the response to the crimes has improved. In reference to the urgent work needed in this domain, Lagarde y de los Ríos declared recently, '*la ley no es suficiente pero la ley es imprescindible*' [the law is not enough but it is essential].[19] In addition to national law, the '*sistema nacional para prevenir, atender, sancionar y erradicar la violencia contra las mujeres*' [national system to prevent, attend to, sanction and eradicate violence against women] was introduced with a 'gender alert system' [*alerta de género*] that could be activated to draw police attention to women at risk or experiencing violence.[20] A citizen observatory, Observatorio Ciudadano Nacional del *Feminicidio* (OCNF) was also established to collate data on violence against women, and as has been pointed out, the observatories, when they are resourced adequately, are important tools for the collation and dissemination of accurate data (Limas Hernández 2016). As already stated, there have been numerous reports issued including those by Amnesty International and the Corte Interamericana de Derechos Humanos. Mexico has also received recommendations from international human rights agencies including demands that the government determine the facts in all of the cases, ensure access to justice for the victims' family members, and increasingly implement policies with a gender perspective (Fregoso and Bejarano 2010: xii). There have been reports and censure from the European Parliament, the Congreso de los Diputados de España and the US Congress as well as local city councils from numerous countries, NGOs, women's networks and many more. The work of activists such as Esther Chávez Cano (now deceased), Marcela Lagarde y de los Ríos, Marisela Ortiz, Lucha Castro, Norma Andrade, Paula Flores and the many others who have toiled to make the issue visible and to hold the authorities to account has also been honoured in various ways.[21] As Lagarde y de los Ríos and others have pointed out, there have been long-term research projects as well as theses, essays, courses and seminars, all motivated by a profound commitment to contribute, through scientific inquiry, to the analysis of the situation in order to take action and eradicate crimes against girls and women. Finally, it is important to note that there is an official memorial park dedicated to victims of *feminicidio* which was inaugurated in 2011 close to the site where the Campo Algodonero bodies were found. This memorial site represented the end point of a prolonged and frequently bitter struggle with the authorities and is testimony to the commitment of the many locally based activists and academics.[22] It should be clear, therefore, that during the decades following the killings, feminicide in Juárez acquired a public visibility, internationally and nationally and the discarded corpses of its victims haunt a global mediascape in a myriad different ways, as we shall see.

Frames of viewing

It should be clear from the discussion thus far how easy it is to become embroiled in questions about the number of victims or the definition of the crimes involved, but what these questions inevitably lead to in any cursory examination of literature about the Ciudad Juárez feminicides is a series of whys. Perhaps it is no surprise that they are often conceptualized as a kind of detective whodunit-style narrative with multiple theories about the perpetrators. Over the course of more than twenty years, the narrative arc accompanying the feminicides has trodden an uneasy path between competing theories and ideologies. This has encompassed subjects as wide-ranging as the radical change in gender roles, the corrosive impact of advanced global capitalism and the emphasis on Ciudad Juárez as an intrinsically monstrous place. Alongside these analyses has been an emphasis on the destructive model of masculinities inflected in Mexico by a culturally embedded notion of redemptive violence traceable to the Aztec deity Huitzilopochtli (Piñeda-Madrid 2011: 55–56).[23] All inter-related, of course, these ideas circulated with varying force and viability and were rehearsed on TV, radio, in the print media, in the activities of NGOs and in the many cultural responses generated by the murders. In this section, I will chart a path through these contested and competing discourses with the goal of mapping the narrative pattern of the Ciudad Juárez feminicidal violence in a way that will enable an illumination of the context within which the cultural responses which are the subject of this study might be best understood.

In the face of inexplicable deficiencies in the investigations into the murders, multiple hypotheses surrounded the killing of the Juárez women. Domínguez-Ruvalcaba and Ravelo Blancas identified a total of thirty-two separate hypotheses that had been invoked to explain them by the year 2010. They included 'narco santeros performing human sacrifices, human organ trafficking, and finally transnational corporations maximizing profits at the cost of the exploitation of women from third World societies, an important sector of the so-called industrial reserve army of labor' (López-Lozano 2010: 133). Theories abounded about serial killers, about 'juniors' and the supposedly out of control offspring of narco drug lords (Washington Valdez 2005). Indeed, as Corchado and Sandoval verify, the hunting of young women for rape and disposal as a form of drug-cartel 'sport' after big sales is commonplace (cited in Staudt 2008: 12). Leading to a state of confusion and bewilderment in the minds of the public, Hayman and Bell observe:

> So after one of the worst cases of femicide in world history, we are left with speculation – powerful politicians or rich businessmen did it, satanic killers did it, a deranged gringo did it, the police did it, copycats did it, all Juárez men hate women, Juárez is a 'city of fear', and so on – but few answers.
> (cited in Corona 2010: 109–110)

Rumours about organ trafficking, about snuff movies, about beauty pageants and catalogues of women from which men could just choose – all fuelled the media frenzy that accompanied the discovery of the corpses and it was particularly acute during those times when multiple corpses were discovered in the same place.

It goes without saying that the feminicidal violence in Juárez has generated a considerable body of interdisciplinary scholarship in the areas of criminology, human rights, political science, sociology, cultural studies and anthropology, to name but just some of the disciplinary areas (Fregoso and Bejarano 2010; Monárrez Fragoso (2000–present); Staudt 2008; Schmidt Camacho (2004–present);

Tabuenca Córdoba (2010); Tabuenca Córdoba and Monárrez Fragoso (2007); Gaspar de Alba and Guzmán 2010; Segato 2006, 2010; Wright 2006). This scholarship is derived from a multiplicity of perspectives as well as distinct ideological and political positions. It can be stated with certainty, however, that much critical work was and continues to be heavily invested in the link between the violent deaths of women in Ciudad Juárez and that city's specific experience of globalization since the early 1990s with 1994 (as the year of NAFTA, the North American Free Trade Agreement) as its fulcrum. This body of work tends to anchor the meanings of the murders, then, on the connection between the exploitation of gendered bodies on a global assembly line and the systematic extermination of those same bodies as part of a singular process brought about by the vagaries of transnational capitalism. This might be labelled the 'globalization argument' and it sees Juárez's problems as the problems of late capitalism magnified and accelerated. Scholarship in this vein posits Juárez as a kind of laboratory, a prototype of unapologetic globalization that, in the words of its critics, is devouring its children.[24] The argument identified the aggressive model of globalization in operation in this part of the world and the misogynistic culture it nurtured as a major element in designating women as corporate garbage, disposable (in labour terms at any rate) and easily replaceable. Following this logic, the *maquiladoras* – whether from critics on the side of an ideological divide that saw them as the trickle-down dividends of neoliberalism through their creation of jobs, or from critics who believed that they represented the worst extremes of inhumanity wrought by global capitalism – were at the heart of the problem. Wright (1999) and the many other scholars to examine the *maquiladora* phenomenon (Carrillo and Hernandez 1985; Salzinger 2003; Arriola 2010; Sánchez Díaz 2011; Sánchez Díaz, Ravelo Blancas and Melgoza Valdivia 2015) pointed to the rapid development of the border region that saw the city's population soar with little accompanying infrastructure and which led to the creation of what might be termed a paradigm of uncompromising globalization.

This model of globalization was particularly gendered, a dimension that has received much scholarly attention (Femenías 2009; Hu-DeHart 2007). Many activists and academics maintain that there would be no killing of women in Juárez without the structurally violent patterns of labour originating with the *maquilas* (Glantz 2003; González Rodríguez 2012), and María Luisa Femenías further points out the extent to which current models of globalization rely on a feminization of existing modes of labour practice.[25] Gendered analyses of the *maquila* as a working environment in this regard are commonplace. Central to these analyses were the ways in which the *maquila* factory programme transformed women's relationship to the public sphere. This line of reasoning suggests that through her movement into the factory, according to Tabuenca Córdoba, '[t]he *maquila* worker came to transgress different spaces in the city's (and the nations's) *usos y costumbres*, defying a social construction of gender' (2010: 97). Much research points to the move from male to female heads of household during this period,[26] and it is important to emphasize the way in which the image of the *obrera* (or public worker) and the *ramera* (or the whore) were interconnected in the cultural imagination (Wright 2011).[27] Advertising sustained this fiction that only 'decent women maintain themselves in private spaces but that women who dare take to public spaces, which are reserved for men, and who like to go dancing "until dawn" put themselves at risk of becoming another statistic' (Tabuenca Córdoba 2010: 102).

That the killings of girls who were 'out at night' were tragically far from the lofty rhetoric of advanced global capitalism with its myth of spatial mobility was evident from the outset and indeed, mobility and other accompanying freedoms became one of the key battlegrounds of this debate.[28] The wealth of studies from this kind of perspective is well established and compelling in many regards. I am struck when I read it about how little comfort such elegant academic abstractions must offer to the grieving families who continue to battle the indifference of a justice system and the unrelenting grief caused by the violent deaths of their daughters, nieces, sisters and cousins, a frustration that might be expressed in terms of the question, 'who's going to put globalization in jail?' The reliance on such theory has been criticized most notably by Rosa Linda Fregoso, who writes that

> [A]lthough there is no doubt that the process of economic globalization is 'out of control', globalism is a monolithic top-down analysis that neither captures nor explains the complexity of feminicide. Nor does conflating the *exploitation* of gendered bodies with their *extermination* offer us the nuanced account of violence that feminicide demands.
>
> (2003: 13)

Fregoso further argues that this theory can erase or elide the importance of women's agency in resisting oppressive work practices (2007: 46–47) and may also have

> worked to absolve the state of its complicity and perhaps even direct involvement in the murders of poor and dark-skinned women in Ciudad Juárez. [. . .] As the master narrative for the Left, globalism generates a problem of interpretation that is unable to account for the consolidation of a new form of state-sanctioned terrorism in Mexico.
>
> (2007: 50)

In spite of these reservations, it is abundantly clear that the patterns of violence associated with feminicide are *linked to* if not *caused by* those economic regimes of globalization signified most powerfully by the *maquila*. Moreover, many of the connections drawn between the experience of the feminicide victims and their positioning within a global world order – as mostly poor and expendable – contributed greatly to the culture of impunity that surrounded the crimes from the beginning.[29] In this regard, the insights from these critiques of neoliberal economic development in the border region are invaluable and of considerable relevance in assessing the crimes. In tandem with this focus on globalization was a wealth of discussion focusing on the nature of the border region as a frontier, binational or denationalized space. In this next section, I trace the development of this scholarship.

Denationalization and the necropolitical order

Accompanying debates about globalization, neoliberal economics and advanced capitalism has been scholarly focus on geopolitics, and indeed the location of Juárez at the US-Mexico border has been central to many of the discussions about feminicide. Alicia Schmidt Camacho posits that the border region, as a denationalized space, has been absolutely central to constructing the notion of disposability – of the labour force, of bodies – but also to creating and sustaining the continuing state of impunity (2005).[30] According to this logic, the crimes are committed in a space that is at once supra-national and in which global multinational companies operate outside of national legal frameworks in a way that renders the space ungovernable and in which impunity is the single most significant and shared characteristic. As Ramona Ortiz asks,

> In what society can one find raped bodies without anything much happening? What makes someone think (be it an occasional or premeditated assassin, a one-timer or serial killer, alone or accompanied, Mexican or foreign) that in Ciudad Juárez you can rape and kill a woman without fear that anything will happen to you?
>
> (Monárrez Fragoso 2010: 68)

Seeking answers to these questions, critics have turned to the work of Giorgio Agamben on the idea of the 'state of exception'. As Stephen Humphreys explains, Agamben identifies the state of exception as a modern institution, with roots in the French Revolution, ascendancy during the First World War leading to dominance by the mid-twentieth century as the 'paradigmatic form of government' (2006: 677–678). Agamben posits that within this mode of governance, conventional politico-juridical structures acquire a status of permanence and the spatial arrangements remain continually outside the normal state of law (1998). In order to develop this logic further and construct an appropriate interpretative framework for the understanding of these crimes, several critics have looked to Achille Mbembe's thoughtful work on necropolitical power (Fregoso 2006; Wright 2011),[31] which in turn is predicated on Agamben's theories of 'Bare Life' and invested in Foucault's ideas on biopolitics (2004).[32] Likening this new global moment to a period he terms late colonial occupation and taking Palestine as the definitive example of such a necropolitical order, Mbembe utilizes the terms necropolitics and necropower

> to account for the various ways in which, in our contemporary world, weapons are deployed in the interest of maximum destruction of persons and the creation of *death-worlds*, new and unique forms of social existence in which vast populations are subjected to conditions of life conferring upon them

the status of *living dead* have argued that contemporary forms of subjugation of life to the power of death (necropolitics) profoundly reconfigure the relations among resistance, sacrifice, and terror.

(2003: 40)

Many of Mbembe's arguments resonate deeply with the experience of life in the border region and the naming of the sites inhabited by Juárez's poor as *colonias* (and therefore directly relating to his ideas about colonial occupation) seem to reinforce the connection even further. The writer Mario Bellatin, in reference to the opera-film he conceived along with composer Marcela Rodriguez, makes this connection explicit when he says,

I believe that there are images that, for me in particular, take me to other parts of the world. I think of Palestine. I feel that this is the horror of postmodernity. I don't know what to call it. I don't want to give it a name, but it is a very particular kind of horror. It is a horror that repeats itself in many parts of the world.

(Driver 2015: 133)

Central to Mbembe's thesis on necropolitics is the idea of a dynamics of territorial fragmentation and a 'splintering occupation' characterized by suburban enclaves and gated communities. The elaborate network of bridges, tunnels and other spatial mechanisms that separate and divide the various sub-sections of society in Juárez are a further factor here. At the heart of his envisioning of this new urban configuration is a proliferation in the sites of violence, in which space is divided along vertical and horizontal axes.[33] This violence, according to Mbembe, is no longer inflicted by the state per se; indeed the entity that is the state ceases to have any real relevance in such new configurations of power exchange; rather he argues that, 'a patchwork of overlapping and incomplete rights to rule emerges, inextricably superimposed and tangled, in which different de facto juridical instances are geographically interwoven and plural allegiances, asymmetrical suzerainties, and enclaves abound' (2003: 31). 'In this heteronymous organization of territorial rights and claims', Mbembe argues that 'it makes little sense to insist on distinctions between "internal" and "external" political realms, separated by clearly demarcated boundaries' (2003: 32). Mbembe does not consider gender as a factor in his analysis, nor do those theorists including Schmitt, Fanon, Foucault, Agamben and others from whose work much of his thinking is derived. In this regard, critical responses such as those from Geraldine Pratt (2005) and her rethinking of Mbembe's work to take account of gender is vital.[34] Sayak Valencia (2010) provides another example of a re-thinking of Mbembe's ideas in the Mexican context, seeking a conceptual vocabulary that can shed light on the specific matrices of gendered border violence. As Melissa Wright has shown in her illuminating analysis, 'gender is central to the violent dynamics linking the production of states to the reproduction of their subjects' (Wright 2011: 710).[35] According to Wright, the politics of death and the politics of gender go hand in hand, linked as they are to a new necropolitical order outside of what has been understood traditionally as a sovereign rule of law (Wright 2011: 710).

There is much to be gained from viewing the feminicidal violence in Juárez through the lens of necropolitics (Avila 2012).[36] The lives of women (and men) in this zone of exception are already being dictated by a global economy that exists in a supra-national sphere and where the vertical relationship between the state and its citizens has been severed. Through NAFTA – and here, perhaps we should recall the words of former US Drug Enforcement Agency (DEA) employee Phil Jordan when he called NAFTA a 'deal made in narco-heaven'[37] (cited in Staudt 2008: 12) – the state survives as part of an ultimately subordinate relationship to the unofficial powers of organized crime and global multinational companies. In this regard, impunity is a logical consequence and sovereignty, as has been pointed out, is reduced to the right to kill, a right wielded by actors, not traditionally conceptualized as part of state apparatuses. Mbembe's ideas have a chilling relevance for the analysis of violence against women and indeed the current wave of drug-related violence unleashed against inhabitants along the border and elsewhere in Mexico.

Ciudad Juárez: the monstrous city

We can see too the way in which ideas around necropolitics and the right to kill are fundamentally connected to location. Linked closely to this in terms of analytical frameworks for the understanding of *feminicidio* in the region has been the circulation of ideas around Juárez as a monstrous locale or a 'feral' city. Naval War College scholar Richard J. Norton's influential concept of the 'feral' city (2003) gained much traction among urban theorists in its description of highly disordered urban areas in the global South which are controlled by violent, non-state militias of various sorts.[38] Applying these ideas to Ciudad Juárez, Sullivan (2014) sees it as a product of an advanced, indifferent and destructive model of neoliberal urban development that enables a city to treble in size with no investment in infrastructure, security or any of the other paraphernalia of modernity. As Sergio González Rodríguez notes,

> Because of its asynchronous historical development, Ciudad Juárez contained an amalgam of pre-modern, modern and ultramodern zones that, around 1990, were being inserted into a new network of global economic relations and information societies. Conditions were set for the rise of the femicide machine.
>
> (2012: 20–21)

The physical topography of monstrosity in Ciudad Juárez has been the subject of much research, including those critics (Driver 2015; Volk and Schlotterbeck 2010; Monárrez Fragoso 2009) who draw attention to the ways in which the monstrous nature of the crimes is replicated through its geography. Alice Driver examines how citizens have marked public space as a way of countering an official narrative of silence (2015: 25) and her use of the term *ecotestimonio* is illuminating as she charts the ways in which the physical environment of Ciudad Juárez bears testimony to the crimes against women. An example of this is the proliferation of *lotes baldíos* or empty lots which function literally as containers for the bodies and figuratively as the spaces in which the excesses of cruelty in the city are displayed. Monárrez Fragoso (2009: 271) is similarly struck by the way in which the bodies are staged as part of the urban environment. Driver further asserts that

> It is difficult to imagine how integral such empty lots are part of the geography of Juárez without seeing a map of the city. These lots are not just on the periphery; they form a patchwork of no man's land all throughout the city and are often controlled by gangs. [. . .] Given that many women walk long distances during the early hours of the morning or late hours of the night to reach public transportation, these vacant lots represent danger zones.
>
> (2015: 110)

The 'geographies of danger' (González Rodríguez in Rodríguez 2009: 183) described here contribute to the idea of the city itself as a mechanism of violence, an idea that was quite pronounced among research conducted among Juárez citizens. Staudt notes in relation to a study by Pablo Vila, that citizens of Juárez spoke of their city invoking 'disparaging images: "banditry, gangs, homicides, drugs, and prostitution"' (Staudt 2008: 118). Similarly, she reports a very high awareness of violence from research conducted in 2005 among Juárez residents who

> talked about changing their everyday behaviour to avoid violence and/or kidnapping. More parents than usual walked children to school and back home; some husbands walked wives to the buses; some women wore slacks and/or running shoes to facilitate escape.
>
> (Staudt 2008: 64)

This awareness of danger exhibited by the subjects of this research demonstrates the extent to which notions of the 'bad' city became profoundly ingrained in the community.[39] This is further seen in the efforts from 2001 onwards to radically 'clean up' the city and which received its clearest manifestation in the Plan Juárez. This plan included, among its many lofty aims, 'the need to drastically reduce crime levels and to end the image of impunity' (Staudt 2008: 103). In posters circulated in late 2003 and early 2004, a clear message was communicated to residents through its pompous-sounding *Los 10 puntos de Juárez* [The Juárez 10-point plan]. Monárrez Fragoso shows how the authorities invited its citizens to share the message that '*Ciudad Juárez es y seguirá siendo una de las ciudades más dinámicas e importantes de América*' (2004: 12) [Ciudad Juárez is and will continue to be one of the most dynamic and important cities of America]. Furthermore, the authorities presented the figures of *feminicidio* as highly exaggerated, comparing them favourably to Philadelphia, for example (Monárrez Fragoso 2004: 12).

This discourse of monstrosity is clearly located in such overdetermined efforts on the part of the authorities. It is heavily present in media reportage and also the behaviour of local authorities. Indeed, the mayor of Juárez seems to invoke this implicitly when he said in 1998: 'I want Ciudad Juárez to go to sleep early; I want everyone to be home by 2:00 am' (cited in Tabuenca Córdoba 2010: 108–109).

As Tabuenca Córdoba points out, in pronouncements such as these, 'all that is associated with night's negative image and its black legend is constructed as though it were natural' (2010: 109), and the city itself is isolated for blame for the annihilation of its young women. This idea of Juárez as intrinsically monstrous has deep historical roots, and it is well acknowledged that cities along the US-Mexico border traditionally enjoyed a reputation for vice and lawlessness beginning with the tumultuous geopolitical separation of the two nations in 1848 (Tabuenca Córdoba 2010). The depiction of Juárez as a grotesque parody of the civilized modern city, then, is culturally embedded; indeed Monsiváis's description of the border region generally as the 'garbage can of Mexico' (cited in Staudt 2008: 118) is a conviction deeply held nationally, and the idea of the city itself as the problem is manifested at various points during the narrative arc of the feminicides.[40]

Victim-blaming and counter-narratives

Accompanying this seam of scholarship that isolated the globalization discourse in which all the problems of Juárez are based on the impact of late capitalism, Rosa Linda Fregoso categorized another interpretative strand regarding the *feminicidios* and which she termed the moralizing discourse in which, because of their behaviour, the victims are blamed for their own demise (2000: 138). This schematic division is also shared by other scholars of the phenomenon including Nancy Piñeda-Madrid (2011), Kathleen Staudt (2008), Edward A. Avila (2012) and Miguel López-Lozano (2010). The evidence for the systematic victim-blaming is overwhelming in media reportage, in oral histories, in testimony from the victims' families and in statements and pronouncements from the Chihuahua government and the mayors of Juárez and nearby towns. It is perhaps most effectively illustrated through the prevention campaigns that circulated in two local newspapers, *El Diario* and *Norte*, in Ciudad Juárez in 1995 and that exhorted women not to dress provocatively (Tabuenca Córdoba 2010: 101), as well as through oral testimonies by the families that exemplify the moralizing, judgemental and in most cases wholly inaccurate assumptions brought to bear on the cases of the young victims. Many studies (Nathan 1999; Wright 1999) confirm the frequency with which the explanation of the *doble vida* [double life] was offered by police as reason for the disappearances and murders. Indeed, the governing authorities urged families to keep track of their female members' whereabouts so as to discourage them from leading double lives, as workers or students by day and prostitutes by night Activist Esther Chávez Cano bluntly synthesized the mentality:

> The police say the dead women and girls were hookers, or that they were heroin-users. Their whole point is that it's somehow the fault of these girls. . . . We are supposed to believe these women are responsible for their own deaths.
> (cited in Wright 2011: 714)

Studies by journalists Washington Valdez (2005), González Rodríguez (2002) and Teresa Rodriguez (2007) also make plain the appalling treatment received by the families at the hands of the police. Indeed it was largely through the women's family members, primarily their mothers who began to mobilize and share personal stories about experiences with the police, that this official reaction to the victims began to be recorded (Staudt 2008).[41]

To counter such reportage, a wave of testimonies, protest marches and other events were organized, as described by Piñeda-Madrid who argues that due to the pressure from hundreds of national, international and transnational human rights groups, the state was forced to modify its account of these killings (2011: 31). This, she contends, led to a new strategy of damage limitation in which the authorities invested much energy in disputing the statistics and undermining the NGOs and other activist groups (2011: 31).[42] All of this occurred at the same time as the shocking deficiencies in the investigations of the crimes were emerging.[43] The assumptions that underpin the kind of victim-blaming discourse stemmed, of course, from rigid distinctions between public/private spheres, positing moral differences between the women who were safely ensconced at home (where they should be) and the women or the 'working girls' who were out roaming the streets at night (by definition transgressing patriarchal norms and therefore punishable by society) (Tabuenca Córdoba 2010). Nevertheless, the impact of the early victim-blaming strategy was clearly evident in how quickly the narrative took hold in the public imagination and, linked to scholars who were heavily invested in isolating globalization as the root of the violence unleashed in Juárez, it provided yet another convenient set of theories about women's lives as the inevitable by-product of a system that was morally bankrupt and patently misogynistic. In this sense, Fregoso neatly captures the polarizing extremes of debates around the killings: on the one hand, the widespread demonization of the victims inculcated through ideas about a *doble vida* and an academic emphasis on what was considered globalization's toxic impact on the other. Small wonder that with such differing accounts of the victims, the perpetrators, the causes and the criminal acts themselves, the bewilderment to which Hayman and Bell refer and mentioned earlier (Corona 2010) characterized to such an extent the public response as the citizens of Juárez struggled to comprehend the truths at the heart of Juárez's so-called women-killing spree.[44]

What was indisputably the case, however, was that by the end of the twentieth century, due to sustained activism and grassroots campaigns as well as international and national and regional media scrutiny, Ciudad Juárez (and the border region) was registered gradually, but nevertheless dramatically, as a space of violent death. Its visualization as a death site was further complicated by the feminized nature of death in operation. The erection of scores of pink crosses throughout Juárez and the desert region beyond (where many of the girls' bodies were dumped) bear poignant testimony to this as the appropriation of pink as the quintessential 'feminine' colour saturated the visual landscape. The campaign to erect crosses has been well documented, as have the attempts by activist

Guillermina Flores, sister of victim Sagrario González Flores, through the grassroots organization Voces sin Eco (Voices without Echo), to paint black crosses on a pink background throughout the city. This feminization of death in the borderlands has had a pronounced effect and it is interesting to note the extent to which borderlands violence is still frequently feminized even when the victims of violence are not necessarily female. While many of the pink crosses have disappeared or been removed from the cityscape today, they remain a potent emblem of feminicidal violence and continue to figure prominently in cultural responses to the violence as well as reportage and scholarship more generally.[45]

Continuing the journey through the narrative trajectory of the feminicides, it can be seen that through the mid-1990s, reports in Juárez impugned the victims' reputations. Subsequently however, with social movement activism and its criticism of police impunity, the tide turned in media reports on feminicide (Staudt 2008). This tide-turning had a significant impact in terms of feminist responses to the atrocities that insisted on more complex examinations of the context in which the murders are being committed. This, as well as the intervention of multiple feminist scholars (such as Marcela Lagarde y de los Ríos), saw the debate move to a more sustained campaign to take the issue out of Juárez and away from the border and to focus on the endemic nature of gender violence regionally, nationally and on a continental basis in the Americas. The global reach of this debate is also now indisputable as recent horrific cases in India, Argentina, and elsewhere exemplify.[46] Rossana Reguillo (2010, 2011), Sergio González Rodríguez, and many other writers in Mexico bear witness to the depraved extremes that define violence in the neoliberal age,[47] and it is certainly the notion of excess that has most shaped perceptions of the crime of feminicide globally. This idea is problematic in many regards; on the one hand, the excessive nature of death by feminicide – particularly in cases that involve mutilation, torture or multiple rape – ensures that the crimes continue to be visible in a global mediasphere. On the other hand, they can fetishize and sexualize the murders as the actions of 'sick' individuals, emphasizing the pathological dimension that feminist scholars have sought to avoid in favour of structural interpretations. In this regard, discussion that has now extended to feminicide in other areas of Mexico and elsewhere and what is denounced as the endemic nature of gender violence within Mexican society is welcome. Following this, the state most under the spotlight in recent years has been Edumex or el Estado de Mexico (Mexico State) in which, according to the Citizen Observatory, there were 263 cases of femicide in 2016 alone.[48] Sharing many characteristics with the border region in terms of the speed of its development as well as population growth (with large numbers of people displaced from other areas of Mexico), it has seen a concomitant rise in violence against women that is deeply troubling. As this book goes to press, further attention is directed towards the particularity of gender violence in this enormously urbanized state.

It can be seen from this overview of scholarship on feminicide the extent to which feminist critics like Marcela Lagarde y de los Ríos, Julia Monárrez Fragoso, Rita Laura Segato, Rosa Linda Fregoso, Alfredo Limas Hernández, Ignacio Corona, Patricia Ravelo Blancas, Héctor Domínguez-Ruvalcaba, Alicia Gaspar de Alba, Melissa Wright and Alicia Schmidt Camacho, among many others, have contributed to a more advanced understanding of the rise of feminicidal violence. They have crafted sophisticated interpretative frameworks that might pave a way towards justice for the families as well as suggesting innovative ways of shifting deeply embedded structural patterns that nurture cultures of violence against women. One of the most forceful analyses from within this body of work has been by anthropologist Rita Laura Segato, whose arguments about the destructive model of masculinity in operation can be used to try and understand the paradigmatic nature of the crimes.[49] Segato's transcultural perspective on masculinity speaks to this complexity when she qualifies it as

> a status that is only conditionally achieved and as such has to be reconfirmed with certain regularity throughout life. This is done through a process of tests or conquests and is above all dependent on the exaction of tribute from another that, because of the naturalized position in this status order, is perceived as the provider of the repertoire of gestures that nourish virility.
> (2010: 76)

She clarifies:

> I do not doubt that misogyny, in the strict sense of intense hatred of women, is common in the environment in which the crimes take place and constitute a precondition for their occurrence. Yet I am convinced that the victim is the waste product of the process, a discardable piece, and that extreme conditions and requirements for being accepted into a group of peers are behind the enigma of Ciudad Juárez. Those who give meaning to the scene are other men, not the victim, whose role is to be consumed to satisfy the group's demands to become and remain cohesive as a group. The privileged interlocutors in this scene are the peers: the members of this mafia fraternity, to guarantee and seal their covenant; its opponents, to exhibit power before their business competitors, local authorities, federal authorities, activists, scholars and journalists who dare to get mixed up in their sacred domain; or the victims' fathers, brothers, or male friends. These requirements and forms of exhibitionism are characteristics of the patriarchal regime of a mafia order.
> (2010: 77)

Here, familiar tropes from the narratives around *feminicidio* including the idea of female bodies as waste[50] are given a different inflection in the sense that the resulting violence is not so much dependent on their position within the globalized labour force but rather emerges from a toxic model of masculinity that ensures their demise as units of exchange between men. This is not to suggest of course that they are not linked; indeed many would argue that toxic models of masculinity are a central component of neoliberalism's entrenchment. Nevertheless, her insights accentuate an analysis of gender that goes beyond neoliberalism in the sense that while these economic regimes may account for the particular manifestation of violence, they can hardly be said to be its root cause. In this regard, it is important to underscore that gender violence – violence produced by men in positions of relative power towards women in varying positions of subordination – is a disturbing constant throughout all historical periods, all geopolitical contexts and across vastly different political ideologies. This emphasis, therefore, on the conditions within which virility is produced and sustained is an essential part of any interpretative toolkit in relation to the crime of *feminicidio*. Segato's work, which draws from her fieldwork in other parts of the globe including Brazil, offers a suggestive lens through which answers to the 'why' questions that plague the Juárez feminicides might be found.

This overview has sketched the many different contours that make up the narrative trajectory of *feminicidio* in Juárez: from the early victim-blaming through the focus on the *maquila* as the cause as well as the site of brutality, through to considerations that foreground the important interconnections of geopolitics, feminism, misogyny and the many other elements that shape and determine the pathways of the crimes. The messy picture that emerges from this account serves to underline the complex web of lies, counter-lies and contradictory assertions that plagued discourses around the crimes from the beginning. For example, while some of the victims were workers in the *maquiladoras* and many of the victims were found dumped in the desert, raped, often strangled, frequently tortured as well as sexually mutilated, many others were not (Fregoso and Bejarano 2010: 6). The fact that these were the circumstances of only some of the victims should not have detracted attention, however from full investigations into the circumstances of all of the deaths nor, it should be pointed out, should it have allowed or enabled dismissal of any cases simply because it had been shown that the so-called Juárez feminicide prototype did not hold true in all circumstances. José Pérez-Espino has shown the extent to which the media (local, national, international) including TV and print sources colluded in constructing powerful myths and stereotypes about the crimes and their victims/perpetrators that still persist (2004).[51] It is these convenient half-truths, however, that helped to cement the murders in Ciudad Juárez in the national and international imaginary and to a certain extent, those same half-truths prompted the extensive cultural responses to the phenomenon, as we shall see. What the cases of these women undoubtedly do share is the decided lack of action by the judicial authorities that has seen accusation and counter-accusation regarding corruption within the police forces, the federal agencies, the political system and endless speculation about the embedded nature of the 'out-of-control' drug cartels with the official authorities of the Mexican state. In this regard, impunity or *la impunidad* has become a code word for the failure of the apparatuses of officialdom to bring those responsible to justice.

In spite of, or perhaps because of all the interconnecting, bewildering and contradictory strands that make up the narrative of *feminicidio* in Ciudad Juárez, there was something about these stories of violent horror that struck a chord within Mexico and beyond. One could argue, of course, that this was as the result of lurid media coverage or a consequence of the public's fascination with torn or wounded bodies. Ileana Rodríguez vividly pinpoints what she sees as the way in which the prototypical murder pierced the imagination of the public, saying that 'The frequency of their appearances, the spectral character of the carriers of crime and bodies, the perversity of their mutilations, the age and profile of the abducted, tortured and murdered drives the essence of power into the open' (2009: 164). This idea of an essential power at the heart of feminicidal violence is key to understanding the grip it held on the public imagination and also to the outpouring of cultural expressions on the subject. Ignacio Corona argues that 'Unlike the wanton murder, the targeted assassination, or the proven crimes of a serial murderer, the reiterative killing of women suggests a political reading, as it defies the legal and political bases of society' (2010: 122). Feminicide, then, exposed these societal bases – the bedrocks of modern democracy – as at best fictions, or worse, as active conspirators in a world that extinguished women's lives in an endlessly repeating cycle of horror. Corona's insistence on a political reading means that it is now, at least, widely acknowledged that *feminicidio* is part of a global system of violence that is highly gendered. Its psychic, cultural and societal impact is yet to be fully determined, though in this regard Rodríguez describes how the crimes brought about the 'serious and perhaps irreparable tear of the social fabric' (2009: 164). As the following chapters will seek to show, it is through the cultural works produced as a response to the crimes – the dance, theatre, artworks, writing and film-making – that the tearing and wounding of the social fabric referred to by Rodríguez here, is most vividly communicated. It is on these cultural products that the remaining chapters will focus.

Notes

1 Robert Young's reference to violence, 'as a phenomenon that has a history', is cited by Simon Critchley in conversation with Brad Evans, 'Humans in Dark Times' (2017). For more information, see https://opinionator.blogs.nytimes.com/2016/03/14/the-theater-of-violence/ [Accessed 7 February 2018].
2 The Wikipedia entry – probably many 'ordinary' citizens' first entry into information surrounding the crimes – attests to the confusion over figures citing multiple sources and alerting the reader about accuracy and neutrality. Available at https://en.wikipedia.org/wiki/Female_homicides_in_Ciudad_Ju%C3%A1rez. [Accessed 7 February 2018].
3 Jacques Rancière offers valuable insights here into the process of counting, which according to his reasoning always involves exclusions: whereby the uncounted are outside of what he calls the 'police logic' or the ordering of society in certain 'ways of doing, ways of being, and ways of saying' (Rancière 1999: 29).
4 *Ni una más* is a documentary film directed by Alejandra Sánchez (2002) which features wide-ranging coverage of this particular crime. Sánchez's follow-up film project, *Bajo Juárez: la ciudad devorando a sus hijos*, with collaborator Antonio Cordero (2006), also features her story. Lilia Alejandra García Andrade's case remains open and continues to be the subject of attention. For more information, see, for example www.jornada.unam.mx/2003/11/29/038n1soc.php?printver=1&fly= [Accessed 7 February 2018].
5 In January 2012 the remains of 21 young women between the ages of 15 and 21 were found in a dry stream bed called Arroyo del Navajo, 80 miles southeast of the city in the Juárez Valley. These cases re-ignited international attention to feminicidal violence in Ciudad Juárez and the court cases that followed attracted huge media interest.

6 Emilio Gines Sanchidrian offers an overview of the judgement (2013).
7 During a class with students on the *Maestría de género* [Masters in Gender Studies] at the Universidad Autónoma de Ciudad Juárez (UACJ), I was struck by the extent to which the case of Airis continued to dominate their framing of *feminicidio*.
8 I am indebted to Alfredo and Myrna Limas Hernández for sharing their work on the subject.
9 By way of example of this cultural visibility, the Museo de Memoria y Tolerancia in Mexico City curated an exhibition titled *Feminicidio* en México: Ya Basta (January–May 2017). In the sphere of public protest, it is important to remember that there were mass marches against gender violence in April 2016. Organized under the hashtag #*vivasnosqueremos*, the march garnered international headlines.This public disquiet has continued and indeed there is continuing outrage surrounding various examples of *feminicidio*. Notable incidences in the summer of 2017 included the case of Lesvy Berlín in the National Autonomous University of Mexico (UNAM) in May 2017, the disembowelling of Mariana Joselín Baltierra in August and the rape and murder of eleven-year-old Valeria Teresa Gutiérrez Ortiz in June, both in Mexico State (Edumex).
10 The murder of Dutch citizen Hester van Nierop in 1998 caused international headlines and constituted one of Ciudad Juárez's more high-profile murder cases. In response to the brutal murder, the Hester Foundation was established by the victim's mother. For more information, see www.hester.nu/english/about-hester-foundation [Accessed 8 February 2018].
11 As Adriana Martínez points out, Monárrez Fragoso provides evidence that 60% of the victims of feminicide were actually natives to the State of Chihuahua (2005: 358) which 'contradicts the popular perception of the victims as "lonely migrants from the South"' (2011: 107).
12 There was a media outcry following the discovery of these bodies, and Gaspar de Alba attests to the swarm of media attention from the US in particular (2014: 139). It is these cases that led in turn to the investigation by the Corte Interamericana de Derechos Humanos which produced the critical judgement, already mentioned.
13 Cited by Gaspar de Alba and Guzmán (2010: 5). In line with this envisioning of the crimes, 'The Maquiladora Murders, Or, Who Is Killing the Women of Juárez?', was the title of a major international conference organized at the University of California, Los Angeles (UCLA) in 2003.
14 This was cited on the website of the organization Justicia para Nuestras Hijas 2003. Available at www.geocities.ws/justhijas/ [Accessed 7 February 2018].
15 It was nominated for a Pulitzer Prize and received a Texas APME First Place Award.
16 Sergio González Rodríguez continued to write about violence in Mexico until his untimely death in April 2017. His books, *El hombre sin cabeza* [The Headless Man] (2009) and *Campo de Guerra* [Battlefield] (2014) have been critically acclaimed. See also *The Femicide Machine* (2012).
17 Ensler visited Juárez for a solidarity rally at the state judicial police office in the city, and participated in honouring human rights and gender violence activist, Esther Chávez Cano, as one of 21 international leaders for the twenty-first century. See Rojas (2010) for a trenchant critique and contextualization of this event.
18 Animosity developed during this visit between Caraveo and the Amnesty International activists over numbers. This tension is further elucidated in Alicia Gaspar de Alba's account of the conference at UCLA in 2003 (2014) and by conference participants (personal conversation with Kathleen Staudt, 1 March 2017). For the most comprehensive account of grassroots organizing against *feminicidio* in Juárez, see Patricia Ravelo Blancas (2011).
19 This affirmation came from Lagarde y de los Ríos in response to questioning about the utility of legislation as a feminist strategic response in a context in which the law is demonstrably impotent. Research symposium, 'Globalización, violencias y

feminismos: Desafíos actuales, Reunión Binacional sobre Violencia de Género'. "*Cátedra Internacional Marcela Lagarde y de los Ríos*" y Seminario Binacional "*Diversidad sin Violencia*", 24–25 November 2016, Centro de Investigación y Estudios Superiores en Antropología social (CIESAS), Tlalpan, Mexico. It is generally recognized that the law has had little impact, due to lack of enforcement at different governmental levels. See the *Amnesty International* report (2009). Available at www.amnesty.org/es/press-releases/2009/01/mexico-dos-anos-ley-proteccion-mujeres-sin-impacto-20090129/ [Accessed 8 February 2018].

20 Lagarde y de los Ríos (Avila 2014) talks about the failure of this alert system in many states currently in an interview in *El universal*. Other measures in place to ensure that hate crimes against women are properly investigated include the *Fiscalía Especial para los Delitos de Violencia contra las Mujeres y Trata de Personas* [Office of the Special Prosecutor for Crimes against Women and People Trafficking, or *Fevimtra*] and *La Alerta de Violencia de Género contra las Mujeres* [Gender Violence Alert System]. On the specific failures of the alert system in Mexico State, see http://internacional.elpais.com/internacional/2013/07/20/actualidad/1374278479_808201.html [Accessed 8 February 2018].

21 Esther Chávez Cano, the human rights activist and founder of Casa Amiga in Ciudad Juárez, died from cancer in 2009. A collection of her papers and records of her activities is held by New Mexico State University and numerous memorial events were held to pay tribute to her legacy. A Cátedra or research agreement was established between the University of Texas, El Paso (UTEP); Universidad Autónoma de Ciudad Juárez (UACJ); Centro de Investigación y Estudios Superiores en Antropología social (CIESAS); Universidad Autónoma de México (UAM) and others to pay tribute to the theoretical and political contributions of Marcela Lagarde y de los Ríos whose primary contribution has been the insertion into public discourse of the term *feminicidio* with its insistence on the complicity of the state in the crime. Paula Flores has been honoured for her work in promoting justice for the victims of *feminicidio* in diverse ways; through the documentary film, *La carta* (2010), which charts her biography; and through the presentation of an artwork to her on the occasion of the research symposium '*Globalización, violencias y feminismos: Desafíos actuales, Reunión Binacional sobre Violencia de Género*', already mentioned (24–25 November 2016).

22 Alfredo Limas Hernández attests to the extent to which there was dialogue between the families and the Chilean sculptor Veronica Leytón whose finished piece, 'Rosa del Desierto', is located in the park (personal conversation, 28 February 2017).

23 In certain circles, it is axiomatic to assert that violence is somehow inherent to the Mexican psyche. Alan Knight (2013) takes issue with this viewpoint in a vigorously argued piece.

24 The idea of Juárez as a laboratory is explicitly referenced in work by US journalist and writer Charles Bowden, *Juárez: Laboratory of Our Future*. The image of devouring or consuming its young is also captured by Bowden's work and can be seen in the title of the 2006 documentary, *Bajo Juárez: La ciudad devorando a sus hijos* (Dir. José Antonio Cordero and Alejandra Sánchez). It is further exemplified by the opera-musical documentary film by Marcela Rodríguez about Ciudad Juárez based on Mario Bellatin's short story, 'Bola negra', the central character of which gorges himself alive. Bellatin explains this in the musical in a striking scene in which the children's choir sings the line 'they gorged themselves' over and over again. For more information, see Informador.mx, 4 January 2013. Available at www.informador.com.mx/entretenimiento/2013/428035/6/bola-negra-una-metafora-de-una-ciudad-que-se-devora-a-si-misma.htm. [Accessed 7 February 2018].

25 She argues that (2009: 55) the sub-standard working conditions ensure that Mexico's *maquila* regime has acquired the qualities and characters of the domestic economy outside of the home noting that the extension of these working conditions to both men and children simply exhibits the power of feminization as a strategy of globalization.

44 *Framing* feminicidio

26 Of interest here is the myth that *maquilas* employed predominantly female workforces, a point reinforced by Martínez-Fernández (2011: 48). As Sánchez Díaz points out (2011:125), by 2004, of a 250,000 strong *maquila* workforce, approximately half were men.
27 He writes about the labels of promiscuity and 'looseness' that attached themselves to the women *maquila* workers. (Sánchez Díaz 2011: 125).
28 See Victor Ballina, '*Padecen violencia familiar 10 millones de mexicanas cada día*', *La Jornada*, 27 October 2003, when he affirms that none of the murder victims owned cars. Public transport featured prominently in narratives around the feminicidal violence in Juárez from the arrest of a gang of bus drivers nicknamed *Los choferes* (The drivers) to the academic emphasis on poverty (and therefore lack of private transport) as a primary driving factor in the rise of violence against women.
29 Sánchez Prado urges us to interpret the logic underpinning feminicide as 'related to this imperative of compulsive modernization at the level of the body and its assemblages. The first logic that needs to be further theorized is therefore the (de)construction of the body of the citizen into a link in the chains of production of the post-fordist economy' (2016: 11).
30 Schmidt Camacho's work (2004, 2005, 2006) is particularly insightful on the biopolitical framework underpinning the crimes.
31 Roberto Esposito (2008) shares with Agamben the interest in the transition from biopolitics to thanatopolitics in the modern era. For a useful comparison, see Miguel Vatter (2010) and his article, 'Eternal Life and Biopower'.
32 For an excellent discussion of the application of some of these ideas to the Latin American context, see Abraham Acosta (2014) and Moraña and Sánchez Prado (2014).
33 In this account, Mbembe relies heavily on Frantz Fanon's brilliant analysis of the processes of colonization (2003). He is further indebted to the insights of Eyal Weizman, 'The Politics of Verticality' (2002).
34 The gender blindness of much biopolitical theory has been noted. In the book *The Agamben Effect*, Penelope Deutscher (2008: 55) asks whether it is 'possible to open a debate with Giorgio Agamben concerning the role of women's bodies in the politicization of life? What different inflections of life and of politicized life would result from an intermittent insertion 'born of women's bodies?' See also a critique from a legal perspective, Cerwonka and Loutfi (2011), and in the Mexican context, Janzen (2017).
35 For examples of the transition of Mbembe and Agamben's ideas to gender violence elsewhere in the world, see Geraldine Pratt (2005). Edward A. Avila also draws on research on 'gendered zones of death' in Turkey (2012: 45). See also Jiwani (2013) on cases of missing and murdered women in Vancouver.
36 For a fascinating and detailed study of the application of necropolitics to the examination of cultural products about *feminicidio* in Ciudad Juárez, see Avila (2012).
37 This is cited in a number of studies including Kathleen Staudt (2008) and Rafael Luévano (2012: 133).
38 For an analysis of Ciudad Juárez using the same analytical tools and contrasting ideas around failed, fragile and feral cities, see Sullivan (2014). The work of Robert Muggah (2014) and Paul Virilio (2005) is also helpful in understanding the wider framework within which cities are managed and controlled. Sergio González Rodríguez's essay, *The Femicide Machine* (2012), which combines a number of his previous studies but for the first time in English translation, offers a cogent analysis of the emergence of Ciudad Juárez as a monstrous locale.
39 See also Tabuenca Córdoba on the construction of perverse cities and Ciudad Juárez's stigmatization as a border town (2010: 96).
40 Since what is seen as the most intense period (2008–2012) of violence has passed, there have been major attempts to rehabilitate Ciudad Juárez's image abroad. This can be seen in the major feature by Sam Quiñones in *National Geographic* (June 2016), in which the narrative is that of a city with the worst of excessive violence behind

it. It can also be seen in the uproar generated in Ciudad Juárez by the release of the Hollywood film *Sicario* in 2015, in which the city is predictably portrayed as a site of grotesque violence. Indeed the mayor of Juárez, Enrique Serrano Escobar, led protests and a campaign to boycott the film and threatened to sue the producers.

41 Staudt writes, 'Mostly ignored and with their daughters' reputations impugned, mourning mothers began to share personal stories about their daughters' tragic deaths and their own experiences with the police: sent from office to office; asked for bribes to pursue cases; told that evidence was lost or misplaced; and worse yet, threatened' (2008: 81–82).

42 In addition, as already noted, there were publicity campaigns aimed at repairing the image of the city and an active downplaying of the murder figures. In this regard, the governor of Chihuahua, Francisco Barrio, insisted in 1995 that the murder numbers fell within normal ranges for the city (Diebel 1997). Moreover, there was general resistance to the idea of the violence as either a political or economic problem and sustained attempts to degrade the victims and their families.

43 Domínguez-Ruvalcaba and Ravelo Blancas provide an excellent overview of these deficiencies with reference to the report by María López Urbina, special prosecutor for women's homicides in 2004 in her review of over 150 cases (in Fregoso and Bejarano 2010: 184).

44 The denomination of the killing of women in Ciudad Juárez as a 'spree' or *asesinos de juerga* came from the FBI agent, Robert Ressler, charged with investigating the crimes (González Rodríguez 2002). Available at www.letraslibres.com/mexico-espana/las-muertas-juárez [Accessed 12 February 2018]. Julia Monárrez Fragoso also discusses the typologies of *feminicidio*, including 'spree-killings' in her study, *Trama de una injusticia* (2009).

45 Pink crosses were also utilized outside Mexico to signal *feminicidio*. Alice Driver notes that the symbol of the cross has proved a difficult image for some victims' mothers and quotes Juana Rodríguez Bermudez, mother of Brenda Berenice, who writes about her difficulty with them: 'I took down the crosses, I took down everything that had to do with God . . . I became very angry, I took down the crosses, I didn't want the crosses, I didn't want anything' (cited in Driver 2015: 128). The crosses are, nevertheless, hypervisible in cultural representations about Ciudad Juárez and violence and continue to be a site of contestation and ambiguity. For example, in advance of the visit by Pope Francisco in 2016, the crosses on the lampposts on the Pan-American highway were painted over. Many of them are also painted over in the town centre, illustrating the way in which the battle for visual control of the cityscape continues.

46 The gang rape and murder of a young woman, Jyoti Singh, on a bus in Delhi, India, in December 2012 captured international headlines and was one of many incidents that prompted a more global debate around gender violence, misogyny and rape culture. In Argentina the murder and impalement of sixteen-year-old Lucía Pérez prompted marches with the slogan, Ni Una Menos, throughout the country and elsewhere in Latin America in October 2016.

47 Given the extent to which *narcotráfico* and organized crime have come to define public discourse in Mexico since 2006, it is no surprise that a great number of writers have attempted and continue to attempt to unravel its complexities, reveal its roots, denounce its depravity and analyze its expressive forms. Writers of note within this large body of work include Cristina Rivera Garza (2013, 2015), Sergio González Rodríguez (2009, 2012, 2014), Ioan Grillo (2011), and Rossana Reguillo (2010, 2011).

48 The Comisión Mexicana de Defensa y Promoción de los Derechos Humanos registers a figure of 922 homicides with 'feminicidal characteristics' from 2005–2011.See http://cmdpdh.org/temas/violencia-contra-las-mujeres/alerta-de-genero-edomex/ [Accessed 12 February 2018]. Figures on feminicidal violence in Edumex in 2017 show a figure of 301. In addition, the widely publicized alert system (*La alerta de violencia de género contra las mujeres*) was declared in respect of the Estado de Mexico in 2015. For a comprehensive account, see Humberto Padgett (2012).

49 Segato's views about the toxicity of the model of *lo macho* are also explored in the work of feminist critics, María Luisa Femenías (2009) and Celia Amorós (2008). There is much scholarship on the topic of masculinity in the Mexican context. Héctor Domínguez-Ruvalcaba's work on institutions that produce violent masculinities is a case in this regard (2013) See also Gutmann (1996), Harris and Thakkar (2010), among others. For an illuminating reading of masculinity and violence in contemporary Mexico, see Biron (2012).

50 Geoffrey Kantaris offers an interesting analytical overview of the distinct ethics and morality of ideas of 'waste', 'trash' and 'garbage' (2016).

51 For a good discussion also on this aspect, see Sabine Pflegger (2015).

Works cited

Acosta, Abraham, 2014. *Thresholds of Illiteracy: Theory, Latin America, and the Crisis of Resistance*. New York: Fordham Press.

Agamben, Giorgio, 1998. *Homo Sacer: Sovereign Power and Bare Life*. Trans. by Daniel Heller-Roazen. Stanford: Stanford University Press.

Amnesty International, 2003. *Mexico: Intolerable Killings. Ten years of abductions and murders in Ciudad Juárez and Chihuahua*. Available at:

https://www.amnesty.org/download/Documents/104000/amr410272003en.pdf [Accessed 14 May 2018].

Amnesty International, 2009. *Mexico: A dos años de aprobada, ley de protección de mujeres sin impacto en estados*. 29 January. Available at: www.amnesty.org/es/press-releases/2009/01/mexico-dos-anos-ley-proteccion-mujeres-sin-impacto-20090129/ [Accessed 12 February 2018].

Amorós, Celia, 2008. *Mujeres e imaginarios de la globalizacion: Reflexiones para una agenda teórica global del feminismo*. Rosario, Argentina: Homo Sapiens.

Arriola, Elvia, 2010. Accountability for Murder in the Maquiladoras: Linking Corporate Indifference to Gender Violence at the U.S.-Mexico border. In Alicia Gaspar de Alba and Georgina Guzman, eds. *Making a Killing: Femicide, Free Trade and La Frontera*. Austin: University of Texas Press, 25–62.

Avila, Edward A., 2012. *Conditions of (Im)possibility: Necropolitics, Neoliberalism and the Cultural Politics of Death in Contemporary Chicano/a Film and Literature*. Thesis (Ph.D). University of San Diego. [online]. Available at: https://cloudfront.escholarship.org/dist/prd/content/qt7sh1f55b/qt7sh1f55b.pdf?t=ml5m0g [Accessed 15 February 2018].

Bajo Juárez: la ciudad devorando a sus hijas, 2006. [Film]. Directed by Antonio Cordero and Alejandra Sánchez.

Biron, Rebecca E., 2012. It's a Living: Hit Men in the Mexican Narco War. *PMLA*, 127 (4) (Oct), 820–834.

Bola negra: El musical de Ciudad Juárez, 2012. [Film]. Directed by Mario Bellatin with composer Marcela Rodríguez.

Bolaño, Roberto, 2004. 2666. Barcelona: Anagrama.

Carrillo, Jorge V., and Hernández, Alberto, 1985. *Mujeres fronterizas en la industria maquiladora*. Mexico: Secretaría de Educación Pública.

Cerwonka, Allaine, and Loutfi, Anna, 2011. Biopolitics and the Female Reproductive Body as the New Subject of Law. *feminists@law*, 1 (1). [online]. Available at: http://journals.kent.ac.uk/index.php/feministsatlaw/article/view/18/77 [Accessed 24 January 2018].

Corona, Ignacio, 2010. Over Their Dead Bodies: Reading the Newspapers on Gender Violence. In Ignacio Corona and Héctor Domínguez-Ruvalcaba, eds., *Gender Violence at the U.S.-Mexico Border: Media Representation and Public Response*. Tucson: University of Arizona Press, 104–127.

Deutscher, Penelope, 2008. The Inversion of Exceptionality: Foucault, Agamben, and "Reproductive Rights". In Alison Ross, ed., *The Agamben Effect*. Durham, NC: Duke University Press, 55–70.

Diebel, Linda, 1997. Macabre Murders Bewilder Mexicans: More than 100 Women Slain near Border Since 1993. *Toronto Star*, 7 Dec 1997.

Domínguez-Ruvalcaba, Héctor, 2013. *De la sensualidad a la violencia de género: La modernidad y la nación en las representaciones de la masculinidad en el México contemporáneo*. México: Centro de Investigaciones y Estudios Superiores en Antropología Social.

———, and Ravelo Blancas, Patricia, 2010. Obedience Without Compliance: The Role of the Government, Organized Crime, and NGOs in the System of Impunity That Murders the Women of Ciudad Juárez. In Rosa Linda Fregoso and Cynthia Bejarano, eds., *Terrorizing Women: Feminicide in the Americas*. Durham, NC: Duke University Press, 182–196.

Driver, Alice, 2015. *More or Less Dead: Feminicide, Haunting, and the Ethics of Representation*. Tucson: University of Arizona Press.

Esposito, Robert, 2008. *Bíos: Biopolitics and Philosophy*. Trans. by T. Campbell. Minneapolis: University of Minnesota Press.

Evans, Brad, and Critchley, Simon, 2016. The Theater of Violence. *The Stone*, 14 March [online]. Available at: https://opinionator.blogs.nytimes.com/2016/03/14/the-theater-of-violence/ [Accessed 12 February 2018].

Fanon, Frantz, 1991. *The Wretched of the Earth*. Trans. by C. Farrington. New York: Grove Weidenfeld.

Female Homicides in Ciudad Juárez. *Wikipedia Entry*. [online]. Available at: https://en.wikipedia.org/wiki/Female_homicides_in_Ciudad_Ju%C3%A1rez [Accessed 7 Feb 2018].

Femenías, Maria Luisa, 2009. Poder y violencia sobre el cuerpo de las mujeres. *Sociologias, Porto Alegre*, 11 (21), 42–65.

Feminicidio en México: Ya Basta, 2017. [Exhibition]. Museo de Memoria y Tolerancia, Mexico. Jan–Mar.

Foucault, Michel, 2004. *Society Must be Defended: Lectures at the Collège de France, 1975–1976*. Trans. by David Macey. Mauro Bertani and Alessandro Fontano, eds. London: Allen Lane.

Fregoso, Rosa Linda, 2000. Voices without Echo: The Global Gendered Apartheid. *Emergences: Journal for the Study of Media and Composite Cultures*, 10 (1), 137–155.

———, 2003. *MeXicana Encounters: The Making of Social Identities on the Borderlands*. Berkeley: University of California Press.

———, 2006. 'We Want Them Alive!': The Politics and Culture of Human Rights. *Journal for the Study of Race, Nation and Culture*, 12 (2), 105–138.

———, 2007. Toward a Planetary Civil Society. In Denise A. Segura and Patricia Zavella, eds., *Women and Migration in the U.S.-Mexico Borderlands: A Reader*. Durham, NC: Duke University Press, 33–66.

Fregoso, Rosa Linda and Bejarano, Cynthia, 2010. Introduction: A Cartography of Feminicide in the Américas. In Rosa Linda Fregoso and Cynthia Bejarano, eds., *Terrorizing Women: Feminicide in the Américas*. Durham, NC: Duke University Press, 1–44.

Gaspar de Alba, Alicia, 2014. *[Un]Framing the "Bad Woman": Sor Juana, Malinche, Coyolxauhqui and Other Rebels with a Cause*. Austin: University of Texas Press.

———, and Guzmán, Georgina, 2010. *Making a Killing: Femicide, Free Trade and La Frontera*. Austin: University of Texas Press.

Gines Sanchidrian, Emilio, 2013. La sentencia de la Corte Interamericana de Derechos Humanos en el Feminicidio del Campo Algodonero de Ciudad Juárez, como instrumento jurídico y búsqueda de propuestas para su ejecución efectiva. In Fernando M. Marino, Amparo Alcoceba Gallego y Florabel Quispe Remon, coord., *Feminicidio: El fin de la Impunidad Direccion*. Valencia: Tirant lo blanch, 281–295.

González Rodríguez, Sergio, 2002. Las Muertas de Juarez. *Letras Libres*, 31 December. [online]. Available at: www.letraslibres.com/mexico-espana/las-muertas-juárez [Accessed 8 February 2018].

———, 2009. *El hombre sin cabeza*. Barcelona: Editorial Anagrama.

———, 2012. *The Femicide Machine*. Los Angeles: Semiotext(e).

———, 2014. *Campo de Guerra*. Barcelona: Anagrama.

Glantz, Margo, 2003. También la muerte se maquila. In *Las muertas de Juárez*, special issue of Metapolítica, 61–62.

Grillo, Ioan, 2011. *El Narco: Inside Mexico's Criminal Insurgency*. London: Bloomsbury.

Guidotti-Hernández, Nicole M., 2011. *Unspeakable Violence: Remapping U.S. and Mexican National Imaginaries*. Durham, NC: Duke University Press.

Gutmann, Matthew C., 1996. *The Meaning of Macho: Being a Man in Mexico City*. Berkeley, London: University of California Press.

Harris, Christopher, and Thakkar, Amit, 2010. *Men, Power and Liberation: Readings of Masculinities in Spanish American Literatures*. London: Routledge.

Hester Foundation, 2014. Press Release, 24 January. [online]. Available at: www.hester.nu/english/about-hester-foundation [Accessed 8 February 2018].

Hu-Dehart, Evelyn, 2007. Globalization and Its Discontents: Exposing the Underside. In Antonia Castañeda, Susan H. Armitage, Patricia Hart and Karen Weathermon, eds., *Gender on the Borderlands: The Frontiers Reader*. Omaha: University of Nebraska Press, 244–260.

Humphreys, Stephen, 2006. Legalizing Lawlessness: On Giorgio Agamben's State of Exception. *The European Journal of International Law*, 17 (3), 677–687.

Janzen, Rebecca, 2017. Embodiment Envy: Love, Sex and Death in Pedro Ángel Palou's Con la muerte en los puños. In Ignacio M. Sánchez Prado, ed., *Mexican Literature in Theory*. London: Bloomsbury, 237–252.

Jiwani, Yasmin, 2013. 'Bare Life': Disposable Bodies, Race, and Femicide in the Trial Coverage of Vancouver's Murdered 'Missing' Women? *Synaesthesia: Communication Across Cultures*, 1 (4), 140–158.

Justicia para Nuestras Hijas, 2003. [online]. Available at: www.geocities.ws/justhijas/ [Accessed 7 Feb 2018].

Kantaris, Geoffrey, 2016. Waste Not, Want Not: Garbage and the Philosopher of the Dump (Waste Land and Estamira). In Christopher Lindner and Miriam Meissner, eds., *Global Garbage: Urban Imaginaries of Waste, Excess, and Abandonment*. Abingdon, New York: Routledge, 52–67.

Knight, Alan, 2013. War, Violence and Homicide in Modern Mexico. *Bulletin of Latin American Research*, 32 (1), 12–48.

Limas Hernández, Alfredo, and Limas Hernández, Myrna, 2016. *Trata de Personas y Violencia Feminicida: Factores de vulnerabilidad ante la desaparición de niñas y mujeres jóvenes en Juárez*. [Presentation]. Globalización, violencias y feminismos: Desafíos actuales, Reunión Binacional sobre Violencia de Género "Cátedra Internacional Marcela Lagarde y de los Ríos" y Seminario Binacional "Diversidad sin Violencia", 24–25 Nov. Centro de Investigación y Estudios Superiores en Antropología social (CIESAS), Mexico. (Unpublished).

López-Lozano, Miguel, 2010. Women in the Global Machine: Patrick Bard's *La frontera*, Carmen Galán Benítez's *Tierra marchita*, and Alicia Gaspar de Alba's *Desert Blood: The Juárez Murders*. In Héctor Domínguez-Ruvalcaba and Ignacio Corona, eds., *Gender Violence at the U.S.-Mexico Border: Media Representation and Public Response*. Tucson: University of Arizona Press, 128–151.

Luévano, Rafael, 2012. *Women-Killing in Juarez: Theodicy at the Border*. New York: Orbis Books.

Martínez-Fernández, Adriana, 2011. *Las mujeres del otro lado: A critique of the representations of Mexican women at the U.S.-Mexico border*. Thesis (Ph.D). University of Michigan.

Mbembe, Achille, 2003. Necropolitics. *Public Culture*, 15 (1), 11–40.

Monárrez Fragoso, Julia Estela, 2000. La cultura del feminicidio en Ciudad Juárez, 1993–1999. *Frontera Norte*, 12 (23), 87–117.

———, 2002. Serial Sexual Femicide in Ciudad Juárez: 1993–2001. *Debate Feminista*, 13 (25), 279–305.

———, 2004. Elementos de análisis del feminicidio sexual sistémico en Ciudad Juárez para su viabilidad jurídica. Presentation. International Seminar, *Feminicidio, Derecho y Justicia, Congreso de la Unión, LIX Legislatura, Mexico City,* 8–9 December. La Comisión Especial para Conocer y Dar Seguimiento a las Investigaciones Relacionadas con los Feminicidios en la República Mexicana y a la Procuración de Justicia Vinculada. Available online at: http://mujeresdeguatemala.org/wp-content/uploads/2014/06/Elementos-del-feminicidio-sexual-siste%CC%81mico.pdf [Accessed 14 May 2018].

———, 2005a. Elementos de análisis del Feminicidio sexual sistémico en Ciudad Juárez para su viabilidad juridical. In Feminicidio, justicia y derecho, ed., *Comisión Especial para Conocer y Dar Seguimiento a las Investigaciones Relacionadas con los Feminicidios en la Republic Mexicana y a la Procuración de Justicia Vinculada, Cámara de Diputados, H. Congreso de la Unión, LIX Legislatura, Mexico City,* 4–18.

———, 2005b. Las Diversas Representaciones del Feminicidio y los Asesinatos de Mujeres en Ciudad Juárez, 1993–2005. In *Sistema Socio-Económico y Geo-Referencial sobre la Violencia de Género en Ciudad Juárez*. Chihuahua: Propuestas para su Prevención. [CD-ROM]. Ciudad Juárez: El Colegio de la Frontera Norte, 353–398.

———, 2006. Violencia sexual en Ciudad Juarez. Percepción de trabajadoras y trabajadores de la maquila sobre el sistema de gobierno. In Patricia Ravelo Blancas and Héctor Domínguez-Ruvalcaba, eds., *Entre las duras aristas de las armas: Violencia y Victimización en Ciudad Juárez*. Mexico: CIESAS, Publicaciones de la Casa Chata, 21–54.

———, 2009. *La ciudad y el Feminicidio. Trama de una injusticia: Feminicidio sexual sistémico en Ciudad Juárez*. Mexico: El Colegio de la Frontera Norte y Miguel Ángel Porrúa.

———, 2010. The Victims of Ciudad Juárez Feminicide: Sexually Fetishized Commodities. In Cynthia Bejarano and Rosa Linda Fregoso, eds., *Terrorizing Women: Feminicide in the Americas*. Durham, NC: University of Duke Press, 59–69.

Moraña, Mabel, and Sánchez Prado, Ignacio, 2014. *Heridas abiertas: biopolítica y representación en América Latina*. Madrid: Iberomaericana/Frankfurt am Main: Iberoamericana.

Muggah, Robert, 2014. Deconstructing the Fragile City: Exploring Insecurity, Violence and Resilience. *Environment & Urbanization*, 26 (2), 1–14.

Nathan, Debbie, 1999. Work, Sex and Danger in Ciudad Juárez. *NACLA Report on the Americas*, 33 (3), 24–30.

Ni una mas, 2002. [Film]. Directed by Alejandra Sánchez.

Norton, Richard J., 2003. Feral Cities. *Naval War College Review*, 56 (4), 97–106.
Padgett, Humberto, 2012. *Las muertas del Estado: Feminicidios durante la administración mexiquense de Enrique Peña Nieto*. Mexico: Grijalbo.
Pérez-Espinoso, José, 2004. Homicidio de Mujeres en Ciudad Juárez: La invención de mitos en los medios y la lucrativa teoria de la conspiración. In Griselda Gutiérrez Castañeda, coord., *Violencia Sexista: Algunas Claves para comprender el Feminicidio en Ciudad Juárez*. Mexico: Universidad Nacional Autónoma de México, 85–102.
Pflegger, Sabine, 2015. *La construcción narrativa-mediática del Feminicidio en Ciudad Juárez: Frontera, Mujeres y Hombres Oscuros*. Vigo: Editorial Academia del Hispanismo.
Piñeda-Madrid, Nancy, 2011. *Suffering and Salvation in Ciudad Juárez*. Minneapolis: Fortress Press.
Pratt, Geraldine, 2005. Abandoned Women and Spaces of Exception. *Antipode*, 37, 1052–1078.
Quiñones, Sam, 1998. *The Maquiladora Murders*. Ms. May–June.
———, 2016. Once the World's Most Dangerous City, Juárez Returns to Life. *National Geographic*, June. [online]. Available at: www.nationalgeographic.com/magazine/2016/06/juarez-mexico-border-city-drug-cartels-murder-revival/ [Accessed 8 Feb 2018].
Rancière, Jacques, 1999. *Disagreement, Politics and Philosophy*. Trans. by Julie Rose. Minneapolis: University of Minnesota Press.
Ravelo Blancas, Patricia, 2011. *Miradas etnológicas: Violencia sexual y de género en Ciudad Juárez, Chihuahua: Estructura, política, cultura y subjetividad*. Mexico City: Universidad Autónoma Metropolitana, Ediciones Eón.
Reguillo, Rossana, 2010. Retóricas de la seguridad la in-visibilidad resguardada: violencias(s) y gestión de la paralegalidad en la era del colapso. In *Diálogos Transdisciplinarios en la sociedad de la informacion*, 33–43. [online]. Available at: http://fundacionredes.org/phocadownload/revista_ii.pdf#page=33 [Accessed 8 Feb 2018].
———, 2011. La narcomáquina y el trabajo de la violencia: Apuntes para su decodificación. *E-misférica*, 8 (2) #narcomachine. [online]. Available at: http://hemisphericinstitute.org/hemi/es/e-misferica-82/reguillo [Accessed 10 February 2018].
Rivera Garza, Cristina, 2013. *Los muertos indóciles: necroescrituras y desapropiación*. Mexico: Tusquets Editores.
———, 2015. *Dolerse: textos desde un país herido*. Mexico: Surplus Ediciones.
Rodríguez, Ileana, 2009. *Liberalism at Its Limits: Crime and Terror in the Latin American Cultural Text*. Pittsburgh: University of Pittsburgh Press.
Rodriguez, Teresa, 2007. *Daughters of Juárez: A True Story of Serial Murder South of the Border*. New York: Atria Books.
Rojas, Clara E., 2005. Voces que silencia y silencios que enuncian. In Pequeño Rodríguez and Báez Ayala, coords., *Género, feminismo(s) y violencias desde la frontera norte*, special issue of *Noésis*, 15 (28) July–December, 15–32.
———, 2010. The V-Day March in Mexico: Appropriation and Misuse of Local Women's Activism. In Alicia Gaspar de Alba and Georgina Guzmán, eds., *Making a Killing: Femicide, Free Trade and la Frontera*. Austin: University of Texas Press, 201–210.
Salzinger, Leslie, 2003. *Genders in Production: Making Workers in Mexico's Global Factories*. Berkeley: University of California Press.
Sánchez Díaz, Sergio Guadalupe, 2011. *Diálogos desde la subalternidad, la resistencia y la resiliencia: Cultura obrera en las maquiladoras de Ciudad Juárez*. Mexico: Universidad Autónoma Metropolitana. Ediciones Eón.

———, Ravelo Blancas, Patricia, and Melgoza Valdivia, Javier, 2015. Violencia en la ciudad, en el trabajo maquilador y la subjetividad de obreras y obreros en Ciudad Juárez. *El Cotidiano*, 191 (mayo–junio), 87–96.

Sánchez Prado, Ignacio, 2016. *War and the Neo-Liberal Condition: Death and Vulnerability in Contemporary Mexico.* [Presentation]. University of Florida, 15 September (Unpublished).

Schmidt Camacho, Alicia, 2004. Body Counts on the Mexico-U.S. Border: Feminicidio, Reification, and the Theft of Mexicana Subjectivity. *Chicana/Latina Studies*, 4 (1) (Fall), 22–60.

———, 2005. Ciudadana X: Gender Violence and the Denationalization of Women's Rights in Ciudad Juárez, Mexico. *The New Centennial Review: Interdisciplinary Perspectives on the Americas*, 5 (1).

———, 2006. Integral Bodies: Cuerpos Integros: Impunity and the Pursuit of Justice in the Chihuahuan Feminicidio. e-misférica, 3 (1). [online]. Available at: http://hemispheric institute.org/journal/3.1/eng/en31_pg_camacho.html [Accessed 10 February 2018].

Segato, Rita Laura, 2006. La escritura en el cuerpo de las mujeres asesinadas en Ciudad Juárez. In *Territorio, soberanía y crímenes de segundo estado*. Mexico: Universidad del Claustro de Sor Juana.

———, 2010. Territory, Sovereignty, and the Crimes of the Second State: The Writing on the Body of Murdered Women. In Rosa Linda Fregoso and Cynthia Bejarano, eds., *Terrorizing Women: Feminicide in the Américas*. Durham, NC: Duke University Press, 70–92.

Staudt, Kathleen, 2008. *Violence and Activism at the Border: Gender, Fear and Everyday Life in Ciudad Juárez*. Austin: University of Texas Press.

Sullivan, John P., 2014. Narco-Cities: Mexico and Beyond. *Small Wars Journal*, 31 (Mar). [online]. Available at: http://smallwarsjournal.com/jrnl/art/narco-cities-mexico-and-beyond [Accessed 7 Feb 2018].

Tabuenca Córdoba, María Socorro, 2010. Ghost Dance in Ciudad Juárez at the End/Beginning of the Millenium. In Alicia Gaspar de Alba and Georgina Guzmán, eds., *Making a Killing: Femicide, Free Trade and La Frontera*. Austin: University of Texas Press, 95–119.

———, and Monárrez Fragoso, Julia Estela, 2007. *Bordeando la violencia contra las mujeres en la frontera norte de Mexico/Violence Against Women in the Mexican Northern Border*. Ciudad Juárez: Colegio de la Frontera Norte.

The Vagina Monologues by Eve Ensler, 1996. [Play].

Valencia, Triana Sayak, 2010. *Capitalismos gore y necropolítica en México contemporáneo*. Tenerife: Editorial Melusina.

Vatter, Miguel, 2010. Eternal Life and Biopower. *The New Centennial Review*, 10 (3) (Winter), 217–249.

Virilio, Paul, 2005. *City of Panic*. Trans. by Julie Rose. Oxford: Berg Books.

Washington Valdez, Diana, 2005. *La cosecha de mujeres: Safari en el desierto mexicano*. Mexico: Océano.

———, 2006. *The Killing Fields: Harvest of Women*. Burbank: Peace at the Border.

Weizman, Eyal, 2002. The Politics of Verticality. *OpenDemocracy*, 25 April [online]. Available at: www.openDemocracy.net.

Wright, Melissa, 1999. The Dialetics of Still Life: Murder, Women and the Maquiladoras. *Public Culture*, 11 (3), 453–473.

———, 2006. *Disposable Women and Other Myths of Global Capitalism*. New York: Routledge.

———, 2007. Femicide, Mother-Activism and the Geography of Protest in Northern Mexico. *Urban Geography*, 28 (5), 401–425.

———, 2009. Justice and the Geographies of Moral Protest, Environment and Planning. *Society and Space*, 27, 216–233.

———, 2010. Paradoxes, Protests, and the Mujeres de Negro of Northern Mexico. In Rosa Linda Fregoso and Cynthia Bejarano, eds., *Terrorizing Women: Feminicide in the Americas*. Durham, NC: Duke University Press, 312–330.

———, 2011. Necropolitics, Narcopolitics, and Femicide: Gendered Violence on the Mexico-U.S. Border. *Signs*, 36 (3) (Spring), 707–731.

2 Sacrificial screams

Excess in Àlex Rigola's stage adaptation of 2666

Ciudad Juárez theatre

In 1998, an image featuring the corpse of a sixteen-year-old girl who had been kidnapped, raped and murdered, taken by the Ciudad Juárez-based photographer Jaime Bailleres, was included in the book *Juárez: Laboratory of Our Future* by the North American writer Charles Bowden.[1] In reference to a local newspaper's refusal to publish the image, Bowden explains that, 'The reason for this decision is very loud: the lips of the girl pull back, revealing her clean white teeth. Sound pours forth from her mouth. She is screaming, and screaming and screaming' (Bowden 1998: 67). The image's attempt to capture the sounds made by a victim of feminicide before death problematizes the very essence of the ethics of representation that haunts artistic responses to the crimes.[2] This chapter focuses on the screaming of another feminicide victim, the character of Rosita Méndez, played by Catalan actor Alba Pujol in Àlex Rigola's stage version of Roberto Bolaño's novel, *2666*. Arguing that the scream forms part of a trope of sacrifice that, in its most excessive performative dimension, permeates discourses of *feminicidio* on the US-Mexico border, I analyze the ways in which feminicidal pain is inscribed in both the sound and movement of Pujol's agonizing body.

The sacrificial screams uttered by Pujol resonate throughout the multiple plays, performances and theatre pieces that have been staged as a response to the Ciudad Juárez outrages, both within the city and beyond. They are echoed at theatre festivals in Latin America and elsewhere: through digital interventions; avant-garde theatrical expression and what might be seen as more traditional dramatic approaches. There is a rich body of theatre about feminicide in the State of Chihuahua and the region surrounding the city of Ciudad Juárez. Indeed, it is arguably in the realm of theatre that the most profound cultural interventions about *feminicidio* in Ciudad Juárez have been forged. Evidence for this can be seen in the many community theatre projects based in the city and wider region that have creatively reimagined the horrors of feminicide while attempting to stage public acts of mourning and commemoration. The theatre anthology, *Hotel Juárez: Dramaturgia de feminicidios* (2008) amply showcases the range of techniques, modalities and expressive forms utilized by playwrights when exploring the inhumanity, pain and injustice associated with the crimes. Durango playwright Enrique Mijares's play, *Jauría* [Pack of Dogs], uses a cast of animals to depict Ciudad Juárez's underworld, and playwrights Virginia Hernández (*La ciudad de las moscas*) [City of Flies] and Demetrio Avila (*Sirenas del río*) [Mermaids of the River] effectively employ mythical, biblical and topographical symbolism to convey the deeper truths that sustain structural, economic and symbolic violence against women. The work emanating from activist, actor and director Perla de la Rosa's company Telón de Arena through the plays *Antígona: las voces que incendian el desierto* [Antigone: The Voices That Set the Desert on Fire] (2005)[3] and *Justicia negada* [Justice Denied] (2013), has also been significant in projecting the complex lived realities for women in Ciudad Juárez to audiences outside the region. In tune with this approach, Susana Báez Ayala's scholarly work on theatre from the US-Mexico border region (2006) signals the way in which the work of Chihuahuan playwrights exposed the culture of fear that had taken hold in Juárez. She pays tribute to the contributions of regional or state-wide theatre and its impact on local grassroots, on policy and policing and on public discourse. Focusing in particular on the dramaturgs Victor Rascón Banda, Edelberto Galindo and Antonio Zuñiga, she emphasizes their role as part of a broader civil insurgency [*insurgencia civil*] (Báez 2006: 261), drawing attention to theatre's powerful political charge.

It is difficult to summarize the dynamic body of theatre and performance that exists about *feminicidio* in Juárez, and there are many plays that have dealt with the violence in provocative and disturbing ways, like for example Galindo's *Lomas de Poleo*, which opens with the rape of its victim, Maty, on stage.[4] Performance pieces on the subject have often embraced the opportunity to dissolve divisions between activism and art, and marches, along with other collaborative exercises of protest, have frequently taken this form.[5] *La procesión de las muertas de Juárez* was held in Mexico City and drew attention to the cultural politics of spectacle in collective demonstrations against gender violence. Other examples of the blurring of lines between traditional theatrical modes and more experimental interventions include the virtual protest organized by the Teatro del Disturbio Electrónico [Theatre of Electronic Disturbance], in which more than eleven thousand people from fifty-nine different countries participated and which consisted of large-scale sending of protest letters to the Chihuahua government and the Organization of American States (OAS). It constituted an innovative example of artivism, commonly understood as a way of combining conventional modes of activism with creative energy and expression.[6] Aligning the local and the global in an innovative way, the project sought to establish a platform of digital solidarity in the pursuit of justice.

Alongside some of the examples of theatre production in Ciudad Juárez as well as the wider state of Chihuahua, already noted, there are many other striking interventions by Mexican playwrights or actors based elsewhere in the country and committed to theatre as a mode of political resistance and consciousness-raising.[7] The play, *Mujeres de arena* [Women of Sand], by Humberto Robles, is probably the best known theatrical response to the crimes and has been performed in multiple locations nationally and internationally.[8] A poignant example of documentary theatre, it utilizes the testimony of four different feminicide victims interspersed with poetic fragments and has been staged and re-staged extensively to critical acclaim. Cristina Michaus's one-woman show *Mujeres de Ciudad Juárez* [Women of Ciudad Juárez] (2001) constitutes another interesting example of a theatrical response and it has been performed in numerous locations.[9] Beyond Mexico, on the international stage, there have also been some remarkable forays into the world of theatre conceived as a particularly expressive vehicle through which to explore the horrors of *feminicidio*.[10] These include productions by the Welsh playwright, Jill Greenhalgh, whose project, *The Acts – Vigia*, consisted of a series of devised performances directed, staged and presented in collaboration with groups of young female performers in the UK and internationally.[11] Eve Ensler makes reference to the feminicidal violence in the monologue 'Memory of Her Face', part of her famous hit play *The Vagina Monologues*, which has been performed throughout the world since 1996.[12] Caridad Svich's psychedelic, experimental play *Iphigenia Crash Land Falls on the Neon Shell That Was Once Her Heart* (2004) rather controversially utilized male actors in drag to portray *maquiladora* workers when it was performed in Chicago,[13] and the Ecuadorian, Mercedes Hernández, whose piece titled *Murmullos en el Páramo* [Whispers in the Wasteland] integrated poetry, testimony and narrative in a dance performance. In all of these examples the expressive, experiential terrain of the body on stage works to re-calibrate understanding of ongoing questions of agency, action and subjectivity. Taken together, they might be seen as a kind of collective mutiny in the way imagined by Báez Ayala when she speaks of civil insurgency (2006: 261). Perhaps the experiential quality of theatre as well as its formal versatility lent it a particular urgency in terms of bringing home the 'truths' of *feminicidio* in Ciudad Juárez. Robles invokes the Brechtian concept of 'useful theatre' [*teatro útil*] as a way of drawing attention to the place of theatre within activism and the struggle for justice for victims of feminicide. Following this, he names theatre as the modality through which the concept of *emergencia* can best be transmitted. The complex and politically fraught positioning of actors/characters as complicit witnesses to the horrors they reveal signals theatre's particular role in foregrounding the bodily horror invoked by a feminicidal violence that is all too often characterized by dismemberment and bodily defilement as well as rape. Through this theatre, the dead themselves are frequently positioned as agents in the revelation of their pain and suffering, a concept explored by Joseph Roach, in his evaluation of those performative instances and processes of substitution (labelled surrogation in his study), that come to fill the voids left by death and destruction in the circum-Atlantic world (1996). This concept is vividly taken up by Àlex Rigola and Pablo Ley in their approach to the staging of *2666*. In the next section, I would like to briefly outline the background to the Rigola production and explore the particular challenges of a project that conjoins two giants on the Hispanic cultural stage, Roberto Bolaño and Àlex Rigola, in a re-imagining of the former's internationally acclaimed novel.[14]

Roberto Bolaño's 2666

In a chapter on the work of Valeria Luiselli and innovation in the contemporary Mexican novel, Emilio Sauri remarks that 'we never read a novel like *2666*; we always read Roberto Bolaño's *2666*' (2017: 339). And in a similar, if rather playful take on the same theme, Brett Levinson observes that, '*2666* refers to nothing but itself, to the Bolaño *ouevre* it names' (2009: 187). These comments serve to underscore the way in which it has become impossible to separate the text(s) of *2666* from the layers of myth-making, media hype, literary and publishing history that subtend the figure of Roberto Bolaño.[15] Roberto Bolaño's celebrity status in the Spanish-speaking world was secured long before his premature death at the age of fifty in 2003, but his positioning as literary legend continues to grow apace with each passing year. He straddles the Hispanic literary world in interesting ways: born in Chile, living for a period in Mexico and latterly in Catalonia, Spain, he is undoubtedly the first pan-Hispanic writerly 'brand', even if he has only ever really been considered Latin American in the Spanish literary marketplace. He thus represents a publishing phenomenon that was quite unprecedented in Hispanic literature, 'a successful case of genius and glamour, coolness and literary power' (Villalobos-Ruminott 2009: 194). In the English-speaking world, he is similarly applauded and celebrated, as well as being subject to strategic positioning by a range of cultural exchange brokers albeit in different ways.[16] Indeed, ever since his novel, *Los Detectives Salvajes* [*The Savage Detectives*] was eagerly embraced by the publishing house Farrar, Straus and Giroux (FSG) and reviewed with enthusiasm, in some cases likening its author to García Márquez (Stavans 2007), he has been enthusiastically welcomed by an English-language market and is now a bona fide literary cult figure. As Daniel Crimmins writes, 'Meet the Kurt Cobain of Latin American literature' (2007); he has also been compared to Jim Morrison, Jack Kerouac and other tormented souls of contemporary North American culture (Castellanos Moya 2009). Viewed in this English-language market light, he is constructed as the archetypal *poète maudit* in the Romantic tradition and represents a fitting antidote to the coterie of Latin American left-leaning *boom* writers, such as Gabriel García Márquez and Carlos Fuentes, about whom he was so utterly scathing.[17]

The blurb advertising a book on Bolaño and his authorial positioning within the spectrum of 'World Literature' (Birns and De Castro 2017), describes *2666* as 'a monumental global five-part masterpiece'. Published in Spanish in 2004, a year after the death of its author, and in English in 2008, the title of the manuscript was rescued from Bolaño's desk after his passing and there is famously no reference to it in the novel.[18] Moreover, there is the fraught question of its genesis to consider. According to Jorge Herralde, Bolaño's long-standing collaborator, confidant and publisher, Bolaño's wish was that it would be published as one novel, but in the face of his imminent death, it seemed to him to be more economically viable as five separate books (some short, some medium-sized) so as to better provide for his young family (Echevarría in Bolaño 2004: 1122). Indeed, as Brett Levinson reminds us, 'bound and unbound, *2666* is as much about its binding as it is about its content' (2009: 185). This then is a book about death by an author who was dying, and it is divided into five loosely connected sections. The section that concerns us in this chapter is Part IV, '*La parte de los crímenes*' [The Part about the Crimes], which is almost three hundred pages long and comprises an epic reconstruction of the murders of women in a fictionalized border town called Santa Teresa in forensic detail. The murders are narrated chronologically, describing in the cold, hard language of the forensic report the locations where each body was found, the state of decomposition and cause of death, among other aspects. The narrative continues in this vein, a ruthless catalogue of brutality told in a mode that remains mostly detached. As the bodies mount up and all the investigations come to nothing, one critic reminds us that 'it is hard to think of a grislier sequence in literature' (Skidelsky 2009). Multiple critics have grappled with the cruelty and complexity of 2666; it remains the only so-called serious novel of literary worth to examine the cases of feminicidal violence in Ciudad Juárez and is furthermore easily the best-known literary text on the topic. For this reason alone, it continues to deserve scholarly attention.

My concern with Bolaño in this chapter, then, forms part of my aim to (re) assess his magnum opus, 2666, as part of a much wider corpus of cultural responses to the historical incidences of feminicide in Ciudad Juárez from the early 1990s onwards. I am not interested in adding my voice to the already crowded field of scholarship on the novel, nor am I drawn to studying the novel from within an exclusively literary studies framework. Rather, I am compelled to study the theatre version of 2666 as a cultural response to the Juárez atrocities alongside many other theatrical performances on the subject. In this regard, and as noted already, while there is a rich body of theatre about feminicidal violence in Juárez which has had a particular impact for its regional audiences, this piece of work speaks to the transnational appeal of the subject matter. Indeed, given its global reach, 2666 makes for an illuminating test case to study the mechanisms of representation employed in conveying the horrors of feminicidal crime. I nevertheless experience a significant degree of unease in dedicating extended space to Bolaño who is such a polarizing figure in many ways. Furthermore, I am sympathetic to views held by many that critics should prioritize work that emerges from the communities that suffer from *feminicidio* firsthand. Added to this, of course, is the fact that this study focuses on a theatrical interpretation of the degradations of feminicidal violence by a white European male speaking from a position of cultural power, albeit inflected with the complexity of language positioning and the politics of minorising that comes from staging work in a Catalan theatre, however central it may be to that cultural stage. However, I would argue that it is also politically necessary to study the ways in which narratives about *feminicidio* in Ciudad Juárez are re-imagined and re-presented by other voices, including those of white Europeans. What is more, the novel has become something of a touchstone in global consciousness about feminicidal violence in Ciudad Juárez, and it is no exaggeration either to say that it approaches something akin to an international literary 'talking point'. Ultimately, 2666 – like few other cultural products before it or since – has managed to pierce global consciousness and this means that it remains the vehicle through which the majority of readers outside of Latin America learn about feminicidal violence and Ciudad Juárez. In this regard, whatever one's view of Bolaño's literature – and there are many conflicting views – 2666 has shone a light on the crime of *feminicidio* in a way that is absolutely unparalleled in the cultural sphere. It, thus, demands our attention.

Àlex Rigola's 2666

The novel was transposed to stage by Àlex Rigola, director of the renowned Teatre Lliure in Barcelona (2003–2011), working in collaboration with Pablo Ley. It was shown as part of the Festival de Barcelona Grec in 2007 and later in other key places on the international theatrical circuit including the Schaubühne Theatre in Berlin in 2014.[19] Àlex Rigola, while not as internationally well-known as Bolaño, is frequently positioned in cultural discourses in similar ways as something of an *enfant terrible*. A master of controversy and particularly interested in the avant-garde European theatre tradition, he is drawn also to political engagement and human rights activism, like Bolaño, and has a history of adapting great European theatre classics, especially Shakespeare, to the Catalan stage.[20] Rigola also has a track record of representing graphic violence on stage, as seen in his productions of *Titus Andronicus* (2001) and *Richard III* (2005), for example. Rigola's ambitious adaptation of 2666, a production lasting more than five hours, received what might be described as almost ecstatic reviews from the national and regional press and also numerous prizes.[21] The play makes use of many of the motifs that characterize Rigola's theatrical interpretations including the prominence of screens along with the use of multimedia devices and remediation techniques. Indeed the third section, '*La parte de Fate*' [The Part about Fate] takes place entirely inside a box projected onto a screen. Given these staging decisions, it is interesting to scrutinize its generic transition from a text that is so hermetic and embedded within a discourse of literariness to the stage of a public theatre, such as the Teatre Lliure in Barcelona. Multiple shifts are discernible in the novel's transition to the stage, as might be expected from any attempt to 'translate' or adapt a novel of approximately 1,100 pages. My analysis does not concern itself particularly with the differences between the written and performative texts,[22] and is more interested in the processes of adaptation, an approach that involves looking at the product as part of a lateral rather than a vertical relationship with the original (Hutcheon 2013: xv). Having due consideration for the complexity of the adaptation process and the history of criticism in this area, nevertheless it should be clear that it is in Parts III and IV where Rigola most emphatically rejects the source text to explore alternative mechanisms of representation. Indeed, as Rigola outlines, it is the fourth section of Bolaño's novel, when he 'exhaustingly enumerates' (Pearson 2014) the murders of women from the fictionalized town of Santa Teresa (standing in for Ciudad Juárez), which constitutes the biggest trial for stage adaptation.[23] Playing with the desert space as an 'infinite cemetery' (Pearson 2014), the description of the 108 bodies in Part IV of the novel is translated to the stage via a masterclass in compression in the form of one body, the character Rosita Méndez, played by actor Alba Pujol. Part IV commences with a short exposition by four policemen over a corpse and is followed by a monologue enunciated by Klaus Hass, the presumed murderer (played by Joan Carreras). Following this, another sequence of actions occurs, constructed around three central axes of representation, all of which happen at the same time.

The first axis of action involves the corpse itself which 'wakes up' and re-enacts her rape, torture and death conveyed through a series of noises, shouts, moans and a few coherent words. Some of the only ones that can be made out are an anguished, stuttered, *'por favor'* [please]. After three minutes, Beethoven's Seventh Symphony[24] begins to play during which a sound battle commences between the two noises, one singular, agonizing (the body), the other in synthesis and harmony (the soundtrack). The action in this sequence – which lasts approximately ten minutes – culminates in silence: the silenced body returns to its inert state while the music crescendos gradually to a climax. The scene is bookended by the policemen who re-enter the stage at the end to tell a series of clichéd *'chistes machistas'* [sexist jokes], and that function to illuminate the wider culture of symbolic, verbal and systemic violence which enables the murder of women to continue. Their words chime in our ears here as we listen uneasily to the jokes, many of which, in similar cross-cultural versions, we have heard before.

The second axis of interest involves a giant screen which appears during the sequence of screams and on which is projected an extended list of victims' names. In this regard at least, it might be argued that the stage version resembles the novel but with several distinctive characteristics. The list of names projected here is not fictional or fictionalized but rather is taken from *El informe de la Comisión Nacional de Derechos Humanos en México* [Report from the National Commission for Human Rights in Mexico] presented on 25 November 2003. Furthermore, Santa Teresa, the fictionalized town of the novel has disappeared and appears here very explicitly as CIUDAD JUÁREZ. This shift in focus situates us within the real socio-historical context as well as signalling a clearly demarcated testimonial dimension to the project, a dimension I shall return to in the last section of the chapter. The third feature to highlight in the adaptation of Part IV to the stage is the strategic placement of multiple pink crosses (approximately sixty) as a gesture of inscription, commemoration and mourning. Resembling the process of sowing (of seeds), it also serves to foreground the stage play as a live testimonial act, bearing witness to violent death.

Excessive death

It hardly requires stating that the action in this section might be categorized as excessive: excessive in the names that spill over the frames of the screen; excessive in its use of noise and screaming; excessive in the tortured and tortuous gestures of the female victim that accompany our contemplation of the chaotic multiplication of the crosses. As Rodríguez Serrano affirms: '2666 *resulta, por cierto, una obra excesiva desde casi todos los puntos de vista*' (2008: n.p.) [2666 is an excessive work from almost every point of view]. In the next section, I would like to filter my exploration of the meanings generated by the writhing body of Pujol through related frames, all of which hinge on the central analytical category of excess. Excess, of course, as articulated as philosophical concept, and centrally

60 Sacrificial screams

associated with the work of Georges Bataille, has always been concerned with the relationship between death and power. Moreover, excess permeates the ideas of necropolitics and necropower so crucial to discussions about the violence of contemporary Mexican society and is a key part of Mbembe's theorizations on the subject, examined in Chapter 1.[25] Following these articulations of the concept, I consider the sexual excess and discourses of hysteria in this adaptation of 2666 in so far as they relate to the representation of the female body; excess conceived as sacrificial noise, through which the victims of *feminicidio* are ultimately offered up; and finally a consideration of the excessive nature par excellence of the genre of testimony, to which the stage version so clearly belongs.

The writhing body

The first layer of signification that concerns us with this adaptation of 2666's '*La parte de los crímenes*' [The Part about the Crimes] involves the displacement of the novel's 108 dead bodies and their transformation into a single cadaver that starts to come alive: to writhe and move as well as shout and scream. Naked, blood-spattered and seemingly re-enacting her own rape and death, this is a portrayal of a female body as chaotic and out of control. Unable to contain its own movement, the portrayal of the female body as somehow outside of the natural order, inviting control, domination and destruction, connects to a complex gender politics present

Figure 2.1 Photographic image from Part IV of the stage version of Roberto Bolaño's 2666 performed at Teatre Lliure in Barcelona in 2007

Directed by Àlex Rigola. Image courtesy of Teatre Lliure.

in both texts that is decidedly problematic. In this section, I would like to unpick some of the levels of meaning generated by this representation as a way of teasing through the dynamics of authorial responsibility as well as audience response.

On one level, we might view the incoherent enunciation of Rosita Méndez as in alignment with feminist critic, Luce Irigaray's paradigm of *parler femme*, defined as an incoherent, chaotic discourse, rooted in feminine sexuality and whereby the hysterical/the irrational *is* the feminine. According to Irigaray (1987), this is due to the position of women within the patriarchal order which fixes her as a subject that is in-between, or in the process of becoming: 'Her economy is that of the *between-subjects*, and not that of the subject-object relation' (1987: 211). Of course, the feminist force of Irigaray's argument is derived from her harnessing of this inbetweenness as a way of registering female agency and power. There are risks, too, however, with this privileging of meaning held by the female body as well as in the female body, a body that is figured as inherently unstable. Schmidt Camacho – while making no reference to Irigaray – also notes the problematic way that discourses about Mexican women's bodies 'have come to inhabit the space between humanity and non-humanity, between subjectivity and absence' (2004: 32).

This depiction of Rosita Méndez places her in a long and pervasive tradition of constructions of the hysterical, uncontrollable female body that is worthy of further exploration. Indeed, we might link this more widely to a technique of representation of the 'third world' woman, that frequently posits her as outside discourse both reified and conceptually frozen within a monolithic framework in which she is constructed as irrational and not quite fully human. That these dominant constructions frequently invoke ideas around poverty, precarious existence as well as racialized and highly gendered labour practices means also that they evoke an image of a third world woman who inhabits a murky threshold between life and death. Schmidt Camacho writes eloquently about this dimension in the context of international solidarity campaigns about *feminicidio*, saying that they 'are undermined by their inability to displace, or their collusion with, dominant constructions of poor Mexican women as bodies made for violence' (2004: 22). Arguing cogently that this reification of subjectivity can potentially undercut or destabilize networks of feminist coalition, Schmidt Camacho's insights are a timely reminder of the ethical and artistic risks associated with the representation of bodies from the 'elsewheres' of the world, an issue that is subject to further exploration in Chapter 3. She is right to draw attention to the ethics surrounding the presence of the body in discourses about *feminicidio* and to warn us that 'the proliferating figure of the dead body, which invites identification with their wounded femininity after death', may in fact also 'displace any recognition of poor women's subjectivity in life' (2004: 37). Elsewhere she states that

> precisely because the *feminicidio* entails a social fantasy that certain women are made for killing, that is, to be used up to the point of extinction, those invested in stopping the crimes must not collude with any depiction of vulnerable Mexican women as less than fully human, less than fully alive.
>
> (2004: 24)

Arguably, Rigola's decision to use the body in this way does leave him open to charges of collusion in the way referenced by Schmidt Camacho and, furthermore, opens him up to accusations of the kind of re-victimization that is so loudly critiqued by activists and grassroots organizations in the region.[26] In this way, Rigola participates as one more voice in a line of representational approaches that seeks meaning *from* and *in* the tortured and discarded female body. And while we might accept that he seeks to disrupt dominant constructions of victims, he can also be accused, quite legitimately if not a little ungenerously, of simply re-inscribing the body of the poor Mexican woman as spectacle.

In connection with this, it is important to underscore the extent to which masculine dominance and violence, frequently portrayed against women, are central tropes of Catalan performance spectacle since the 1970s and throughout the *destape* period from 1975 onwards. Both the groundbreaking work from Albert Boadella's Els Joglars and the experimental Fura dels Baus feature striking examples of violence against women.[27] Moreover, naked female bodies are very much a feature of the work of key directors Calixto Bieito and Àlex Rigola throughout the 1990s and the early part of the twentieth century, as are graphic representations of rape and sexual violence against women set against an active focus and exploration of masculine performance.[28] This theatre has relied extensively on ideas of excessive femininity in which female subjects are presented as intrinsically othered and through which the 'crazy' woman is fetishized and placed centre stage. There is also, however, a strong tradition of theatre from and about Latin America in Catalonia populated by Latin American directors and actors. This theatre also tends to place the body at its epicentre though in different ways. We can see this, for example, in the work of *Teatro de los sentidos* [Theatre of the Senses], located in Barcelona and founded by the Colombian anthropologist and playwright Enrique Vargas, in which the body is central to its evocation of female subjectivity.[29] This preponderance of physicality is further exemplified by the theatre collective, *Teatro laboratorio* [Theatre Laboratory]. Also based in Barcelona and made up of collaborators from Chile, Argentina, Mexico, France and Spain, the tour-de-force physical performance by the Catalan actor Julia Rabadán in the company's production of *Altazor*, based on the Chilean poetry of Vicente Huidobro, is derived from the same approach to the expressive terrain of the female body as a vehicle for the communication of horror.[30] We should also recall that the year 2006 saw the first Festival of Latin American Theatre in Barcelona showcasing work by the company, Fábrica Teatro who presented *Fábrica 7*, a play based on female factory workers in a bean canning factory in Brazil and therefore shedding light on the gendered work practices that are accused of producing violence so similar to those explored in the Juárez cases. Linked to this is an unequivocal ethical commitment by a number of diverse companies to a performative practice inspired by and rooted in Augusto Boal's ideas about a 'theatre of the oppressed'. For example, the Brazilian practitioner and theorist's revolutionary methodology underpins the work of the company, uTOpía Barcelona, and also Pa'tothom, a theatre practice that is linked explicitly to the defence of Human Rights using artistic tools developed by Boal and the work of Colombian playwrights, Santiago García and Enrique Buenaventura.[31]

These examples serve to illustrate the extent to which a performative practice – rooted in the body and emerging from Latin American revolutionary politics – is firmly embedded within the rich theatre traditions of Barcelona. We can see too how this connects to Rigola's more recent work which seems to want to move to a space beyond language, a privileging of the body *as* narrative as well as the body *in* narrative.[32] This dimension is further linked with a trend towards the use of surrogation in recent Catalan theatre, identified by Helena Buffery (2017) and understood as the process whereby 'live actors stand in for the dead', seen by performance anthropologists as one of the principal means by which communities ensure their continuity and/or legitimise change' (2017: 866). It is here that Rigola's construction of the *feminicidio* victim might be seen to adhere to '[p]revailing international discourse about the *feminicidio*' that 'has shown itself so willing to recirculate the construct of poor Mexican women as the living dead, natural extensions of a harsh border landscape that cannot support meaningful existence' (Schmidt Camacho 2004: 25). In this regard, the movement of the actor Alba Pujol, while surging beyond the rigidly linguistic contours of the novel, locks it into another problematic discourse of the essentialising, exoticizing and othering of women from the so-called third world. With this in mind, it is possible to trace a line of continuity between 2666 and a diverse set of theatre practices in the region that includes the excessive portrayals of femininity and graphic representations of rape and sexual violence typical of Els Joglars or Calixto Bieito and what you might term a social, anthropological or ethnographically inflected theatre tradition in Catalonia that has been particularly invested in certain narratives about political violence in Latin America.[33]

The noise of pain

We have seen the ways in which the movement of the actor's body in this part of Rigola's interpretation of 2666 might be usefully located within a tradition of representation of the female body as incoherent and hysterical. I would like to turn my attention now to the noises she emits – also incoherent – that might easily be incorporated within that same interpretative framework. However, rather than view them as some extension of the hysterical, irrational body, I think that the noise and screaming of the female corpse in this part of the production might be more usefully linked to a trope of sacrifice and located within a specific Mexican historiography. Here, while the noise is ultimately extinguished on stage, it is done in such a way that it reinstates the body's centrality, subjectivity and agency. In this way too, we can chart a connection with the renowned Argentine playwright Griselda Gambaro, another figure linked to Barcelona, having taken up residence there between 1977 and 1980 when she found herself in exile from Argentina's 'Dirty War'. Gambaro's repertoire also involves extensive use of the female body as a vehicle for storytelling, often in graphic ways. What is of interest in her work, however, is the way she aligns the female body with ideas around agency, action and resistance.[34] We could argue that the same patterns of alignment between body, action and agency are discernible in the anguished jerks of Alba Pujol's body, a body that acquires power, agency and, most critically, life (if only momentarily). It is necessary here also to register the agency and artistry of the actor involved in bringing about this portrayal of the dying female body. While it is clear that meanings are etched on her body, it is also imperative to recognize that she is central to the creation of those meanings through her performance.[35] In this way the body's movement tells the unspeakable, unrepresentable story, eloquently illustrating the ways in which the horrors of *feminicidio* are ultimately always inscribed on and in the body. As the mother of Lilia Andrade perceptively notes, 'when we found her, my daughter's body told of everything that had been done to her' (cited in Schmidt Camacho 2004: 36). In this next section, I would like to consider some of these registers of meaning and in particular the articulation of pain through noise and sound, especially screaming.

We have already claimed Rigola's 2666 as a production that is reliant on excess in terms of the execution of its mise-en-abyme. Whereas in the novel the bodies are converted into inert things lacking life and identity except for their fictitious names, here the body is resuscitated in an explosion of pain and anguish. Its excessive quality draws me to the work of French theorist Georges Bataille. Bataille's theory of what he calls 'General Economy', founded on the violent consumption and exchange of flesh (among other commodities), is developed by him at length in the first volume of *The Accursed Share*. Waste is the governing principle (Hegarty 2000) in this riveting text, in which Bataille describes the coping strategies devised by human cultures to confront the profuse excesses of modern life and which include the performance of the waste of excess objects, produce and human life. As theorized by Bataille, excess implies a profound loss – loss of life, of meaning, of the body, of being. Paul Hegarty writes in his insightful analyses of *Noise Music* that 'Bataille's notion of excess is not about goodness, about communion or some sort of realization of nothingness: it is a principle of evil, apathetic evil. Excess cannot be about gain, but instead involves loss: the loss of self' (Hegarty 2006: 2). In this way, excess becomes a vehicle through which the most extreme loss of selfhood might be communicated. But as well as the connection with loss, Bataille's linking of excess with noise is also of interest here; 'Noise is offered as that which cannot be appropriated, mastered, made musical – whilst all the while occurring in the place of music, without allowing dwelling in that place' (Hegarty 2006: 1).

These thoughts are curiously apposite in the context of the body's performance on stage in 2666 where the noise, as already explained, quite literally occurs in the place of music, competing with it, strangling it and ultimately being defeated by it. Indeed, we might argue that the sexualized, screaming female body portrayed here participates in a gendered battle of sound that pits the hysterical, stuttering female voice against the ordered noise of Beethoven's symphony, or in other words, against a figure who embodies the epitome of Western white male cultural privilege. A feminist Irigarayan reading would see this as a way of the female voice talking back or over the dominant voice of the European classical tradition of music. Or we might see it as a modality of performance that seeks to annul both the excessive literariness of the source text (which, lest we forget, consists of over 1,100 pages) as well as the verbal overload of the stage production where the sheer volume of words enunciated exceeds five hours and twenty minutes. In this sense, the actor's voice also does battle with the parallel discourses of literary language and the Western classical music tradition. Furthermore, the distinction here between the active, dynamic voice that struggles against the potent music of Beethoven and the naked body, bloody and hysterical, incapable of rational movement, reminds us of the pertinent analysis of Elaine Scarry (1985) in her examination of the effects of state torture on citizens' bodies. In her brilliant study, Scarry alerts us to the violent divorce between body and voice at the moment of forced suffering and pain. Viewed through this lens, the voice may seem hysterical and incoherent in the same way as the body, but in fact, actually functions as a vehicle of communication. While this communication might not be categorized as rational (in the Cartesian sense of the word), it is certainly coherent in the sense that it forms a unified whole, accumulating power (in the sense of volume) and also presence in the room (in the sense of its total occupation of sonic space). Thus we can see how the voice, and the moans, noises and screams it emits, affectively structures that story not through imaginary identification so much as through sensual assault. In this way, the entanglement of the different dimensions of *feminicidio* resonate through the different noises produced by Pujol's body as well as they are expressed through other modes.[36]

Bataille's illuminating reflections on the nature of noise as excess explain that noise is 'always that which is excluded as waste' (Hegarty 2006: 2). Following this logic, the anguished noise in 2666 therefore functions metonymically as the waste product that is the body of the impoverished feminicide victim in Juárez. And waste, as we have seen, is centrally connected to discourses about disposability and globalization that have inflected narratives about *feminicidio* since the beginning. The actor's body then functions as a sign of waste, a contaminated body, superfluous material that must be expelled. Moreover, '[a]s the exclusion is brought under control (e.g. by ears adjusting at a performance, or by getting some familiarity with a recording), noise fades, so must endlessly be resuscitated, to be killed again, over and over' (Hegarty 2006: 2). This vividly captures the excruciating experience of listening to the screaming body of Pujol/Méndez in the sense that just when you think you have adjusted, it resuscitates itself again with renewed vigour and power. Furthermore, the idea of 'killing over and over' alerts us to the way that excess is embedded within the act of feminicidal violence itself which is frequently marked by its excessive, repetitive nature including not only death, but torture, dismemberment or mutilation. Joseph Roach, in his influential study, reminds us that performances always 'propose possible candidates for succession. They raise the possibility of the replacement of the authors of the representations by those whom they imagine into existence as their definitive opposites' (1996: 6). A similar process may be discerned here and indeed is central to the power of this portrayal because replacement is so fundamental to the logic of *feminicidio*, which unfolds through its numbing and repetitive concatenation of destroyed female flesh, one narrative replacing another in an unbearable cycle of death.[37] Most importantly, Bataille contends that noise represents 'always

66 *Sacrificial screams*

a momentary sacrificial experience' (cited in Hegarty 2006: 2), and it is on this notion of sacrifice that I would like to concentrate now as it is a recurring trope employed when describing, narrativizing or representing the feminicidal crime wave in Ciudad Juárez.

Screams of sacrifice: the daughters of Coyalxauhqui

Bataille, as Roach notes, was drawn to images of Mesoamerica for suitable 'dramatizations of the terrors of excess' (1996: 123) and he devoted a significant section of his essay *The Accursed Share* to a discussion of Aztec sacrifice. In a section titled 'Sacrifices and Wars of the Aztecs', he sees his ideas perfectly synthesized in their ritualized performances of waste expulsion signified through their reliance on human sacrifice.[38] For Bataille, the sacrificial victim *is* the 'accursed share':

> The victim is a surplus taken from the mass of useful wealth. And he can only be withdrawn from it in order to be consumed profitlessly, and therefore utterly destroyed. Once chosen, he is the accursed share, destined for violent consumption.
>
> (1991: 59)[39]

There is an eerie parallel we may draw here between Bataille's assertions about sacrificial victims being chosen and early narratives about the feminicidal crimes in Juárez that alleged that the victims too were chosen from catalogues.[40] Sergio González Rodríguez identifies the *maquila* as a sacrificial culture in his powerful essay on *The Femicide Machine*.[41] Making reference to the 'repetitive, reflective, compulsive, integrating, stylized, collective and generative tasks' undertaken by the workers, he speaks of the 'ritualization of labour' adding that the workers 'allow themselves to be assimilated into the productive apparatus in an endless flux of sacrifice and self-sacrifice' (2012: 29–30). He also explores the notion of sacrificial violence in depth in his study, *El hombre sin cabeza* [The Headless Man]. I have already signalled the ways in which the alignment of symbolically violent gendered labour practices with feminicidal killing practices (the exploitation/ extermination parallel) is problematic on a number of levels (Schmidt Camacho 2004; Fregoso 2003). Here what is of interest is the way in which both of these practices – the body used for labour and the body used for killing – are identified as sacrificial in the sense that they involve the loss of personhood and subjectivity. Elsewhere, scholars Patricia Ravelo Blancas and Alfredo Limas Hernández invoke the idea of a sacrificial civilization as a way of explaining the feminicidal impulse in Juárez (2002) and Diana Washington identifies a 'culture of sacrifice' [*cultura del sacrificio*] in the city (2007).[42]

It is in the work of Alicia Gaspar de Alba, however, that the idea of sacrifice receives its most complete consideration in the context of the feminicidal crimes that assailed Ciudad Juárez. In her chapter 'Re-Membering the Sacrificed Daughters of Ciudad Juárez',[43] Gaspar de Alba traces a line from Coyolxauhqui, the Aztec goddess of the moon, who was famously dismembered by her brother

Huitzilopochtli, to the female bodies discarded in the deserts beyond Juárez. Citing insights from Gloria Anzaldúa who 'interpreted Coyolxauhqui as "the first sacrificial victim" of the Aztec patriarchal military state that developed under Huitzilopochtli's reign as the patron god of the Mexica' (2014: 132), Gaspar de Alba looks to various versions of the myth, particularly the pictographic records from the Florentine Codex (1561–1565), generally acknowledged to be recorded by Bernardino de Sahagún (2014: 131). For Gaspar de Alba,

> Coyolxauhqui is the first femicide victim in Mexico, her ritual beheading and dismembering reenacted on the tortured female bodies on the U.S.-Mexico border, such as the victim found in a public place in Ciudad Juárez in October 2009, with her head inside a plastic bag beside the torso.
> (2014: 132)

Ultimately, Gaspar de Alba advocates for a view that sees the murders as

> 'a form of ritual blood sacrifice, a modern enactment of the core patriarchal myth of Goddess murder' as explained by Caputi who points 'to examples of other patriarchal cultures across the world that encourage and condone misogynistic rituals such as witch hunt, widow burnings, public stonings of "bad women" and genital mutilations of girls'.
> (cited in Gaspar de Alba 2014: 171)

Central to discussions about sacrificial culture is the notion of substitution explored through the idea of the 'monstrous double' (Girard 1977), or surrogation as theorized by Roach (1996). René Girard's work on sacrifice resonates here, in particular, his contention that sacrificial violence is a kind of societal expenditure necessary to preserve its internal coherence and meaning (1977). Accompanying this is the parallel – strongly present in certain narratives about the crime – between the killings in Ciudad Juárez with satanic ritualistic practices. Drawing on the work of Davíd Carrasco on the sacrificial customs of the Aztecs (1999), Gaspar de Alba interprets the way in which the killings, 'replicate the overtly sacrificial goal of taking a victim's energies and making them the killer's own' (Gaspar de Alba and Guzmán 2010: 286). Sacrifice is also part of the lexicon employed when interpreting the current wave of extreme violence in Mexico. Samuel Steinberg (2016) takes the issue of sacrifice to task in his fascinating reading of cultural texts about the massacre at Tlatelolco and Sánchez Prado criticizes the reliance of the testimonial mode on a sacrificial logic that normalizes mass acts of killing (2016). Reading through these illuminating interpretations, we may discern many of the narratives, explanations and myths that have circulated since the beginning about feminicidal violence in Ciudad Juárez.

This association between the feminicidal victims and indigenous goddesses from Mexican history, however, might also be viewed as a re-positioning of the victims, removing them from a discourse in which they are the fossilized third world waste products from the periphery and reinstating them at the centre of a historical narrative that places the sacrifice of worthy citizens at its centre. By this I mean that Aztec historiography displays evidence of its practice of the selection of people for sacrifice believing that those people needed to be worthy of the Gods (Carrasco 1999). Linked to this was the worldview that sacrifice was a 'good' death (along with war and childbirth). I do not mean to suggest in any facile way that the deaths of women in Ciudad Juárez can be interpreted as positive acts nor enter into a debate about the morality surrounding the belief systems of the Aztec community.[44] I simply wish to underscore the ways in which the idea of sacrifice, one that is consistently linked to the victims in legal, journalistic and cultural narratives about the crime, has a long historical trajectory that is replete with meanings about individual self-worth and the relationship between individual and community.[45] In this sense, it represents a counter-narrative to those discourses that see the feminicidal victims as collateral damage from a periphery zone utterly disconnected from the centres of power charged with their protection (the Mexican State or the US or other multinational employers in the case of *maquila* victims). In this regard, a sacrificial reading positions them differently. A further connection can be detected here. We have seen how Giorgio Agamben's ideas about 'bare life' (1998) and biopolitics have been deployed to explain the border as some kind of death zone or state of exception, and defined by Mbembe as a necropolitical order (2003). This reliance on the biopolitical in understanding the border region can, however, potentially occlude readings that allow for agency and resistance by the communities who call it home. Taking this into account, it is possible to read the noisy sacrificing of the body in Rigola's *2666* as a reversal of the biopolitical – that doctrine rooted in the life of *homo sacer* [sacred man], 'who may be killed and yet not sacrificed' (Agamben 1998: 8). Following this line of argument, the victims of feminicide in Juárez have been excluded from the polis, deemed unworthy of sacrifice, and are thus disposed of with impunity. Reinstating them as sacrificial victims loudly displaces Agamben's idea of homo sacer and provides a valuable counterpoint to the widely circulating idea of the victims as waste products.

Testimonial excess

It is now time to consider the other representational axes in the analysis and, in this regard, it has been clear from the beginning that the series of bodily movements and noises are interconnected with other aspects of the scene. These include the increasingly frenzied placing of crosses by the rest of the actors alongside the accelerated presentation of real victims' names on a screen behind the stage, set against the deepening crescendo of the Beethoven symphony. Here not only do the names spill over the frame of the screen both above and below, but also the letters of the names become illuminated on the surface of the crosses and on the body of the inert woman. In this way, she becomes bathed in a pink light as though she were one more cross. The physical marking of the stage with the traces of crosses brings me to consider the testimonial dimension of Rigola's theatre spectacle that is clearly signalled on various levels and at various points.

First, it can be seen in the change from the fictitious name, Santa Teresa as well as the refusal to use fictitious names, already mentioned. Instead, the list of names is communicated via a screen bearing the title 'DOCUMENTACIÓN REAL DE MUJERES MUERTAS EN CIUDAD JUÁREZ DESDE 1993' [Real records of dead women in Ciudad Juárez since 1993]. The engagement by Rigola with the subject matter is also left in no doubt and can be seen in the interview reproduced in the programme notes in which he describes his visit to the city. During the week of his stay, from 7 in the morning until 10 at night, he photographed what he described as 'the pulse of the border town' and further insists that some of those photographs be displayed in the theatre before, during and after the performances (Tramullas 2007: n.p.). In this way, the textual activism also overflows or goes beyond the stage to occupy the theatre space and the programme notes. In addition, there is a need to focus for a moment on the context of the performance's timing in 2007 and the total indifference of the Mexican authorities to the feminicidal crimes as they found themselves in the middle of a campaign of unanticipated, unprecedented and unparalleled ferocity against organized crime brought about by the escalation in hyperviolent activities on the part of the major drug cartels locked in combat with the Mexican state. In this context, it might be affirmed that any act of *concientización* or critical consciousness in relation to the forgotten crimes of Juárez contributes to the resuscitation of this issue at the national level in Mexico. Furthermore, the act of planting of crosses again in the metaphorical earth of the Catalan theatre stage may be interpreted as an act of re-inscription that accompanies the list of real victims' names projected on screen.

The third element to consider here involves the production context of Barcelona and in this regard, it is important to note that the year of the first performance of 2666 coincides with the introduction of the Ley de Memoria Histórica [Law of Historical Memory] in Spain. This took place, as is well-known, against the backdrop of a highly charged debate about the disappeared and forgotten victims of the Civil War and the legacy of Franco in broader terms. In the realm of theatre, Alison Guzmán (2012) identifies the presence of '*muertos vivientes*' [the living dead] as a unifying theme across a significant number of plays by contemporary playwrights, from José Sanchis Sinisterra to Jerónimo López-Mozo, Itziar Pascual, Juan Copete and Laila Ripoll, who return persistently to the question of the Civil War's continuing impact on the present. 2666 is but another production in which a figure who might be described as part of the living dead, raises the spectre of historical injustice and the violation of human rights. What is more, in Catalonia, given its Republican past and where the debate about the law of historical memory was particularly tense, it should be noted that the Catalan government introduced a legislative instrument, the Memorial Democrático at the end of 2007, which outlined explicitly its commitment to the fight against fascism and totalitarianism and to a project of the recuperation of memory derived from a bedrock of plurality.[46] Roberto Bolaño is centrally involved in this discourse about the recuperation of the past and famously appears as a character in Javier Cercas's celebrated testimonial novel about the war and its legacy, *Soldados de Salamina*, and which forms part of the extended literary corpus on this topic. Indeed, perhaps it is when viewed within the context of its reception in Catalonia in 2007 that we can best appreciate how the theatre adaptation might be situated as a living organism in interrelationship with a particular environment. In this regard, the competing narratives about the deaths of women in Ciudad Juárez, historical memory in Spain and the nuances of that debate refracted in Catalonia, as well as the recurring spectre of the Holocaust and a European history of atrocity (that is laid bare in section 5), operate in a kind of polyphonic chaos. We might do well here to recall Linda Hutcheon when she challenges us to look at cultural adaptation the way we would look at biological adaptation (2013: xvi) and the extent to which the adapted product 'takes' to its new environment and is accepted there. I ask myself, therefore, what meanings do Rigola's honest and 'real' confrontation with the violation of human rights in Mexico generate in a wider debate about human rights, forgetting and re-inscription in Catalonia and the Spanish state?

It can be seen even from this brief outline, the extent to which the testimonial or activist dimension saturates the adaptation, an activism that is, not surprisingly, present in many other cultural responses to the crimes. Of course, there are many who might question the activism and commitment of a director who spent such a short length of time in the city. The literature on activism is wide-ranging and can be defined in different ways. In Latin America activists are often referred to as 'militantes' and the broader literature points to the feelings of melancholia and exhaustion that can accompany lengthy campaigns.[47] It is certainly the case that many artistic practitioners immerse themselves in the environment they are hoping to intervene in and that this immersion is a critical part of the artistic/creative process. However, their methods are not the same as those invested either in social science research or those who commit energy and time to work for non-governmental organizations (NGOs) or grassroots organizations. Linked always to political action, artistic interventions or activism frequently sit uneasily on the threshold between the search for aesthetic innovation and the necessity for political change; indeed, arguably it is this time-honoured tension that animates artistic and cultural creativity in this sphere. Rigola is not an activist in any traditionally understood sense of that term though social responsibility was at the heart of much of the work produced by Teatre Lliure during his directorship exemplified most poignantly, perhaps, by its engagement with the refugee crisis. In line with Rigola's activist trajectory then, this production is energized by a sense of urgency and makes certain demands of its audience, insisting (through excessive sensual assault among other mechanisms) that they become informed and engaged. The excessiveness, already noted, is also absolutely key to the testimonial genre in its diverse manifestations. Indeed, I would argue that this activist dimension locates *2666* within an ever expanding tradition of experimental testimonial writing and performance from the twenty-first century (Detwiler and Breckenridge 2012). As is well established, since 1969 when the prize for the best testimonial work was first established by the Casa de las Américas publishing house, testimony has been central to the debate about the positioning of the

Latin American intellectual and the tension referenced already between aesthetics and politics. Carmen Ochando Aymerich, in her analysis of the Casa de las Américas prize observed the tendency by authors to submit texts '*cuyas características textuales salían* fuera de los cauces *de las modalidades tradicionales*' [whose textual characteristics went beyond the boundaries of traditional modalities] (Detwiler and Breckenridge 2012: 242, my emphasis). From this, we might affirm that the essence of the genre was in some senses always derived from its excessive capacity, the drive to identify new ways of telling stories of incalculable loss and pain. *Testimonio*, then, has always found it necessary to transgress generic boundaries, indeed to question the very notion of *literatura* itself (Beverley 2004). In this sense, the excess of 2666 corresponds to the excess of the testimonial genre in general and its very excessiveness reveals the testimonial impulse that drives it.

Conclusion

The chaotic wails that resound throughout the theatre as part of Rigola's response to Bolaño's 2666 bear witness to the conditions of accelerated globalization and its consequences for the bodies of impoverished women who inhabit the peripheries or border zones of this new global world order. The protagonist in South African writer Zoë Wicomb's acclaimed novel, *David's Story* (2001), also emits a series of wails though they signify a longing for a world in which there is order and justice:

> Dulcie knows that there is only a point to screaming if you can imagine someone coming to your rescue; that a scream is an appeal to a world of order and justice – and that there is no such order to which she can appeal.
> (2001: 134)

The sacrificial screams of Rosita Méndez also appeal to a 'world of order and justice' that ultimately extinguishes and crushes them. In this sense, and returning to Bataille, noise is nothing (Hegarty 2006: 3). Amy Hughes has emphasized the political charge of excess, especially in its manifestation as body spectacle: 'This is why spectacles of excess – bold, un-self-conscious displays; bodies in extremity; demonstrations of extraordinary skill – are inherently radical. Excess is always, already political, too' (2012: 18). And so, from this, and notwithstanding the play's participation in a discourse that frames the Mexican female body in certain problematic ways, it is also possible to see how the register of the voice and the display of this body in extremity convert the play into an act of dynamism, expressed through a body that is transformed into a live testimony of its own death. Furthermore, by linking the performance to ideas around sacrifice and ritual, it is also possible to see that this approach to Part IV rather than just utilize the body of the Mexican female as spectacle does indeed attempt to rupture those static interpretative frameworks that reify representations of Latin American women more generally. Alba Pujol's work is really important, of course, in this context given that representational power depends on live agency. In this way, her performance draws attention to the salient features of the sacrificial economy and enacts its excess, that remainder that cannot be contained within the pink crosses or any other form of representation.

Finally, it is important to point out that the dynamism of the approach that combines voice, movement, screens, reading, planting of crosses among many other techniques, stands in direct contrast to the dead 'things' that populate the novel's exploration of the topic and unsettle in other ways key motifs that have characterized the feminicide debate since it began. These include those rigid binary oppositions that lock the narrative into one either about globalization and late capitalism and/or about the crisis in gender roles, filtered through the Agamben script of exceptionality, a narrative that is unsettled by a consideration of the trope of sacrifice. If we accept, on the other hand, Kate Lacey's idea that 'acoustic space sits somewhere between the physical and the virtual, just as the public sits somewhere between the real and the imaginary' (2013: n.p.), then this gendered expression of horror in sonic terms while highly mediated in this in-between chaotic, frequently incoherent space, may well be the vehicle through which the feminicidal horrors of Juárez are best approximated. At the very least, we can perhaps see how the body of Alba Pujol and the sounds she emits foreground questions of agency and resistance as it tells its own story of pain, wounding and sacrifice.

Notes

1 Taken in 1996, the image was initially refused publication and reproduced later in *Harpers* magazine before being used by Bowden for this publication. Schmidt Camacho elaborates on the history of misrepresentation behind the image, explaining that it was taken by Bailleres in a Mexico City morgue and is confused by Bowden in being part of his other work on the Juárez murders (2004). See also Fregoso (2007).
2 Schmidt Camacho tackles some of the issues raised by the image, remarking that neither the photographer (Bailleres) nor the journalist (Bowden), concerns himself with 'what the dead girl might be saying' (2004: 39). For illuminating readings of the image and its multiple reading contexts, see Jochum (2015), Driver (2015) and Rodríguez (2009: 188–189).
3 This play was selected for the Programa Nacional de Teatro Escolar and toured extensively around Mexico. For an analysis, see Pianacci (2009).
4 Iani del Rosario Moreno provides a lucid reading of the play in *Theatre of the Borderlands: Conflict, Violence and Healing* (2015).
5 The Cuban-American performance artist Coco Fusco's involvement with the peace network, *Women in Black* is one such example. This particular performance demonstration which took place in Washington D.C in August 2002 brought together artists from different disciplines along with activists to call for women to transform themselves into 'women in black' and to perform '*una actitud luctuosa*' [an attitude of mourning] as part of their act.
6 Chela Sandoval and Guisela Latorre define artivism as a 'hybrid neologism that signifies work created by individuals who see an organic relationship between art and activism' (2008: 82). In reference to the work of chicana artivist and digital muralist, Judy Baca, they interpret artivism as an expression of Chicana feminist philosopher Gloria Anzaldúa's theory of liberatory consciousness (2008: 82). Baca organized an exhibition on feminicide in Ciudad Juárez held at the Social and Public Art Resource Center (SPARC) in Los Angeles and was a founding member of that workspace for artivists in the region.

Sacrificial screams 73

7 Other examples include *Los Trazos del Viento* [Traces of the Wind] by Alan Aguilar; *Las muertas de Juárez* performed by Grupo Sinergía during V-Day celebrations in Texas in 2004; *Rumor de Viento* [Murmur of the Wind] by Norma Barroso (2004); *La ciudad de las moscas* [City of Flies] by Virginia Hernández (2008); *Sirenas del Río* [Mermaids of the River] by Demetrio Avila; *Justicia light* by Ernesto García; *Tlatoani (Las Muertas de Suárez)* by Juan Tovar; *Gritos de Justicia* [Cries of Justice] by Leopoldo Ibarra Saucedo; and *Desere (El desierto)* [Desert] by Cruz Robles (2007), as well as numerous dance pieces including Rossana Filomarino's *Ni una más*. In addition, the most acclaimed feature film to explore *feminicidio* in Ciudad Juárez – *El traspatio* [Backyard] – had a screenplay written by established playwright Sabina Berman. I am grateful to Enrique Mijares for generously speaking to me about the evolution of his anthology of theatre about *feminicidio* in Juárez. For further review, see Misemer (2009). For an excellent web resource, consult the project '*Dramaturgías y feminicidios*' compiled by Alejandra G. Rebelo. www.dramaturgiasyfeminicidios.com/textos [Accessed 10 February 2018].

8 First performed as part of a suite of activities for the Day of Non-Violence against Women and Children [Día de no Violencia contra las Mujeres y las Niñas] in April 2002 in Mexico City's main square, other activities included a performance by Mitrago, a music recital, the presentation of Sergio González Rodríguez's *Huesos en el desierto* [Bones in the Desert], a video installation by Canadian-Colombian artist Claudia Bernal and paintings and poetry from Mexican artist Maritza Morilla. *Mujeres de arena* has since played extensively throughout many of the Mexican states. Performances outside Mexico include Uruguay, Germany, Argentina, Australia, Canada, the US, Spain, Cuba, Costa Rica, Colombia, the UK, Peru, Italy and the Dominican Republic. It is also available in translation in multiple languages.

9 *Mujeres de Ciudad Juárez* was a one-woman show written and performed by Cristina Michaus. It was translated by Jimmy Noriega and began its production in 2011 with Teatro Travieso from 2014 onwards. According to Katherine Zien, by 2015, it had been performed twenty times in fourteen locations across the US and Canada, for over 4,100 people, mostly at the invitation of universities (2015).

10 Lorena Wolffer's *Mientras dormíamos: el caso Juárez* [While we slept: The Case of Juárez] (2001–2004) is an interesting example. In 2003, Coco Fusco dedicated her play *The Incredible Disappearing Woman* to the victims of *feminicidio*. Albuquerque-based collective Las Meganenas visit the subject of feminicidal violence in their play *River of Tears/Río de Lágrimas*, performed at the National Hispanic Cultural Center in New Mexico in 2012. J. Jiménez-Smith (pen name of J. P. Smith)'s play *Among the Sand and Smog* was directed by Jamie Keener and played to audiences in Texas in 2006. Hilary Bettis's *The Ghosts of Lote Bravo*, developed at the Juilliard playlab, was well received when performed at different locations in the US in 2015–2017.

11 Conceived as part of a performance research project, 'The central aim of the research has been to investigate appropriate practices for the preparation and exposition of performance work in relation to such contemporary issues and ways in which performances constitute acts of protest, provocation and intervention in the public domain. Each version of "The Acts – Vigia" was created over a four-day period. Stagings have included Bogotá, Colombia (Nov 2006); Lima, Peru (Nov 2006); Barcelona, Spain (April 2007) and the Hemispheric Institute of Performance and Politics, Buenos Aires, Argentina (June 2007). Aberystwyth (Sept 2007) Santa Clara, Cuba (Jan 2008), Cardiff (2008), Brazil (July 2008), Mexico (Aug 2008). Supported by an Arts Council of Wales "Creative Wales" award in March 2007'. For more information, see http://cadair.aber.ac.uk/dspace/handle/2160/1092?locale-attribute=en [Accessed 13 February 2018].

12 As mentioned, Ensler famously performed *The Vagina Monologues* to help fight a decade of rapes and murders on the US-Mexico border in Mexico City in 2003. Indeed, Ensler dedicated a personal performance of the play in Mexico City to human rights activist Esther Chávez Cano and to collect funds for Chávez's centre, Casa Amiga, which helps rape and abuse victims in Ciudad Juárez.

74 Sacrificial screams

13 The play received very mixed reviews when it opened. See, for example, Reid (2011). Clumsy Bodies Theatre performed a version of Svich's play in The Space @ Niddry St, Edinburgh, Scotland in August 2017.
14 The novel, 2666, has since been adapted for stage by Robert Fall and received its premier in Chicago in the Goodman Theatre in 2016.
15 There is an impressive array of scholarship on the work of Roberto Bolaño, some of it locating his work specifically within the framework of 'world literature', including the volume of essays, *Roberto Bolaño as World Literature* (2017). On the place of Latin America within the paradigm of World Literature, Ignacio Sánchez Prado's work is indispensable (2006). A special edition of the *Journal of Latin American Cultural Studies: Travesía* (2009) was devoted to the work of Bolaño gathering studies by Alice Driver, Gareth Williams, Jean Franco and Brett Levinson, among others. See also Oswaldo Zavala (2015).
16 Citing Casanova's work on cultural brokers, Sarah Pollack's fascinating article (2009) on the trajectory from Spanish to English-language market for the novel *The Savage Detectives* is a must-read.
17 Bolaño famously wrote an email to his friend, the Honduran writer Horacio Castellanos Moya, saying of the Latin American boom writers that they comprised 'a rancid private club full of cobwebs presided over by Vargas Llosa, García Márquez, Fuentes and other pterodactyls' (Castellanos Moya 2009: n.p.).
18 The reference to 2666 can be found, instead, in Bolaño's novel *Amuleto*, published in 1999 and in English in 2006. Here, in a cryptic sentence describing the Colonia Guerrero in Mexico City, it is imagined as a cemetery, 'Guerrero, at that time of night, is more like a cemetery than an avenue, not a cemetery in 1974 or 1968, or 1975, but a cemetery in the year 2666, a forgotten cemetery under the eyelid of a corpse or an unborn child, bathed in the dispassionate fluids of an eye that tried so hard to forget one particular thing that it ended up forgetting everything else' (2006: 86).
19 It was also performed as a co-production between Teatre Lliure, Festival de Barcelona Grec 2007 and Teatro Cuyas del Cabildo in Gran Canaria. It has been staged in Paris, Santiago de Chile, Madrid, Girona, Granada and Berlin.
20 Other European theatre classics include Shakespeare's *Titus Andrònic* [*Titus Andronicus*] (2000), *Juli Cèsar* (2002) and *Ricard III* (2005), *Mcbth* [*Macbeth*] (2015) and *Coriola* [*Coriolanus*] (2015). He has also staged Chekhov's *Ivanov* (2017).
21 See reviews by Marcos Ordoñez, *El País*; Sergi Doria, *ABC*, Santi Fondevila, *La Vanguardia*, María Jose Ragué Arias, *El Mundo* and Juan Carlos Olivares, *Avui*, among others. (Rigola 2007–2008: 5). Available online: www.teatrelliure.com/webantiga/1213/documents/temp0910/2666_cat.pdf [Accessed 10 February 2018]. On the basis of its Teatre Lliure production, it won the Barcelona Critics Prize for the Best Drama Performance, Best Dramaturgy and Best Set 2008, the International Terenci Moix Prize of Scenic Arts 2008, the Qwerty Prize 2008 for the Best Adaptation from a Novel to Another Format, and the Max 2009 Awards for the Best Theatre Show and Best Scenography.
22 The time-honoured tendency to privilege the source text over the adaptation has been well acknowledged within the critical field on adaptation (Leitch 2008). See also Hutcheon (2006, 2013) and Sanders (2016).
23 Rigola and his set designer Max Glaenzel discuss the challenges of adaptation in an interview on the Berlin production: 'This crime space is our translation of the fourth part of the book, which is crime after crime after crime after crime – it is really exhausting', says Glaenzel. 'We are translating this part into an infinite cemetery which is a desert' (Pearson 2014).
24 *Irreversible* (2002) by director Gaspar Noé also uses Beethoven's Seventh Symphony as the backdrop to the rape of its protagonist, Alex (Monica Belluci). Laura Wilson (2015), provides a fascinating insight into the ways in which films frequently communicate narratives of mutilation through their soundscape.

25 Within recent cultural criticism in Mexico, Andrea Noble (2015) explores the idea of baroque excess in relation to the visual foregrounding of beheadings and bodily dismemberment as part of cultural representations and mediations of the conflict around drug-trafficking and organized crime. Lucy Bollington's Ph.D thesis (2018) is an excellent examination of the concept of excess applied to a range of literary and visual outputs in Mexico.

26 This was precisely the accusation levelled at Rigola in discussions of the stage version of 2666 during classes with the students on the *Maestría de género* [Masters in Gender Studies] at the Universidad Autónoma de Ciudad Juárez (UACJ) in February 2017.

27 This type of representation has tended to be read in terms of visual bodily resistance to the repression of the Franco regime (and the concomitant silencing of the Catalan language). I am deeply indebted to Helena Buffery for her guidance in the preparation of this analysis and in helping me to unpick the nuanced layers of meaning surrounding the bodily transmission of violent memory in Catalan theatre and performance.

28 Bieito's play *Forests*, for example features a scene during which there is a 'solo' performance of a naked violated body pinned to a wall on stage. *Forests* was a collaboration between the Birmingham Repertory Company and Barcelona Internacional Teatre in association with the Royal Shakespeare Company in 2012. Indeed, Rigola's Shakespearean adaptations are generally characterized by the presence of viscerally violent scenes.

29 Based for over twenty years in Barcelona, Teatro de los Sentidos is dedicated to exploring a poetics of the senses in its multiple theatre productions inspired by the playwright and anthropologist Enrique Vargas. For more information, see http://teatrodelossentidos.com/ [Accessed 15 February 2018].

30 Altazor won a number of awards at the VII CENIT Certamen de Nuevos Investigadores Teatrales [New Theatrical Researcher Competition] in Seville in 2015 including the Best Actor award for Julia Rabadán, whose performance in her monologue, according to the jury, 'made the spectators present shudder' [*cuyo monólogo hizo estremecer a los espectadores asistentes*]. See www.atalaya-tnt.com/altazor-gana-el-vii-cenit/ [Accessed 13 February 2018].

31 uTOpía Barcelona is an NGO with a theatre platform that tries to disseminate Boal's theories about a Theatre of the Oppressed to wider society, to generate creative, artistic spaces for dialogue as well as social change. http://utopiabarcelona.org/ For more information on Pa'tothom, see www.patothom.org/index.html [Accessed 15 February 2018].

32 *Migranland* (2013), for example, conjoins social activism, song and performance in a searing filmic, musical and theatrical exploration of the life of fourteen recently arrived refugees in the Catalan town of Salt. The insertion of the dancing body of Laia Duran (in the part of the Molinera) in Rigola's adaptation of Joan Sales's classic novel *Incerta Glòria* in 2015 is another example of his interest in exploring meaning through the unsettling movement of female bodies. See Buffery (2017).

33 2666 is also part of this narrative. As Marcela Valdés writes, 'In his 1998 acceptance speech for the Rómulo Gallego's Prize, Bolaño revealed that in some way everything he wrote was "a letter of love or of goodbye" to the young people who died in the dirty wars of Latin America. His previous novels memorialized the dead of the 1960s and '70s. His ambitions for 2666 were greater: to write a postmortem for the dead of the past, the present and the future' (2008: n.p.).

34 *Après Moi, déluge* (2007) by renowned Catalan playwright Lluïsa Canillé is a good example of where Catalan theatre has grappled with the staging dilemmas of representing violence. Indeed, there have been many Catalan women dramatists, performers and directors who have sought ethical, sensitive and politically charged ways of dramatizing sexual violence and violence against women. In addition, there have been stagings of international plays on the same theme including the British playwright, Sarah Kane's controversial play about gender violence, *Blasted (Rebentats)*,

which was shown at the Teatre Nacional de Catalunya in 2018. Similarly, Eve Ensler's *The Vagina Monologues* [*Monólogos de la vágina*] was shown at various theatres throughout Barcelona.

35 When presenting on this as part of a performance studies colloquium ('BodyStories' at University College Cork, 18 June 2016), a member of the audience, who was a film director and actor, remarked that all she could think about when viewing the clip from the play that I had shown were the director's notes that would have been passed to the actor about how to convey the pain and horror of gang rape – both vaginal and anal.

36 Finally, we can link the emission of excessive noise in the stage production to the noises of the novel that function as a way of evoking the irreality of the atrocities. Sharae Deckard argues that noise is a key 'lynchian trope' in the novel citing the passage from Part V in which Klaus, who has been imprisoned having been suspected of the crimes, outlines his experience in prison: 'It's like a noise you hear in a dream. The dream, like everything dreamed in enclosed spaces, is contagious. Suddenly someone dreams it and after a while half the prisoners dream it. But the noise you hear isn't part of the dream, it's real. The noise belongs to a separate order of things' (Bolaño 2009: 490). Deckard writes that, 'in perceiving the noise, Klaus shares with the other prisoners a collective consciousness from below of systemic violence, which seems to supersede narrative – hence its rendering as noise, as sound, rather than words – yet which is after all "real life"' (2012: 360). In the same way as imagined here, the noise on stage works here as part of a separate order that might be seen too as an expression of collective consciousness embedded within a ritualized performance of horror.

37 While writing this chapter, the case of Mariana Joselín became the subject of intense media scrutiny when her body was found disembowelled in a butcher's shop in the neighbourhood of Ecatepec, Mexico State, in August 2017.

38 Adriana Cavarero critiques Bataille's focus on the erotic ecstasy of horror, as explored in his book, *The Tears of Eros*. Cavarero cautions against the way his exposure of the 'profound nucleus of horror [. . .] shuts off the vision of the other side of the vulnerable, the side that yearns for care' (2009: 56). Lucy Bollington notes also Cavarero's re-introduction of Hannah Arendt's concerns 'in relation to Bataille's surrealist emphasis on sacrificial destruction underscoring in particular the ways in which such an outlook both mirrored and ran the risk of normalising or conditioning the forms of historical sacrifice and mass disposability that characterised World War I' (2018: 47).

39 See Roach (1996: 123–131) for an interesting reflection on Bataille's theories in *The Accursed Share* and their relevance for the examination of performance rites of abundance, reproduction and sacrifice.

40 See, for example, the testimony of Judith Galarza in Lourdes Portillo's documentary film *Señorita Extraviada* [Missing Young Woman] (2001). Here she notes the custom in the *maquilas* for photographs of the workers to be taken, alleging that these images were later collated and distributed as catalogues of female flesh for consumption.

41 Rosa Linda Fregoso ominously describes feminicide as 'the "blood price" the nation pays for globalization' (2000: 142).

42 Diana Washington Váldez writes an article titled '*Ciudad Juárez y la cultura del sacrificio*' in Melgar and Beausteguigoitia (2007: 49–65). Molly Molloy also invokes the idea of the bodies of feminicidal victims as 'sacrificial host' in a trenchant piece criticizing what she sees as the fetishization of feminicide in Ciudad Juárez (Hooks 2014). See also Segato (2006).

43 Gaspar de Alba also invokes the same trope as a key part of her rationale for the conference she held at the University of California, Los Angeles (UCLA) in 2003 'to re-member the sacrificed daughters of Juárez' (2014: 140).

44 It is important to distinguish, of course, between the distinct types of sacrifice and sacrificial victims who differed enormously in terms of provenance, mode, preparation and other ways. See Laura Rival (2013) and Austin A. López (1998). See also Pennock (2012).

45 Las Casas famously argued that although human sacrifice was seen as aberrant within the Christian worldview, 'the peoples who offered the most precious sacrifices to God (whether the true or a false god) could be regarded as the most religious of all' (cited in Benjamin Keen 1990: 97).
46 The Memorial Democrático (Memorial democràtic de Catalunya) was conceived as an instrument through which the Catalan government should undertake public policy focused on the recuperation of memory of victims of the Civil War and of those people, organizations and institutions that confronted the political, social, cultural and national repression of an ignominious regime.
47 See, for example, Douglas Crimp (2004) or Espinoza and Madrid (2010).

Works cited

2666 by Àlex Rigola, 2003. [Play].
The Acts – Vigia by Jill Greenhalgh and Michael Brookes, 2006–2008. [Performance].
Agamben, Giorgio, 1998. *Homo Sacer: Sovereign Power and Bare Life*. Trans. by Daniel Heller-Roazen. Stanford: Stanford University Press.
Altazor by Teatro Laboratorio, 2015. [Play].
"Altazor" gana el VII CENIT, 2018. Centro Internacional de Investigación Teatral. [online]. Available at www.atalaya-tnt.com/altazor-gana-el-vii-cenit/ [Accessed 13 February 2018].
Among the Sand and the Smog by J. Jiménez-Smith, 2006. [Play].
Antígona: las voces que incendian el desierto, 2005 by Perla de la Rosa. [Play]. In Guadalupe de la Mora, ed., *Cinco dramaturgos chihuahuenses*. Ciudad Juárez: Fondo Municipal Edito Revolvente, 186–228.
Àpres Moi, déluge by Lluïsa Canillé, 2007. [Play].
Báez Ayala, Susana, 2006. Los colores del amanecer: La dramaturgia social en Ciudad Juárez. In Víctor Orozco, ed. *Chihuahua hoy, 2006: Visiones de su economía, política y cultura*. Vol. 4, Chihuahua: Instituto Chihuahuense de la Cultura and Universidad Autónoma de Ciudad Juárez, 255–284.
Bataille, Georges, 1991. *The Accursed Share: An Essay on General Economy*. Vol. 1. Consumption. Trans. by Robert Hurley. New York: Zone Books.
Beverley, John, 2004. *Testimonio: On the Politics of Truth*. Minneapolis: University of Minnesota Press.
Birns, Nicholas, and de Castro, Juan E., eds., 2017. *Roberto Bolaño as World Literature*. New York: Bloomsbury.
Blasted (Rebentats) by Sarah Kane, 2017. [Play].
Bolaño, Roberto, 1998. *Los Detectives Salvajes*. Barcelona: Anagrama.
———, 2004. *2666*. Barcelona: Anagrama.
———, 2006. *Amulet*. New York: New Directions.
———, 2007. *The Savage Detectives*. New York: Farrar, Straus and Giroux.
———, 2009. *2666*. Trans. by Natasha Wimmer. London: Picador.
Bollington, Lucy, 2018. *Reframing Excess: Death and Power in Contemorary Mexican Literary and Visual Culture*. Thesis (Ph.D). University of Cambridge.
Bowden, Charles, 1998. *Juárez: The Laboratory of our Future*. New York: Aperture.
Buffery, Helena, 2017. Bodies of Evidence, Resistance and Protest: Embodying the Spanish Civil War on the Contemporary Spanish Stage. *Bulletin of Hispanic Studies*, 94 (8), 863–882.
Carrasco, Davíd, 1999. *City of Sacrifice: The Aztec Empire and the Role of Violence in Civilization*. Boston: Beacon Press.

Castellanos Moya, Horacio, 2009. Sobre el mito Bolaño. *La Nación*, 19 September [online]. Available at: www.lanacion.com.ar/1176451-sobre-el-mito-bolano [Accessed 26 January 2018].

Cavarero, Adriana, 2009. *Horrorism: Naming Contemporary Violence*. Trans. by William McCuaig. New York: Columbia University Press.

Cercas, Javier, 2001. *Soldados de Salamina*. Spain: Tusquets.

Crimmins, Daniel, 2007. Meet the Kurt Cobain of Latin-American Literature. *Paste*, Issue 30, 19 April [online]. Available at: www.pastemagazine.com/articles/2007/04/roberto-bolano-the-savage-detectives.html [Accessed 26 January 2018].

Crimp, Douglas, 2004. *Melancholy and Moralism: Essays on AIDS and Queer Politics*. Cambridge: MIT Press.

Deckard, Sharae, 2012. Peripheral Realism, Millenial Capitalism and Roberto Bolaño's 2666. *Modern Language Quarterly*, 73 (3), 351–372.

Desere (El desierto) [Desert] by Cruz Robles, 2007. [Play].

Detwiler, Louise, and Breckenridge, Janis, 2012. *Pushing the Boundaries of Latin American Testimony: Meta-morphoses and Migrations*. New York: Palgrave Macmillan.

Dramaturgias y feminicidios, 2017. [online]. Universidad Autónoma Metropolitana-Azcapotzalco, Mexico. Available at: www.dramaturgiasyfeminicidios.com/textos [Accessed 13 February 2018].

Driver, Alice, 2015. *More or Less Dead: Feminicide, Haunting, and the Ethics of Representation in Mexico*. Tucson: University of Arizona Press.

El traspatio [Backyard], 2009. [Film]. Directed by Carlos Carrera. Tardan/Berman.

Espinoza E., Vicente, y Madrid P., Sebastián, 2010. *Trayectoria y eficacia política de los militantes en juventudes políticas: Estudio de la élite política emergente*. Mendoza: Universidad de Cuyo.

Estrellas enterradas by Antonio Zúñiga, 2011. [Play].

Fábrica 7 by Fábrica Teatro, 2006. [Play].

Forests by Calixto Bieito, 2012. [Play].

Fregoso, Rosa Linda, 2000. Voices Without Echo: The Global Gendered Apartheid. *Emergences: Journal for the Study of Media and Composite Cultures*, 10 (1), 137–155.

———, 2003. *MeXicana Encounters: The Making of Social Identities on the Borderlands*. Berkeley, Los Angeles, London: University of California Press.

2007. Toward a Planetary Civil Society. In Denise A. Segura and Patricia Zavella, eds., Women and Migration in the U.S.-Mexico Borderlands: A Reader. Durham, NC: Duke University Press, 33–66.

———, and Cynthia, Bejarano, 2010. Introduction: A Cartography of Feminicide in the Américas. In Rosa Linda Fregoso and Cynthia Bejarano, eds., *Terrorizing Women: Feminicide in the Américas*. Durham, NC: Duke University Press, 1–44.

Gaspar de Alba, Alicia, 2014. *[Un]Framing the "Bad Woman": Sor Juana, Malinche, Coyolxauhqui and Other Rebels with a Cause*. Austin: University of Texas Press.

———, and Guzmán, Georgina, 2010. *Making a Killing: Femicide, Free Trade and La Frontera*. Austin: University of Texas Press.

The Ghosts of Lote Bravo by Hilary Bettis, 2015. [Play].

Girard, René, 1977. *Violence and the Sacred*. Baltimore: John Hopkins University Press.

González Rodríguez, Sergio, 2002. *Huesos en el desierto*. Barcelona: Anagrama.

———, 2009. *El hombre sin cabeza*. Barcelona: Anagrama.

———, 2012. *The Femicide Machine*. Los Angeles: Semiotext(e).

Gritos de Justicia [Cries of Justice] by Leopoldo Ibarra Saucedo, 2008. [Play].

Guzmán, Alison, 2012. Los muertos vivientes de la Guerra Civil en cinco obras de Laila Ripoll: La frontera, Que nos quiten lo bailao, Convoy de los 927, Los niños perdidos, y Santa Perpetua. *Don Galán, Revista de investigación teatral*, 2 (4). [online]. Available at: http://teatro.es/contenidos/donGalan/donGalanNum2/pagina.php?vol=2&doc=2_4&pag=1 [Accessed 31 January 2018].

Hegarty, Paul, 2000. *Georges Bataille: Core Cultural Theorist*. London, Thousand Oaks, New Delhi: Sage.

———, 2006. Noise Music, *The Semiotic Review of Books*, 16 (1–2), 1–15.

Hooks, Christopher, 2014. Q&A with Molly Molloy: The Story of the Juárez Femicides is a 'Myth'. *Texas Observer*. 9 Jan. [online]. Available at: www.texasobserver.org/qa-molly-molloy-story-juarez-femicides-myth/ [Accessed 30 January 2018].

Hughes, Amy E., 2012. *Spectacles of Reform: Theater and Activism in Nineteenth-Century America*. Ann Arbor: The University of Michigan Press.

Hutcheon, Linda, 2006. *A Theory of Adaptation*. London, New York: Routledge.

———, 2013. *A Theory of Adaptation* (Revised Edition). London, New York: Routledge.

Incerta Glòria by Àlex Rigola, 2015. [Play].

The Incredible Disappearing Woman by Coco Fusco, 2003. [Play].

Iphigenia Crash Land Falls on the Neon Shell That Was Once Her Heart by Caridad Svich, 2004. [Play].

Irigaray, Luce, 1987. *Sexes et parentés*. Paris: Editions de Minuit.

Irreversible, 2002. [Film]. Directed by Gaspar Noé. France: Les Cinémas de la Zone Studio Canal.

Ivànov by Anton Chekhov, 1887. [Play]. Directed by Àlex Rigola. [Teatre Lliure, Barcelona, 2017].

Jauría [Pack of Dogs] by Enrique Mijares, 2008 [Play].

Jochum, Tobias, 2015. "The Weight of Words, the Shock of Photos": Poetic Testimony and Elliptical Imagery in Sergio González Rodríguez' The Femicide Machine. *FIAR – Forum for Interamerican Research*, 8 (2 Sep), 92–119. [online]. Available at: http://interamerica.de/volume-8-2/jochum/ [Accessed 24 January 2018].

Journal of Latin American Cultural Studies, 2009, 18 (2–3). On Roberto Bolaño (1953–2003), 125–217.

Julius Caesar by William Shakespeare, 1599 [Play]. *Juli Cèsar*. Directed by Àlex Rigola [Teatre Lliure, Barcelona, 2004–05]

Justicia Light by Ernesto García, 2008.[Play].

Justicia Negada by Perla de la Rosa, 2013. [Play].

Keen, Benjamin, 1990. *The Aztec Image in Western Thought*. New Brunswick: Rutgers University Press.

Lacey, Kate, 2013. *Listening Publics: The Politics and Experience of Listening in the Media Age*. Cambridge: Polity Press.

La ciudad de las moscas [City of Flies] by Virginia Hernández, 2008. [Play].

Las muertas de Juárez by Grupo Sinergía, 2004. [Play].

Leitch, Thomas, 2008. Adaptation, the Genre. *Adaptation*, 1 (2), (1 Sep), 106–120.

Levinson, Brett, 2009. Case Closed: Madness and Dissociation in 2666. *Journal of Latin American Cultural Studies*, 18 (2–3 Dec), 177–191.

Lomas de Poleo by Edeberto "Pilo" Galindo, 2003. [Play].

López, Austin A., 1998. *The Human Body and Ideology: Concepts of the Ancient Nahuas*. Salt Lake City: University of Utah Press.

Los Trazos del Viento [Traces of the Wind] by Alan Aguilar, 2008. [Play].

Mbembe, Achille, 2003. Necropolitics. *Public Culture*, 15 (1), 11–40.
Mientras dormíamos: el caso Juárez [While we slept: The Case of Juárez] by Lorena Wolffer, 2001. [Play].
Migranland by Àlex Rigola, 2013. [Play].
Mijares, Enrique, ed., 2008. *Hotel Juárez: dramaturgia de feminicidios*. Durango, Mexico: Universidad Juárez del Estado de Durango, Union College, Editorial Espacio Vacío.
Misemer, Sarah M., 2009. Hotel Juárez: Dramaturgia de feminicidios (Review), *Latin American Theatre Review*, 43 (1), 218–219.
Mujeres de arena by Humberto Robles, 2002. [Play].
Mujeres de Ciudad Juárez by Cristina Michaus, 2001. [Play].
Murmullos en el Páramo by Mercedes Hernández, 2011. [Play].
Ni una más by Rossana Filomarino, 2014 [Dance]. Available at: www.youtube.com/watch?v=xPcMQTYLmQg [Accessed 10 February 2018].
Noble, Andrea, 2015. History, Modernity and Atrocity in Mexican Visual Culture. *Bulletin of Spanish Studies*, 92 (3), 391–421.
Pearson, Joseph, 2014. Murders in the Desert: Roberto Bolaño in Berlin. *Find*, 14. [online]. Available at: http://find-blog.de/post/79869898506/murders-in-the-desert-roberto-bolaño-in [Accessed 26 January 2018].
Pennock, Caroline Dodds, 2012. Mass Murder or Religious Homicide? Rethinking Human Sacrifice and Interpersonal Violence in Aztec Society. *Historical Social Research/Historische Sozialforschung*, 37 (3) (141), 276–302.
Pianacci, Rómulo, 2009. Teatro, mujer y fronteras: *Antígona; las voces que incendian el desierto* de Perla de la Rosa. In Aurora López and Andrés Pociña Pérez, eds., *En recuerdo de Beatriz Rabaza: Comedias, tragedias y leyendas grecorromanas en el teatro del Siglo XX*. Granada: Editorial Universidad de Granada, 499–508.
Pollack, Sarah, 2009. Latin America Translated (Again): Roberto Bolaño's *The Savage Detectives* in the United States. *Comparative Literature*, 61 (3), 346–365.
Ravelo Blancas, Patricia and Limas Hernández, Alfredo, 2002. Femenicidio en Ciudad Juárez: Una civilización sacrificial. *El Cotidiano*, 18 (11), 47–57.
Reid, Kerry, 2011. New 'Iphigenia' disturbs; 'Feet of Clay' stumbles. *Chicago Tribune*, 24 February [online]. Available at: http://articles.chicagotribune.com/2011-02-24/entertainment/ct-ott-0225-on-the-fringe-20110224_1_mexican-border-city-fresa-fable [Accessed 26 January 2018].
Richard III by William Shakespeare, 2005. [Play]. Directed by Àlex Rigola [Teatre Lliure, Barcelona. 2005].
Rival, Laura, 2013. The Aztec sacrificial complex. In J. Zachhuber and J. Meszaros, eds., *Sacrifice in Modern Thought*. Oxford: Oxford University Press, 163–179.
River of Tears/Río de lágrimas by Las Meganenas, 2012. [Play].
Roach, Joseph, 1996. *Cities of the Dead: Circum-Atlantic Performance*. New York: Columbia University Press.
Rodríguez, Ileana, 2009. *Liberalism at its Limits*. Pittsburg: University of Pittsburg Press.
Rodríguez Serrano, Aarón, 2008. Escena/Cementerio: Sobre 2666 (de Roberto Bolaño) en la versión teatral de Àlex Rigola. *Questión: Revista especializada en periodismo y comunicación*, 1 (18). [online]. Available at: http://perio.unlp.edu.ar/ojs/index.php/question/article/view/544 [Accessed 13 February 2018].
Rosario Moreno, Iani del, 2015. *Theatre of the Borderlands: Conflict, Violence, and Healing*. Lanham, Boulder, New York, London: Lexington.
Rumor de Viento [Murmur of the Wind] by Norma Barroso, 2004. [Play].

Sánchez Prado, Ignacio M., 2006. *América Latina en la "literatura mundial". Instituto Internacional de Literatura Iberoamericana*. Pittsburg: University of Pittsburg.

———, 2016. *War and the Neo-Liberal Condition: Death and Vulnerability in Contemporary Mexico*. [Presentation]. University of Florida, 15 September (Unpublished).

Sanders, Julie, 2016. *Adaptation and Appropriation* (2nd Edition). London, New York: Routledge.

Sandoval, Chela, and Latorre, Guisela, 2008. Chicana/o Artivism: Judy Baca's Digital Work with Youth of Color. In Anna Everett, ed., *Learning Race and Ethnicity: Youth and Digital Media: The John D. and Catherine T. MacArthur Foundation Series on Digital Media and Learning*. Cambridge: MIT Press, 81–108.

Sauri, Emilio, 2017. Dickens + MP3 ÷ Balzac + JPEG or, Art and the Value of Innovation in the Contemporary Mexican Novel. In Ignacio M. Sánchez Prado, ed., *Mexican Literature in Theory*. New York: Bloomsbury, 334–352.

Scarry, Elaine, 1985. *The Body in Pain: The Making and Unmaking of the World*. New York, Oxford: Oxford University Press.

Schmidt Camacho, Alicia, 2004. Body Counts on the Mexico-U.S. Border: Feminicidio, Reification, and the Theft of Mexicana Subjectivity. *Chicana/Latina Studies: The Journal of MALCS*, 4 (1 Fall), 22–60.

Segato, Rita Laura, 2006. *La escritura en el cuerpo de las mujeres asesinadas en Ciudad Juárez. Territorio, soberanía y crímenes de segundo estado*. Mexico City: Universidad del Claustro de Sor Juana.

Señorita Extraviada, 2001. [Film]. Directed by Lourdes Portillo.

Sirenas del Río [Mermaids of the River] by Demetrio Avila, 2008.. [Play].

Skidelsky, William, 2009. Roberto Bolaño's 2666: Latin America's literary outlaw. *The Guardian*, 11 January [online]. Available at: www.theguardian.com/books/2009/jan/11/roberto-bolano-2666 [Accessed 26 January 2018].

Stavans, Ilan, 2007. Willing Outcast. *Washington Post*, 6 May. [online]. Available at: www.washingtonpost.com/wp-dyn/content/article/2007/05/03/AR2007050302008.html [Accessed 26 January 2018].

Steinberg, Samuel, 2016. *Photopoetics at Tlatelolco: Afterimages of Mexico, 1968*. Austin: University of Texas Press.

Titus Andronicus by William Shakespeare, 2000. [Play]. Directed by Àlex Rigola [Teatre Lliure, Barcelona 2000].

Tlatoani: las muertas de Suárez by Juan Tovar, 2006. [Play].

Tramullas, Gemma, 2007. Rigola fotografió el pulso de la ciudad donde transcurre la adaptacion de la novela de Bolaño. *El periodico*, 3 Nov. [online]. Available at: www.elperiodico.com/es/barcelona/20071103/rigola-fotografio-el-pulso-de-la-ciudad-donde-transcurre-la-adaptacion-de-la-novela-de-bolano-5491222 [Accessed 31 January 2018].

The Vagina Monologues by Eve Ensler, 1996. [Play].

Valdés, Marcela, 2008. Alone Among the Ghosts: Roberto Bolano's 2666. *The Nation*, 19 November [online]. Available at: www.thenation.com/article/alone-among-ghosts-roberto-bolanos-2666/ [Accessed 30 January 2018].

Villalobos-Ruminott, Sergio, 2009. A Kind of Hell: Roberto Bolaño and The Return of World Literature. *Journal of Latin American Cultural Studies: Travesía*, 18 (2–3), 193–205.

Washington Váldez, Diana, 2007. Ciudad Juárez y la cultura del sacrificio. In Marisa Belausteguigoitia and Lucía Melgar, coords., *Fronteras, violencia, justicia: nuevos discursos: Programa Universitario de Estudios de Género*. Mexico City: Universidad Nacional Autónoma de México, 49–65.

Wicomb, Zoë, 2001. *David's Story*. New York: The Feminist Press at CUNY.
Wilson, Laura, 2015. *Spectatorship, Embodiment and Physicality in the Contemporary Mutilation Film*. Houndmills, Basingstoke: Palgrave Macmillan.
Zavala, Oswaldo, 2015. *La modernidad insufrible: Roberto Bolaño en los límites de la literatura latinoamericana contemporánea*. Chapel Hill: University of North Carolina Press.
Zien, Katherine, 2015. On the Bleeding Edge of the Real: Women of Ciudad Juárez. *Women & Performance: A Journal of Feminist Theory*, 25 (3), 370–376.

3 Remember them

Ethics and witnessing in artistic responses to feminicide

When searching for examples of ways in which the feminicidal victims from Ciudad Juárez had been sexualized in visual representations in media and other art forms, I came across a set of sixty-four posters that formed an exhibition titled *Las mujeres de Juárez demandan justicia* [The Women of Juárez Demand Justice]. These were displayed in various locations in Mexico City, most notably on International Women's Day (8 March) at the Insurgentes metro station in 2002, to call attention to the ongoing murders occurring on the northern border. It marked but one of myriad attempts to display artworks about feminicide in Ciudad Juárez in public spaces in Mexico. The choice of location in this instance was interesting: Insurgentes takes its name from the independence army led by Miguel Hidalgo y Costilla, already a symbol of nationalist fervour and resistance. Moreover, Avenida Insurgentes is one of Mexico City's focal points and the metro station is located in the Glorieta, a famous shopping mall that constitutes a meeting place for many counter-cultural groups throughout the city. Insurgentes, then, represents a key transit zone, home to an extensive local network of urban transport and an important station for transfer between metro, bus and, more recently, metrobus. Located at the intersection with Chapultepec, it is situated adjacent to Colonia Juárez, all of which made it an ideal location for the display of images protesting the feminicidal violence in the city also taking its name from this critically important national figure. Many of the visual tropes most associated with the imagining of feminicide in Ciudad Juárez are present in these posters: desert locations, images of mutilation and fragmentation, altars. Some of the images also framed the women in almost pornographic terms with one poster featuring a woman naked and tied up. This kind of visual vocabulary which is invested in paradigms about subordination and sexualization, draws attention to the risks and responsibilities associated with any ethical, artistic engagement with violence. And yet, by utilizing the location of Insurgentes – such an everyday site of transit for the city's citizens – the exhibition also offered different possibilities for encounter and engagement with art about gender violence.

Whatever about the pitfalls associated with this particular configuration of images, it is certainly true to say that it is in the arena of the visual that there has been the most pronounced and prolific engagement with the horrors of *feminicidio* in Juárez. Indeed, that the horrors of the feminicidal violence in Juárez from

1993 onwards have seen their re-imagining in visual form across such a diverse range of forms, modes and genres speaks to the ways in which, for reasons examined in the introduction, the Juárez feminicides had a particular role in forging *visibility* for gender violence against women on a global scale. In this regard, for the image-makers and storytellers who seek alternative (his)tories about the city, Ciudad Juárez represents an international starting point for feminicidal violence. Following this, it seems only logical that artists – particularly, but not exclusively, those engaged with projects of social justice – might seek to insert their responses in a global continuum of artwork on the subject. What is less clear is exactly what impact these artworks have had. Indeed, the measuring or evaluation of art's 'impact' is a problematic and challenging terrain. It is this area that I would like to probe in this chapter, focusing specifically on one of the Juárez art projects with which I have had close involvement, that of Irish artist Brian Maguire and his set of portraits of some of the victims of *feminicidio* in Ciudad Juárez shown at various locations in the US and Europe since 2012. Before commencing this analysis, however, a brief overview of art about Ciudad Juárez is warranted by way of contextualizing and locating the Maguire project.

Ciudad Juárez art

The visual responses to the gender violence committed in Juárez have engaged with very different genres and modes of expression including short film, documentary and more commercialized feature productions from both Mexico and the US. There have also been extraordinary photographic responses to the crimes including work by Ciudad Juárez-based photographers, Jaime Bailleres, Julián Cardona, Itzel Aguilera and Lucio Soria among others.[1] Photographers based in Mexico City who have engaged with the *feminicidios* on the Northern border include Maya Goded, who visited Ciudad Juárez to produce her acclaimed photographic series,[2] and Yamina del Real, whose exhibition about the female body including a series of photographs about the victims of *feminicidio* in Ciudad Juárez was held in the Museo archivo de la fotografía in 2011.[3] Photographers from outside Mexico have also been drawn to Ciudad Juárez to capture some of the complexities of *feminicidio* in its locale. They include Irish human rights campaigner and film-maker Mark McLoughlin, the French film-maker and photographer Lanka Haouche Perren[4] and the visual artist, Basil Al-Rawi.[5]

In terms of more formal 'artistic' productions, these have taken many distinct forms and have often involved exhibitions in sanctioned gallery spaces wholly dedicated to the victims of *feminicidio* in the border city. Notable examples of such exhibitions include *Hijas de Juárez*, curated by Rigo Maldonado and Victoria Delgadillo and shown in the Social and Public Art Resource Center (SPARC) in California in 2003.[6] Another US-based exhibition, titled *Rastros y Crónicas: Women of Juárez*, was displayed at the National Museum of Mexican Art in Chicago in 2009–2010. Curated by Linda Xochitl Tortolero and Dolores Mercado, it brought together forty pieces by twenty-six different artists with the explicit goal of drawing attention to the crimes.[7] Teresa Margolles, the internationally acclaimed Mexican artist, has also engaged with the horrors of the Juárez *feminicidios* as part of her wider artistic interest in violence and death.[8] In the arena of graphic design, there have been multiple interventions, like for example, the poster campaign, *Las mujeres de Juárez demandan justicia*, already mentioned.[9] There are examples too of multimedia exhibits, video installations, immersive and interactive digital projects as well as portrait painting. Juárez art has been displayed in Mexico, throughout Latin America, the US, Canada, Ireland, Poland, the UK, Spain, Belgium, the Netherlands, Germany and Italy, to name only a few locations. There have been single artist projects like, for example, Chicana artist Diane Kahlo's *Wall of Memories: The Disappeared Señoritas of Ciudad Juárez*[10] or Mexican artist, Maritza Morillas's evocative series, *CaroDAtaVERnibus en Ciudad Juárez* (2000–2004), displayed in the Metro Station, Pino Suárez, as part of International Women's Day in 2006.[11] There have also been projects that gathered work from multiple artists in response to the Juárez feminicide cases. In this regard some of the more notable exhibitions have been Tamsyn Challenger's *400 women*,[12] *Frontera 450+*, an exhibition of seventeen artists shown in earlier form at the Station Museum Houston, Texas in 2006–2007[13] and the *Ni Una Más, Not One More: The Juárez Murders*, a two-month exhibition featuring more than seventy works of art by twenty international artists in 2010 in Philadelphia in a collaboration with Drexel University.[14] There have been shows that have featured work on the feminicidal violence as collaborative projects working towards global solidarity.[15] In this regard, Norwegian artist, Lise Bjørne Linnert's *Desconocida, Unknown, Ukjent* project is a good example. Shown in multiple locations across the world, it is described as 'A global mass collaboration, protesting continuing murders of women in Ciudad Juárez, Mexico involving approximately 7,900 hand-embroidered name tags (by June 2016)'.[16] In addition, a number of artistic collectives have been established. They include the Mexican multidisciplinary collective, *Movimiento Cultural Techo Blanco* (White Roof Cultural Movement) founded and led by the well-known actress Vanesa Bauche. An artistic project in Los Angeles by Azul Luna and titled '*Viejaskandalosas*' illustrates the extent to which the feminicidal crimes in Juárez generated a sense of feminist solidarity among the latino community north of the border (Delgadillo and Maldonado 2003: 182). Art against feminicidal violence in Juárez has also frequently appeared alongside expressions of protest in other forms such as poetry, theatre, performance and song and of which, the *Primer Encuentro Internacional de Artes sobre el Femicidio en Ciudad Juárez* is an interesting example.[17] The scale and the richness of the art crafted in responses to feminicidal violence in the city can be appreciated thus by this necessarily brief synopsis. It prompts us to reflect on how the dehumanizing experiences of feminicidal violence and its aftermath are transmitted and re-signified via a range of aesthetic practices. In this regard, following Silva Londoño's work on urban art in Ciudad Juárez, perhaps we should ultimately read the artistic interventions in this realm as incantations against silence (2016: 42) and as activation of those invisible and untold stories of pain.

An Oasis of Horror in a Desert of Boredom

By way of starting the discussion on the Maguire project, we might recall Volk and Schlotterbeck's assertion that 'it is precisely because the state has failed so abjectly in stopping these murders that 'fictional' narratives have become both the site where victims are mourned and the means by which justice can be restored' (2010: 121–122). Adding 'artistic' narratives into this consideration, the latter part of this assertion interests me: to what extent can we really know that these artistic responses can become the means by which justice can be restored? On the one hand, it is undeniable that these narratives render the disappeared and mutilated women visible, that is to say that they participate in the 'rhetoric of exposure', as Swanson Goldberg and Schultheis Moore point out, that dominant motif of the global humanitarian project symbolized most powerfully, they maintain, by Amnesty International's candle illuminating the darkness. They write that, 'the rhetoric of exposure has long been a central trope of humanitarian discourse: the promise of revelation presumes that egregious violations are otherwise secret' (2011: 233). They quote Thomas Keenan who elaborates on the symbolic power of such a rhetoric on, 'those agents whose behaviour it wishes to affect – governments, armies, businesses and militias –' and that 'renders them vulnerable to feelings of dishonour, embarrassment, disgrace, or ignominy' (2004: 435). According to this logic, the rhetoric of exposure is deemed politically effective in terms of its assumptions that those agents with the power to effect change (governments; armies; businesses) are part of the same social and cultural milieu as the subjects affected and that therefore they are, to use Keenan's term, 'vulnerable'. However, the degree to which internationally recognized organizations such as Amnesty International and Human Rights Watch, to name but just two, can realistically challenge forms of neoliberal violence of the kind perpetuated in Juárez is subject to wide debate.[18] Furthermore, if we accept that art, like other interventions in the cultural arena, forms part of the rhetoric of exposure referred to earlier, it is less clear how else it might resonate or what function it serves in the political, legal and public spheres where justice is sought. Cara Levey draws our attention to how memory activity, including art, functions as a way of enacting real alternative and radical justice (2016). To return again to the point made in the introduction, perhaps these artistic responses might offer new ways of seeing and thinking about the murders. Certainly, the impact of the artistic production on the Juárez murders, however that might be defined, analyzed or evaluated, depends to large and varying extents on the role played by spectators, readers and consumers of those cultural texts, and it is on the act of seeing and spectatorship that I would like to focus this discussion. In this regard, it is pertinent to ask questions about the conditions that frame the viewing of these artistic responses and in turn, how these frames might shape reactions.

The multi-faceted artistic project by established Irish artist Brian Maguire, comprised a number of distinct parts.[19] The title of the exhibition featuring the Maguire portraits may be recognized as an extract from 'The Voyage', by Charles Baudelaire: 'O bitter is the knowledge that one draws from the voyage!/

Remember them 87

The monotonous and tiny world, today/Yesterday, tomorrow, always, shows us our reflections,/An oasis of horror in a desert of boredom!' (cited in Exhibition Catalogue 2012: 5).[20] This is taken directly from the epigraph to Roberto Bolaño's famous novel, 2666, about which, according to Jean Franco, Bolaño said,

> there is no more lucid diagnosis for the illness of modern man. To escape boredom, to escape deadlock, all we have at hand, though not so close at hand, because even here an effort is required, is horror, or in other words, evil.
>
> (2009: 215)

Completed over a four-year period of frequent visits to Ciudad Juárez (2009–2012), Maguire developed relationships with various family members who had lost daughters to the feminicidal violence in the city. The nub of the project is a series of images of the deceased based on family photographs that Maguire then re-photographed so as not to physically remove the image from the families' possession. Using these images as a basis, he painted two portraits: a large-scale version for exhibition and a smaller version for the family members themselves to keep. Working closely with activist Marisela Ortiz and others,[21] Maguire led art workshops for children affected by violence in Ciudad Juárez 'as a way of giving back something' (personal interview 2014).[22] It is useful to scrutinize the ethical approach adopted by Maguire and to note that his methodology in putting together these portraits was characterized by a determined principled stance. This is illustrated by the extensive time he spent in Juárez, his going back and forth during the time span of the project as well as his commitment to the project following completion.[23] Furthermore, his intense engagement with the families, the emotional connection forged and the decision to paint two portraits, one for display, the other bequeathed to the victims' families demonstrates a certain ethics of artistic responsibility. In this way, his work has a dual function: to publicly expose the cases internationally but also to participate in a project of restorative justice by painting a picture for the families that radically counteracts media portrayals. In the case of the image of Brenda (Figure 3.1), Maguire says 'I allowed my feelings to enter the painting of Brenda' and he painted it in black and white. However, as her mother found it 'too sad', he created a second version for her with colour (Exhibition Catalogue: 85). All this is to say that the singular power of the portraits is derived from the way in which they defiantly inscribe life into the stories of death and destruction. In this regard, of note is the way in which they stand resolutely in contrast to the commodification, sexualization and aestheticization of violent death of women (referenced in the Introduction) and that has so frequently been a characteristic of Juárez coverage and indeed some of the cultural responses they elicit.

The portraits were exhibited in the VISUAL centre in Carlow, Ireland, in 2012–2013, and it is on this display that the reflections in this chapter have been based. As well as Carlow, however, they have been shown in other spaces and in slightly different configurations in a number of other places including

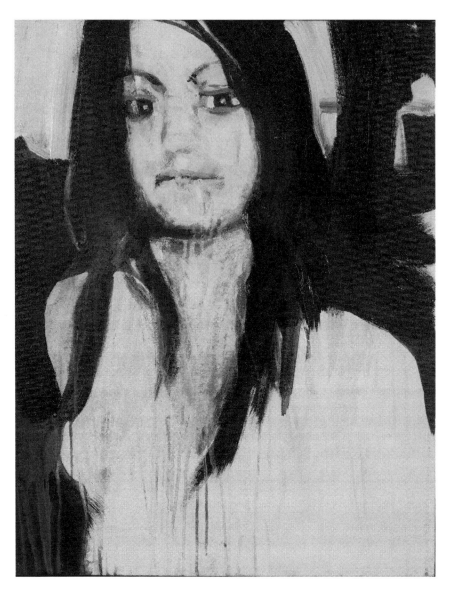

Figure 3.1 Portrait of Brenda Berenice Castillo García, Brian Maguire 2011. Acrylic on canvas. 71 × 55 cm.

Image courtesy of the artist and the Kerlin Gallery, Dublin.

the European Parliament in Brussels (September 2013) and the Victoria Gallery and Museum, University of Liverpool (27 September 2013–1 February 2014). In other showings, a smaller number of portraits were shown including at the Triskel Arts Centre, Cork, Ireland, to accompany the screening of the documentary film, *Blood Rising* (2013), as part of the Cork International Film Festival in

November 2014 and again as part of the exhibition, OUTPOSTS: *global borders and national boundaries*, at the Glucksman Gallery, University College Cork (29 November 2017–11 March 2018) in which I was involved as collaborator. *Blood Rising* was made by the Irish film-maker and human rights campaigner, Mark McLoughlin, and charts the artistic trajectory of the Maguire project as well as exploring the context to the feminicides.[24] The documentary featured sustained footage of the artist himself as it tracked the artistic process that emerged from the relationship with the mothers (and in one case, father) of the victims. The multimedial aspect of the project is crucial also in terms of Maguire's objectives of reaching broad and multiple audiences. Maguire speaks no Spanish and thus the relationship, as it is shown on camera, remains largely non-verbal and in the realm of the emotional. In this regard, it represents a remarkable insight into the communications process involved in the project and bears eloquent testimony to the crucial unspoken dimension of the relationships forged.[25] *Blood Rising* remains to date the only documentary film on the feminicidal violence in Juárez to scrutinize in any depth the role of art and culture as a response to the atrocities. As such, it constitutes a significant contribution to the wide-ranging body of documentary film on the topic and which is the subject of analysis in Chapter 4. In all of the sites of display of the images, Maguire has been active as a presence, attending for question and answer sessions, participating in panel discussions, giving talks and engaging with the public.[26] Finally, Maguire is by no means the only artist to work with portraits of the victims in his response to the feminicidal crimes.[27] In this regard, we might mention the project 'Facing Faces' by Belgian artist and curator, Gino d'Artali, which gathered together eighty-three artists from thirty different countries in an exhibition featuring 162 diptychs.[28] A recent mural project has sought to foreground the faces of victims[29] and in 2008, artists Swoon and Tennessee Jane created an installation titled 'Portrait of Silvia Elena' in reference to Silvia Morales, a victim of feminicide in 1998.[30]

The portraits formed part of a wider exhibition titled *An Oasis of Horror in a Desert of Boredom* and shown at the VISUAL Art Centre in Carlow, Ireland from October 2012–January 2013. It consisted of a series of eight large-scale portraits (of varying dimensions) of victims of the feminicidal violence in Ciudad Juárez displayed in the main gallery space.[31] Each portrait had alongside it a written text with details about the identity of the victim and a brief outline of the circumstances of her death. In addition to the work by Maguire, the exhibition included the project *Desconocida, Unknown, Ukjent* by Lise Bjørne Linnert, two installation pieces by the acclaimed Mexican artist, Teresa Margolles, both of which engaged with urban violence in Mexico;[32] a set of photographs by Lanka Haouche Perren and a section by Mark McLoughlin with images from the process of the documentary making, set against a wall on which the documentary was projected without sound. Alongside the formal exhibits, the Art Centre displayed an extensive series of artworks completed by third level students of art in the nearby Institute of Technology, Carlow and that constituted their response to the Maguire project. Finally, there was a space dedicated to the active work required as part of the *Desconocida, Unknown, Ukjent* display in which spectators were invited to embroider a name onto one of the tags provided.[33] This space also played Lourdes Portillo's acclaimed documentary film on the topic, *Señorita Extraviada* (the subject of analysis in Chapter 4) and displayed a number of books including Kathleen Staudt's *Violence and Activism at the US Mexico Border: Gender, Fear and Everyday Life* (2008) an authoritative account of the topic for English-speaking audiences.

As can be gleaned from the description, this was an exhibition of art but one that was uncompromisingly and unequivocally linked to a human rights activist agenda, participating directly and explicitly in the project of exposing the atrocities to an Irish public utterly unaware of them. It invited active participation from viewers (the *Desconocida* element) and had already engaged significantly with the local community in terms of soliciting the responses from art students. In this regard, the pedagogic, educational and indeed wider community role of human rights art was central to the project's objectives. This area of activism, constructed as an essential part of the exhibition, might be seen in terms defined by Lauren Berlant, as a space for an 'intimate public' as well as a 'place of recognition and reflection' (2008: viii). That it was placed at the end point of the exhibition further reinforced the point about reflection. Furthermore, the exhibition as a whole would seem to adhere to her argument about these intimate spaces in that it 'flourishes as a porous, affective scene of identification among strangers that promises a certain experience of belonging and provides a complex of consolation, confirmation, discipline and discussion about how to live as an *x*' (Berlant 2008: viii). As we shall see later, these kinds of assertions are deeply challenged by Maguire but it is certainly clear that spectators of the images are asked to congregate and be immersed in this environment that is at once a space for learning (signified by the books and the documentary showing) but also a space for political activism where the audience can participate in the *Desconocida* project by sewing. Located in a long artistic line of resistance through traditional feminine activity in Latin America and of which the Chilean *arpilleras*[34] are probably the best known example, the invitation to the spectator/witness to sew name badges and to insert herself into this line is both powerful and moving.

'Remember Them': the power of the face[35]

In what follows, I would like to explore an interpretation of the Maguire portraits and assess the cultural work they perform as a human rights' tool. In doing this, I seek answers to the question posed at the outset about the frames through which first world spectators view the portraits and moreover, the question of our responsibility as first world spectators in – quite literally – the face of these atrocities. In order to work through some of these questions, I will turn to the work of two philosophers utterly unconnected with the situation in Juárez: Emmanuel Levinas and Judith Butler.

French philosopher Emmanuel Levinas's work spans a broad range of areas including religion, politics, aesthetics and ethics but for the purposes of this discussion, I would like to concentrate on his ideas on the *visage* or face, so central to his thinking and which he insists can only be conceptualized as object/encounter (Cooper 2006: 15).[36] Levinas's work on human sociality contends that through the face-to-face relation [*rapport de face à face*], an ethical response is demanded of us. Specifically, Levinas says that the human face 'orders and ordains' us. It calls the subject into 'giving and serving' the Other. Indeed he maintains that, 'no event is as affectively disruptive for a consciousness holding sway in its world than the encounter with another person' (Bergo 2015: n.p.). Here the encounter with the other person is held up as paramount to the subject's sense of being. Levinas maintains that, 'In this encounter (even if it later becomes competitive or instrumental)' and here we might add, 'destructive', 'the "I" first experiences itself as called and liable to account for itself. It responds' (Bergo 2015: n.p.). It would seem that these Levinasian insights might be particularly appropriate in terms of trying to assess the significance of the encounter with the faces of the Maguire project. Indeed, according to Levinas:

> intersubjective experience, as it comes to light, proves 'ethical' in the simple sense that an 'I' discovers its own particularity when it is singled out by the gaze of the other. This gaze is interrogative and imperative. It says 'do not kill me'.
>
> (Bergo 2015)

Furthermore, Levinas encourages us to see the ways in which human faces impact us as 'affective moments', or what he calls 'interruptions'. These powerful insights into the mechanisms of intersubjective or interpersonal encounters challenge us to question our relationship with the faces that confront us during our daily life. At their core, they envision being and subjectivity as constituted directly and unequivocally through its situatedness alongside the Other.

Let us turn now and see how Judith Butler invokes Levinas's take on the face-to-face encounter to further a politics informed by global vulnerability. Butler offers a lengthy critique of Levinas in her work (2004, 2009, 2011) and in particular takes issue with some of what are considered his more controversial views.[37] Her own strategy therefore involves questioning, as she asks, 'can we use Levinas against himself in an articulation of a global ethics?' (Butler 2011).[38] In particular, she is interested in the traditional dichotomies of here/there as well as proximity/distance arguing forcefully that it is possible to reverse these dichotomies. What is perhaps more relevant to our consideration, she argues that, 'certain bonds are wrought through this very reversibility between proximity and distance' (2011). Because, as she puts it,

> what is happening there also happens in some sense here and if what is happening there depends on the event being registered in several elsewheres then it would seem that the ethical claim of the event takes place always in a 'here' and a 'there' that are fundamentally bound to one another.
>
> (2011)

In this sense, the event is always 'emphatically local' and what she calls the 'bodies on the line' registered elsewhere, enable global recognition (2011). Butler insists that witnessing this offers evidence of a certain kind of 'global connectedness', however 'provisional' she says (2011), and to which we could add, 'imperfect'. Her emphasis on the assertion that, 'One's own personal individual boundary is both a limit and a site of adjacency', 'a mode of spatial and temporal nearness and boundedness' and that, moreover, 'the bounded and living appearance of the body is the condition of being exposed to the other' (2011) offer striking ways through which we might reassess our relationships to 'those over there'. Moreover, according to Butler, the ways that 'we are affected and claimed by the face that acts upon us and that the way others act upon us without our will constitutes an ethical appeal' (2011). The resulting ethical relationship within these parameters is asymmetrical and indeed, she insists that reciprocity cannot be the basis of ethics. As she explains, glossing Levinas, 'I am already bound to you and this is what it means to be the self that I am: receptive to you in ways that I cannot fully predict or control' (2011). The most powerful political potential of this position resides perhaps in her insistence on 'an intertwinement between those other lives and my own, that it is also my life or our life, given that since whatever sense our life is already all our lives are dependent on a world of others' (2011).

Let us consider for a moment how the insights from both Levinas and Butler might translate when we contemplate the portraits from the Maguire project. Can we say when we look at the portrait of Airis (Figure 3.2) and learn of the barbaric nature of her abduction and murder at the age of seven, the obscenity of what happened to her, and by extension to her family, that we do not become part of this ethical relationship? Similarly, and looking at a different portrait, that of Brenda (Figure 3.1), do we recognize in the heart-wrenching story of this young mother, an urgent plea for an ethical response? Are we ethically bound to her? To her story? To her mother's story? Are the reactions to a portrait, such as Airis's, primarily emotional and how does emotional affect impact upon the ethical relationships outlined by both Levinas and Butler? The text accompanying the image of Airis in the exhibition, reads as follows:

> Airis Estrella Enriquez Pando was a bright lively cheeky seven-year old in 2005. She was out playing with her sister when they became separated. The young girl was abducted a few streets from her home by two or more men. Terrified for her child's safety, due in part to the killing of a local child earlier that month, Airis's mother immediately organised a search making full use of TV and State politicians. Within a week Airis's abused body was found encased in concrete in an oil drum. The concrete had contracted while drying and the little girl's finger was exposed. The two persons arrested are serving a 90 year sentence. Airis's family are forever marked by the killing.
>
> (Exhibition Catalogue 2012: 72)

As mentioned already, the case of Airis marked one of many turning points in the feminicidal narrative in Juárez, such was the revulsion it provoked in the local community. As well as the mobilization of TV and state politicians referenced here, the family of Airis galvanized local businesses into becoming involved in the search thereby conjoining many sectors hitherto unlinked

Remember them 93

Figure 3.2 Portrait of Airis Estrella Enríquez Pando, Brian Maguire 2005, 2010. Acrylic on canvas. 145 × 120 cm.

Image courtesy of the artist and the Kerlin Gallery, Dublin.

in the feminicidal debates and experiences. In forcing these disparate societal actors to acknowledge their responsibility in tracking down the perpetrators of such a diabolical crime, the family of Airis prompted a new consideration of gender violence in the region. In many ways, this acknowledgement was the embodiment of Levinasian philosophy, forcefully conveyed, that all Juárez citizens were bound to Airis in an intangible but nevertheless painful way. The blackness of Airis's hair and the eyes in the portrait somehow replicate the oily blackness of the liquid normally held in the vat where her body was found or they gesture towards the colour of the concrete material used to encase her little body. That somehow Airis's fingers had managed to escape beyond the concrete that enveloped her is almost too unbearable to assimilate. Focusing on the use of colour in the portrait, Ana Laura Ramírez Vásquez observed that the red colour that pervades the portrait is already a death trace, a signal that she is no longer with us.[39] There is a darkness in Maguire's treatment of Airis's image that reflects that depth of revulsion felt by the community but also seems to touch that sense of 'evil', the aura that pervades discussions and treatment of feminicide more generally and which is explored more fully in Chapters 4 and 5. It is the darkness that seems to dare us to look into another face: the face of a person – a male or males – who could perpetrate this pain and suffering on the body of a little girl.

I cannot disconnect my own viewing experience of Airis from my condition as the mother of a seven-year-old girl. Nor can I prevent feelings of nausea welling up in me alongside the tears that fall when I gaze at her face and read the text. This is further enhanced for me, as it would be for many other viewers, by the extra knowledge I have acquired about the case from reading the graphic details of the abuse suffered by Airis during the period of abduction and recorded in full by the Mexican press. These visceral feelings are located in a realm beyond emotion though they are, of course, mediated by emotions of sadness and grief. As Butler reminds us, 'To grieve, and to make grief itself into a resource for politics, is not to be resigned to inaction, but it may be understood as the slow process by which we develop a point of identification with suffering itself' (2004: 11). In this regard, grief too helps to forge the ethical bond that ensures that we can 'Remember Them'. I would argue that both Levinas and Butler offer urgent ways through which we can understand what Marianne Hirsch has proposed in a similar context, that images such as these ones create or construct 'an affiliative look through which we are sutured into the images and through which we adopt the image' (1997: 93). Furthermore, Hirsch suggests that this 'suturing of the viewer into the affective economy of the image' (1997: 93) is an essential part of the viewing experience. This focus on affiliative memory transmission as a counterpoint to familial modes of transmission is critical as it enables us to feel emotional connections with people we have never met (Hirsch 1997). Jill Bennett's (2005) work on art in the US post-9/11 further prompts us to reflect on the work performed by art that 'makes these interconnections globally, putting distinct traumatic instants into suggestive relationships to provoke empathic encounters' (cited in Luckhurst 2008: 161). According to Roger Luckhurst, for Bennett, 'it is this *relational* affect that distinguishes art practice from other cultural discourses of trauma' (2008: 160, my emphasis).

Remember them 95

Empathic witnessing: the force of Erika

By way of further testing these ideas in relation to the potential for an empathic encounter with portraits such as those in the Maguire project, let us concentrate on one portrait in particular. For the purposes of this discussion, I have chosen the portrait of Erika as a way of unpacking some of the mechanisms suggested by Levinas, Butler and others in relation to spectatorial engagement with narratives of the feminicidal atrocities. What follows, therefore, is an exploration of my own relationship with this particular image and it commences with the

Figure 3.3 Portrait of Erika Pérez Escobedo, Brian Maguire 2012. Acrylic on linen. 81.5 × 73 cm.
Image courtesy of the artist and the Kerlin Gallery, Dublin.

explanation offered of her death. According to the text accompanying the image in the exhibition,

> Erika Pérez Escobedo was 29 years of age and married with two children when she was killed. She worked in a factory making harnesses for cars. Her body was found in the street with her clothes disturbed and her bra around her neck. There was evidence of rape. There were strangulation marks on her neck. The police immediately judged the cause of death to be drug overdose. No investigation followed.
>
> (Exhibition Catalogue 2012: 68)

One of the reasons for selecting this image is that a black-and-white smaller copy of the larger portrait hangs on the wall outside my office. Purchased at the exhibition, a number of these copies were available with all proceeds being donated to the NGO Nuestras Hijas de Regreso a Casa. Through this simple act of consumption, therefore, I was inserted into a relationship with the subject where we were already 'involved'. Following on from this moment, I have personally been contemplating the face of Erika for several years and my relationship with the portrait is coloured by my extensive knowledge of the context, the Maguire project of which it is a part and my own 'real' encounter with the subject's mother, Elia Escobedo García. Taking Butler's dialogue with Levinas's ideas into account:

> To respond to the face, to understand its meaning, means to be awake to what is precarious in another life or, rather, the precariousness of life itself. This cannot be an awakeness, to use his [Levinas] word, to my own life, and then an extrapolation from an understanding of my own precariousness to an understanding of another's precarious life. It has to be an understanding of the precariousness of the Other.
>
> (2004: 134)

Following Butler's discussion of Levinas here, the encounter with Erika can thus be construed as the ultimate awakeness to the other. In addition, this awakeness presupposes or creates the conditions for an understanding of the precariousness of Erika. Given the fact of Erika's death, this seems self-evident in more ways than one. What is perhaps more interesting is the way in which Levinas isolates the face of the precarious other as the 'business' of the first world spectator:

> But that face facing me, in its expression – in its mortality – summons me, demands me, claims me: as if the invisible death faced by the face of the other [...] were 'my business'. As if, unknown by the other whom already, in the nakedness of his face, it concerns, it 'regarded me' before its confrontation with me, before being the death that stares me, myself in the face. The death of the other man puts me on the spot, calls me into question, as if, by my possible indifference, became the accomplice of that death, invisible to

the other who is exposed to it; and as if, even before being condemned to it myself, I had to answer for that death of the other, and not leave the other alone to his deathly solitude.

(1999: 24–25)

If I accept that this encounter with the image of Erika 'puts me on the spot' in the way that Levinas envisions, then in order to avoid complicity I must answer its demands of me, its summons of me. If complicity can be avoided, however, arguably guilt is already there, guilt for living a different life from that of Erika, guilt at my own privilege, guilt for being alive when she is not. This calling of my existence into question thus forces me to face the demands that Erika makes of me. Martina Kopf's theorising of 'empathic witnessing' (2010), underscores again, Hirsch's notion of the suturing together of subjects from different times and spaces into an affective relationship, an empathic encounter. This encounter is further enhanced when we consider that mine and Erika's worlds are also connected through a continuum of violence against women, which, of course, happens over 'here' as well as over 'there', a point made by Mary Anne Franks in her discussion of Adorno's work (2005: 198). Following this, perhaps the faces of the feminicidal victims as part of their ethical solicitation to us also force a process of recognition of similar realities. If this is indeed the process through which my 'here' and Erika's 'there' become part of a global connectedness, then it is clear that the work performed by art installations and exhibitions such as this one is both politically relevant and urgently necessary.

Finally, in this exploration of my ethical relationship with Erika's portrait, I would like to explore Bracha Ettinger's compelling thesis about 'wit(h)nessing' (2006). Ettinger's work invites us to consider that images such as those of Maguire's portrait of Erika construct a 'matrixial alliance', or as Griselda Pollock explains in her exploration of Ettinger's work, that process through which human subjects are brought:

> closer to the possibility of recognizing and being affected by the pain and hence the being of the other, and to assenting to carry some of its burden, to share a borderspace that may become a threshold. This is not sympathy; this is not empathy. This is not about making the viewer feel a good or better person, or a more sensitive one. It is about the specific ways that the aesthetic encounter created by art practice can open up a threshold between now and then, us and them to create a shared borderspace that acknowledges the gap between different beings, times and places, while ethically making each partner vulnerable to the other's trauma and making us want to know it and even able to process it precisely because of the different, matrixial nature of the difference between unknown but co-affecting partners in difference.
>
> (2010: 837–838)

The insistence on a relationship that goes beyond empathy and explicitly involves 'sharing' seems to envision an alliance that can generate productive political change. While the use of the term 'borderspace' by Pollock in the context of art that is generated from the violence emerging from the material border dividing the US and Mexico is perhaps unhelpful here, the idea that my relationship with Erika can go beyond empathy is both persuasive and alluring. As Pollock affirms,

> an unknown other was always a partner-in-difference and co-emergent. Thus we cannot but share the pain or trauma, i.e. the events of the other. We cannot but bear it, transport it, and potentially create a future precisely by such sharing, by recognizing co-humanity.
>
> (2010: 837)

It is important to distinguish, of course, between those who suffer but survive trauma, and the dead – those forever silenced victims of trauma. Erika belongs in the latter category and while no longer suffering, any future that might be created through my sharing her burden will, by definition, not include her. We recall here Levinas's reflections on the face as the ultimate embodiment of the plea for life and the knowledge that it has already failed is another factor to consider in my reaction as spectator, a knowledge that renders me paralyzed and helpless. That this inevitably complicates ideas of wit(h)nessing is another strand to consider when observing the obstacles that inhibit the pathways toward global solidarity. In the next section, I would like to consider how these complications contribute towards an undoing of the ethical viewing frames conceptualized thus far.

Frames undone

Through this rather circuitous exploration of my own relationship with these artworks, we can appreciate that the frames through which spectators view images such as these ones are conditioned necessarily by the other stories, images and contexts that accompany them. Here I would like to consider the ways in which these frames might problematize or unsettle slightly the viewing parameters set out by both Butler and Levinas for the contemplation of the 'other's' humanity. Those viewing parameters through which we apprehend, or indeed, fail to apprehend the lives of others are politically saturated and indisputably conditioned by our socio-political contexts – by our 'here' that is and always probably will be different from their 'there'. In this regard, 'the shared borderspace' visualised by Ettinger is always shot through with what we might call lines of contention, not dissimilar to the barbed wires that proliferate in images of the real US-Mexico border where many of the victims' bodies were discarded. Notwithstanding the force of the claims by both Levinas and Butler then, and the powerful potential for global connectedness that they evoke, I find myself questioning whether this 'empathic encounter' (Bennett 2005) is not a little bit more complicated than that which is suggested by them. Indeed, perhaps the stumbling block in Butler's envisioning of a global ethical coalition is the fact that the affective interruption – the 'interruption by alterity' (Butler 2011) that occurs in the encounter with the other is immediately accompanied by a series of other factors that potentially unsettle its ethical claims.

The first area of doubt that arises can be found in the deeply individual and subjective nature of the spectator's encounter with the other. Might it be argued that because the claim is personal, 'intersubjective' to use Levinas's term, then it could seem to preclude any turn to the sort of collective political action (understood in its traditional sense) that is urgently demanded as a response to the impunity and indifference surrounding the cases in Ciudad Juárez? Lilie Chouliaraki notes in a discussion on what she terms a post-humanitarian sensibility emerging from projects that engage the 'reflexivity of the spectator' (2010: 11) that they may offer 'an alternative vision of agency one whose political implications are deeply ambivalent' (2010: 19). She elaborates: 'this focus on individual judgment further foregrounds the power of personal rather than collective action in making a difference in the lives of vulnerable others' (2010: 19). Taking these insights into account, the emphasis on the spectator's reflexivity, the dependence on the spectator's frames of reference and 'openness' or in Levinas's terms, 'awakeness' to the conditions of the vulnerable other they contemplate, potentially undermines the urgent political action urged by the artist as the appropriate (and politically necessary) response. Chouliaraki contends that the more likely outcome of these kinds of representational practices is 'to expand the domain of politics towards mundane tactics of subversion' (2010: 19). By 'mundane tactics' here, I understand acts of ordinary consumerism and activism like, for example, signing a petition, buying a T-shirt, wearing pink or the other small gestures that signify individual resistance or indeed collective political action. In the case of my empathic encounter with the Maguire exhibition, it involved the purchase of the portrait; the exhibition catalogue and my lengthy interaction with the activities demanded by the *Desconocida* project. Chouliaraki sees these new sets of practices as part of a new 'post-humanitarian sensibility that breaks with [the emotional repertoire of] pity and privileges a short-term and low-intensity form of agency, which is no longer inspired by an intellectual agenda but momentarily engages us in practices of playful consumerism' (2010: 1). In this context, it is interesting to note that she explicitly locates this new set of practices in mixed-media humanitarian projects such as the one exemplified by the exhibition as it was curated at VISUAL, Carlow. Capturing perfectly the experience of the Maguire project for this spectator, the 'playfulness' to which Chouliaraki refers, was amply expressed through the activity of sewing for the *Desconocida* project as well as the signing of the visitor book to express support and outrage and the purchasing of the catalogue and the portrait (already mentioned), the proceeds of which were all donated to one of the primary NGOs. It goes without saying that this new sensibility poses a challenge to the construction of a transnational coalition envisioned by Butler and locates the spectators at once within a system they are invited to critique but of which they are indisputably a part. By definition complicit through their privileged geopolitical positioning, even their capacity to consume suffering in this way radically interrogates the whole notion of the empathic encounter.

Alongside the uneasy positioning of the spectator as playful consumer, as well as empathic witness, is a further problem. By signalling Ciudad Juárez as a space of atrocity in this very graphic manner, artists employ what Swanson Goldberg and

Schultheis Moore denominate, 'an aesthetics of immediacy' (2011: 239). On one level, this is entirely logical and indeed necessary for an art that is demanding or urging political action of its spectators. However, they warn of the possibility that

> the rhetorics and aesthetics of immediacy confound attempts to reread the historical conditions of suffering against the priorities of the state and in light of the long duration of these 'crises', as well as to foreground the possibility of transnational feminist alliances as opposed to humanitarian intervention.
> (2011: 239)

Furthermore, they caution that the deployment of this particular aesthetic approach 'warrants a good deal of critical attention in terms of long-standing debates about the aestheticization of other people's experiences of pain, terror, and atrocity' (2011: 239). The ethical and political issues at stake in this project of aestheticization have, of course, been rehearsed from the perspective of diverse disciplinary fields and are not our specific concern here. Rather, Swanson Goldberg and Schultheis Moore caution that the linking of 'an aesthetics of immediacy with the rhetoric of humanitarian crisis, reasserts the prerogatives of the liberal-capitalist state rather than critiquing its constitutive structural conditions' (2011: 239). In a sense, this returns us to the idea of complicity, or critique from within the very system that sustains us and in which the first world spectator can thrive while the life of the 'vulnerable other' is at risk. Peter Nyers puts it very eloquently when he says that

> To speak of emergencies is to at once enter into a dualistic dance with all that which is taken to constitute a normal and ordered state of affairs . . . A crisis and an ordered existence constitute separate and distinct worlds; their relationship is one of strict difference.
> (2006: 7–8)

In other words here there is a tension between the suturing of the subject into an affective and potentially politically transformative relationship with the other face and an aesthetics of immediacy with its emphasis on exceptionality and difference. The media construction of Ciudad Juárez as a monstrous entity is a good example of the way in which the site's exceptionality was used to reinforce the urgency of the humanitarian situation there. It might be argued that this exceptionality and the notion of excessive violence is what largely characterizes the representation of Mexico in international media since 2006. In cementing these ideas, however, of exceptionality and excess, projects like this one, reinforce their 'over thereness' and potentially dismantle any notion of an unproblematic affective encounter.

A further problem presents itself, relating again, to the positioning of the spectator as active consumer. Does the fact that we consume the portrait as an aesthetic art object further problematize or at the very least unsettle the ethical possibilities suggested by Butler? Can I say that I see the image first as image and second as obliterated subject? First as beautiful art object, second as murder victim? Does it matter whether I read the text or see the image first? And what of our relationship to the tradition into which it has been inserted, namely the tradition of Western portraiture? Of course, historically portrait painting privileged the rich and the powerful and of course we can read the artist's conscious decision to paint portraits of forgotten murder victims on the US-Mexico border as part of a counter tradition that seeks to insert these women into a pantheon of so-called worthy individuals or people whose stories deserve to be seen (and read). The freezing and capturing of the image, so critical to portraiture, captures them at a moment that is charged with life while the fact of their deaths hangs uneasily in the air during any consumption of the texts. To return for a moment though to Levinas: it should be noted that for him, the face does not directly signify the human. As Butler explains:

> Rather, the human is indirectly affirmed in that very disjunction that makes representation impossible, and this disjunction is conveyed in the impossible representation. For representation to convey the human, then, representation must not only fail, but it must show its failure.
>
> (2004: 144)

This is pertinent when applied to the Maguire portraits in that the humanity of the victims is affirmed in the very disjunction that signals the impossibility of representation. By this I mean that for the representation of Erika to convey her humanity in Levinasian terms, the representation must fail and must show that it fails. In this case, failure is most visibly discerned by the fact that all the portraits show their subjects as alive – often smiling or happy. Taking this into account, they are lies in the most literal sense of the word and thus fail as representation even if it is through their failure, that the humanity of their subjects is affirmed. In other words, their humanity is not captured by their representation but rather by their failed representation, the impossibility of their representation as alive. Perhaps the contemplation of subjects after death problematizes the stance adopted by Butler and Levinas for whom the encounter with the other rests on the attentiveness to the plea 'do not kill me' (in Levinas's case) and on the suturing of the disparate experiences from different parts of the globe into a connected whole (in the case of Butler). In this regard, projects that take subjects after death as their source require – as the Maguire project did – the participation of other agents, the grieving family members, the engaged, committed artists, the community, to make sense and to work to piece the humanity of the deceased back together.

This, as alluded to earlier, is probably the ultimate challenge posed by Levinas and Butler in that alongside the affective impact of the encounter, or the interruption of alterity upon us as spectators is the immediate revelation (through the written text) that catapults you as spectator into a simultaneous encounter with death. If we accept Butler's claim that we are somehow 'claimed' by that face, how can we account for the claiming of us by a face who is no longer with us, that most extreme other, who makes an ethical claim on me? This confrontation between alterity in life and death at the same time forms a realization that soon renders any participation in any series of gestures, mundane or otherwise, ultimately redundant. Encountering the face of Erika, or Airis, or Brenda (Figures 3.1–3.3) through this Levinas lens, the knowledge that the plea not to be killed has already fallen on deaf ears, and that a rupture has occurred between the faces that can never be repaired is both paralyzing and irrevocable. There is nothing the spectator can do to help Erika, or Brenda or Rubí or Silvia. And it is perhaps in that dark realization of the utter helplessness of the spectator that the absolute limits of the approaches suggested by Levinas and Butler are most starkly exposed.[40] Perhaps too, this is at the heart of what it means to be a first world witness to atrocity in the Elsewheres of the world in a way that is indelibly connected to the frames – personal, socio-political, collective – through which spectators view the images. In this regard, the exhibition captures some of the epistemological disorientation that Butler refers to, a disorientation that is necessary in her view in order to properly bear global feminist witness. In other words, central to the ability to form the empathic encounter is to recognize the limitations of that encounter, as Swanson Goldberg and Schultheis Moore assert,

> that she cannot fully know the other, that her attempts are limited by her distance in time, place and experience – what Butler might call her 'first-worldism' – and that this *not fully knowing* is an essential component of any possible gesture toward solidarity.
>
> (2011: 247)

The maternal encounter

I want to end my reflections on the exhibition with a consideration of a radically different spectator/participant, namely the mothers and other relatives of the women portrayed here. In 2013, I had the opportunity to meet Elia Escobedo García, mother of Erika, already discussed, and talked specifically about her experiences on the project with both Maguire and McLoughlin.[41] Throughout her interview, Elia exhibits many of the qualities of mother activists including stoicism, bravery as well as quiet determination. She affirms that it is her faith in God and the love for her children and grandchildren that sustain her through the many extreme adversities she faces. Elia's empathic encounter with the image of her dead child is by necessity very different to anybody else's. For her, this is not the encounter with the other, but an encounter with a part of herself and an agonizing challenge to acknowledge the Truth of what happened to her daughter. Elia, like many of the other mothers, has campaigned tirelessly for information in relation to her daughter's murder and to no avail. I asked her specifically about what being involved in Maguire's project meant to her: In response to the question:

> ¿Cómo se siente al ver ese retrato de Erika que tienes ahora en casa o sea la copia que hizo Brian.? ¿Cómo se siente al ver ese retrato todos los días – es un sentido de felicidad, de recuerdo dulce, de dolor profundo, de sufrimiento?
>
> [How do you feel when you see Erika's portrait every day – the portrait you have now at home – is it a feeling of happiness, sweet memories, deep pain, suffering?]

*Una pregunta difícil (empieza a llorar)*⁴²
[(That's) a difficult question (she starts to cry)]
Por las mañanas . . . Hola (tears) . . .
[In the morning . . . hi. . .]
El ver a mis hijos grandes, el ver que este, yo tengo que apurarme por ellos de verla y decirle 'hola hija, buenos días'.
[When I see my children grown up, when I see, you know I have to pull myself together for their sake, to see her and say, 'hi love, how are you?']
Me alienta . . . me alienta. . .

The last words uttered here intrigue me. Etymologically, the verb *alentar* is complex and stems from the latin *alenitāre* (breath) paired with the *-ar* to render it into a verb. Among the many ways you might choose to translate what she says in that final phrase '*me alienta, me alienta*', the one that is most apposite here is perhaps its literal meaning.⁴³ I ask myself whether there can be a more powerful statement about the impact of the artistic object than the one when Elia states that the portrait she holds on her wall, gives her life?⁴⁴ Or indeed, if we interpret it metaphorically, that it emboldens her, cheers her up, encourages her? A further etymological layer reveals the connection between *alentar* and *anhelar*, alluding to a sense of longing or an emotional yearning that is also poignantly germane in its usage here. This particular effort at translation of Elia's words allows us to see that through her experience of the artwork as life-giving; she insists on its generative and transformative potential, a crucial insight into the function of art as a response to atrocity. Indeed, the multiple meanings inherent in the verb *alentar* alert us to the challenges of translation – cultural and linguistic – that the Juárez feminicides present. Butler isolates this challenge as critical:

> We have to consider the demands of cultural translation that we assume to be part of an ethical responsibility [. . .] as we try to think the global dilemmas that women face.
>
> (2004: 49)

Within the plethora of studies on trauma and the affects of trauma, psychiatric discourses emphasize the possibility of a plurality of responses including the all-important one of resilience (to which we might add, resistance). Maguire has repeatedly stated that resistance was never a conscious choice for the victims' families, but rather that it is expressed and experienced as a *necessity* (my emphasis).⁴⁵ An interesting distinction is drawn here, and it is that sense of duty (to her family) and responsibility (to Erika) that is so clearly and intensely reflected in Elia Escobedo García's words. Luckhurst, drawing on the work of Derek Summerfield, suggests that the resilience displayed by victims of trauma and atrocity often 'depends on local traditions and embedded social networks left invisible to the diagnostic criteria parachuted into non-western contexts with psychiatric technicians' (2008: 212). This statement also resonates with Elia's tribute in an earlier section of the interview to those embedded social networks – namely the strength and solidarity she derives from her human rights work and her relationship with the other activist women – Norma Andrade, Marisela Ortiz and others. In this sense, perhaps it is Erika's mother, after all, who is closest to Butler's ideas about the multiple resonances and richness of the encounter with the other face, even when that face signals the most appalling personal tragedy.

And so we return to the questions posed at the outset of this chapter in relation to the function and role of the artistic narratives about Juárez. Notwithstanding the questions raised about the redundancy of art beyond its function as exposure, it is important too not to underestimate this function, nor its power. As the human rights lawyer and activist from Chihuahua, Lucha Castro said in conversation with Maguire, 'for this story to be heard by the governments, it must be told outside Mexico' (Exhibition Catalogue 2012: 9). Thus regardless of how the empathic encounter might be measured or assessed, the simple power of the art object to be able to shape events or political change may suffice.[46] And in the cases of the Juárez feminicides, where, for the most part, conventional legal routes of seeking justice have been exhausted or have expired, then the cultural realm where their pain and loss might be expressed becomes a political tool – not to ensure justice in those specific cases – but to ensure that it cannot happen again. If this sounds hollow, and I have no doubt but that it must sound hollow to the families of victims, then perhaps, it is the best that can be done. Or might the artistic narratives prompt interventions in the realm of transitional justice initiatives or other political gestures, which, however tardy or mealy-mouthed, might still serve as metaphorical compensation and comfort? Or might we get to a point – brought about in part by cultural narratives – when the citizens observatory could pass favourable judgement on the national alert system, the system that has been set up to prevent, sanction and eradicate violence against women in Mexico? Or that the global exposure of the Ciudad Juárez feminicides – ongoing primarily through cultural expression – might be brought to bear on reactions to the current feminicidal wave in the Estado de Mexico? In that state, in 2017, in a case very reminiscent of that of Airis, much media attention was focused on the plight of eleven-year-old Valeria, who was last seen on a bus where she had been placed by her father, anxious to protect her from the heavy rain. Her raped and murdered body was found the next day prompting predictable media outrage but with no sense of anything having changed since Airis's murder in 2005.[47] I have argued elsewhere (Finnegan 2016), that the cases in Edumex (Estado de Mexico) may be seen as part of a cycle of melancholic repetition of feminicidal violence, a cycle as yet unbroken. Indeed perhaps it is the reverberating echoes of feminicidal narratives, their unrelenting repeatability, that constitutes the ultimate challenge to creative practitioners seeking to make a difference with their work.

Having travelled a journey through the particular interpretive challenges represented by the Maguire project, it may seem as though there are more questions than answers. However, I hope, to have signalled at least the possibility that on some very profound level, these images do constitute a solicitation to us the viewers to become part of a global ethical approach to atrocities of this kind. This is not to deny those other aspects of what we might call 'Human Rights' art and/or aesthetics that might be seen as problematic: that the subjective viewing experience might in essence create barriers to meaningful collective action; that the simultaneous encounter with death undoes the political potential of the spectatorial experience; that the aesthetics of immediacy so common in art about Juárez generally copperfastens the dichotomies between here/there rather than dissolve them. Does it matter that artists are inevitably bound to those global circuits of distribution and power that determine who is doing 'good' art, who is doing 'bad' art, which art sells, which art does not sell. Of course. But it doesn't take from the central achievement of the Maguire exhibition which is its ethical solicitation to us. And to return finally to Levinas – that it is our shared vulnerability that ensures that we will continue to be interrupted by alterity, by the claims that others like Erika, like Airis and like Brenda make upon us.

In a wonderfully insightful review of a book on the disappeared students from Ayotzinapa by North American journalist, John Gibler (2016), Guillermo Espinosa Estrada alludes to the existence in Mexico of an unsettling rhetoric of face, or rather of the absence of face ['*una inquietante retórica del rostro o, más bien, de su ausencia*'] (2017: n. p.). In the light of the particular atrocities of Ayotzinapa that included the infamous case of Julio Cesar Mondragón whose body was found with the skin of his face removed, it is, perhaps, not surprising that the dichotomies of face/facelessness, identity/anonymity should be so terrifyingly present in cultural discourse. And it is perhaps as part of this rhetoric of face/facelessness and in the portraits' quiet inscription of life in the face of inexplicable horror that the power of Maguire's portraits might ultimately be discerned.

Notes

1 Julián Cardona has been at the forefront of much photojournalism in Ciudad Juárez and has acted as a critical point of contact for many visiting researchers, artists and human rights activists. For an excellent insight into the work of Ciudad Juárez photographers, see Driver (2015). Driver's documentary film, *If images could fill our empty spaces*, is also based on interviews with Cardona and Bailleres (2015). Lucio Soria is an award-winning photojournalist working for *El Diario de Juárez*. For an interesting overview of his practice see his interview with Darwin Franco Migues (2013).
2 Maya Goded's photographic project, *Desaparecidas*, dates from 2005–2006 and emerged from her concern for the victims of feminicide and their families, particularly the women's children. Haunted by the children's stories, she returned to Juárez in 2015 and produced the video/installations, Ciudad Juárez and Norma, a portrait of one of the mothers of the feminicidal victims. For more information, see http://mayagoded.net/site/portfolios/ciudad-juarez/ [Accessed 24 January 2018].
3 Yamina Del Real's exhibition *El cuerpo deshabitado* was shown in the Museo Archivo de la Fotografía in Mexico City in 2011 and afterwards appeared in book form as *El silencio luminoso*, as part of the series, 'Artes en México', directed by Alberto Ruy Sánchez. The images conjoin visual responses to the victims of *feminicidio* in Ciudad Juárez, imagined as doll-like figures with a broader reflection on the female body constructed through a series of disturbing self-portraits. Emer Clifford presents an excellent discussion of of Del Real's work in '*Otras Miradas: Representations of Gender Violence in Contemporary Mexican Visual Culture*' (Ph.D Thesis, forthcoming 2019). Other projects include acclaimed Mexican photographer, César Saldívar's important series, *Perder el Norte* which was exhibited in Mexico City's Palacio de la Minería in 2010. For an appraisal of this exhibition see Kingsley (2018).

4 Lanka Haouche Perren is a graduate of the Conservatoire Libre du Cinéma Français in Paris. His work has been screened and shown at various festivals and galleries in Ireland, France, England, Finland and Germany.
5 Basil Al-Rawi's work is concerned with 'how art can mediate, rearrange and reconstruct our reality'. His images about feminicide were featured in the exhibition, 'Regarding the Hispanic World', Photo Ireland Festival, Instituto Cervantes, Dublin, Ireland. 2 May–29 June 2017. For further information, see: www.basilalrawi.com/contact/ [Accessed 24 January 2018].
6 This exhibition gathered a large number of visual artists including Adriana Alba-Sanchez, Yolanda Amescua, Judith F. Baca, Raul P. Baltazar, Yreina Cervántez, Victoria Delgadillo, Ofelia and Elena Esparza, Consuelo Flores, Ester Hernández, Jenina, Alma Lopez, Jose Lozano, Azul Luna, Rigoberto Maldonado, Francisco 'Chisco' Ramirez, Martha Ramirez, Victor Rosas, T. Pilar and Martin Sorrondeguy. Thinkagain was Daisy Tonantzin and Patricia A. Valencia. It also involved musical performance with the group Jarocho Candela, whose members are Xochi Flores, Angela Flores, Rocio Marrón, Cecilia Brennan, Angelica Loa, Nikki Campbell, Tianna Paschel and Carolina Sarmiento. Performance artists were Erika Elizondo, Monica Barriga and the group KILSONIC, whose members are Eddika Organista, Frank Luis, Mike Ibarra, Dominique Rodriquez, Brian Walsh, Shane Jordan and Minh Pham. Other participants were Raquel Salinas and Carmen Vega. Spoken word and readings were done by Alicia Gaspar de Alba, Consuelo Flores, and Claudia Rodriguez (Delgadillo and Maldonado 2003) For further information, see http://sparcinla.org/hijas-de-juarez/ [Accessed 19 January 2018].
7 Artists included Adrianna Yadira Gallego, Ana Teresa Hernández, Amalia Benavides, Ambra Polidori, Azul Luna, Carla Rippey, Cecilia Álvarez Muñoz, Consuelo Jiménez Underwood, Ester Hernández, Esperanza Gama, Eva Soliz, Favianna Rodríguez, Judithe Hernández, Karen Musgrave, Linda Vallejo, Monica Huitron Flores, Patricia Acosta, Pilar Acevedo, Rocío Caballero, Rosario Guajardo, Sandra Vista, Stephanie Manríquez, Susan Plum, Veronica Cardoso Nagel and Victoria Delgadillo. The exhibition ran from 16 October 2009–14 February 2010.See http://nationalmuseum ofmexicanart.org/exhibits/rastros-y-cr%C3%B3nicas-women-juarez [Accessed 19 January 2018].
8 Margolles is celebrated internationally for her work in the area of violence, injustice and human rights and courts controversy with her use of real human remains. Possibly the most famous intervention in this regard involves her installation titled '¿De qué otra cosa podríamos hablar?' [What else can we talk about?] featuring human blood recovered from various crime scenes and which formed part of the 53rd Venice Biennial in 2009 where she represented Mexico. For an excellent examination of Margolles's work, see Banwell (2015). Her engagement with *feminicidio* in Ciudad Juárez includes the artworks *Cimbra Framework* and *Lote Bravo*, both exhibited in multiple fora internationally.
9 Other interventions in graphics include the French comic artist Peggy Adam, whose graphic novel, *Luchadoras*, was published in 2006. American cartoonist and illustrator Phoebe Gloeckner's work *La tristeza* (2008) featured as contribution to the project, *I live here*, by Mia Kirshner (2008).
10 This was exhibited at the University of Kentucky's Tuska Center for Contemporary Art in October 2011. Anna Kingsley (2018) provides a compelling reading of the visual paradigms suggested by this project.
11 Another notable example is Elina Chauvet's striking installation, *Zapatos rojos* [Red Shoes] (2009) which has been exhibited in Ciudad Juárez, Mexico City and internationally, including Norway, Italy, Spain, the UK, the US, Chile and Ecuador.
12 Exhibited to date in London, Edinburgh and the Netherlands, the exhibition was inspired by Challenger's trip to Ciudad Juárez in 2006 and her meetings with the

families of missing and murdered women. For more information, see www.tamsyn challenger.com/400-women/ [Accessed 23 January 2018].

13 This show at the Station Museum, Houston (21 October 2006–28 January 2007), directed by James Harithas, was a version of the later Philadelphia show and did important groundwork in gathering together the various artists of relevance. Luis Jimenez, Teresa Serrano, David Krueger, Sharon Kopriva, Lise Bjørne Linnert, Celia Alvárez Muñoz, Sara Maniero, Arturo Rivera, Teresa Margolles, Maya Goded, Carmen Montoya, Kaneem Smith, Susan Plum, Coco Fusco, Margarita Cabrera, Angela Dillon, Laura E. Rosales and Elia Arce. Harithas played a significant role in setting Maguire up with the relevant contacts in Ciudad Juárez and for ensuring his involvement in the Philadelphia project.

14 Frontera 450+ featured seventeen artists, many of whom had participated in the earlier exhibition in Houston: Carmen Montoya, Susan Plu, David Kureger, Celia Alvarez Muñoz, Arturo Rivera, Margarita Cabrera, Teresa Serrano, Sharon Kopriva, Maya Goded, Kaneem Smith, Lise Bjørne Linnert, Teresa Margolles, Sara Maniero, Angela Dillon, Coco Fusco, Elia Arce and Luis Jimenez. *Ni una más* was, according to its description, 'a powerful two-month long exhibition featuring more than 70 works of art by 20 international artists, including works or participation by Yoko Ono, Kiki Smith, Nancy Spero, Irish activist painter Brian Maguire and local artists Arlene Love and Jen Blazina organized by Drexel University through a collaboration of academic, student and institutional departments. Held in 2010, the goal of Ni Una Más is to raise awareness about gender violence and, in particular, crimes against women in the Mexican border town of Juárez'. http://drexel.edu/now/archive/2010/April/ Mass-Murders-of-Women-In-Juarez-Rally-Drexel-to-Art-and-Activism/ [Accessed 19 January 2018].

15 *No nos cabe tanta muerte: Memorial a Ciudad Juárez, Mexico*, for example, mentioned in the introduction, was a collective project led by Mexican artist Paula Laverde involving painting, audiovisual, installation and performance pieces from a range of artists from Europe, Latin America and Japan and shown in Barcelona in 2013. See also the diverse and varied international artistic contributions to the digital project, http:// porlasmujeresasesinadasdejuarez.blogspot.ie/ [Accessed 13 February 2018] as part of *Nuestra aparente rendición*, a digital collective that protests the current violence and ongoing insecurity in Mexico.

16 Each name tag is 2 × 8 cm, and the tags were stitched by 4,800 individuals in about 500 globally arranged workshops. For more details on location, see www.lisebjorne. com/art_projects/desconocida-unknown-ukjent/ [Accessed 23 May 2018].

17 Held from 28 November–10 December 2003 at the Museo de la Ciudad de Mexico.

18 Human rights discourse remains largely and irrevocably tied to the idea and politics of the nation state, a deeply problematic concept in the context of a violence that is largely supra-national. The historical linkages between human rights and nation states has been extensively covered by scholars such as Hannah Arendt. See, for example, 'The Decline of the Nation-State and the End of the Rights of Man' (1951).

19 I am deeply indebted to Brian Maguire for giving of his time to me at various points during the writing of this piece. It is from the many conversations we have had – in Liverpool, Cork, Mexico, Dublin – that the analysis here has emerged. Maguire has also hosted me at his home in Dublin and spoken on multiple occasions with students at University College Cork about the project. I am grateful too to the Kerlin Gallery for the permission to reproduce three of the portraits.

20 Scott Esposito notes that the line has been translated in different ways and writes that 'the one chosen to preface *2666* appears to be from Geoffrey Wanger's translation, found in *Selected Poems of Charles Baudelaire* (Grove Press, 1974). In the Spanish-language edition, the quote is translated into Spanish and largely corresponds to the Grove translation' (2008: n.p.).

21 These workshops came about as the direct result of negotiation with Marisela Ortiz's group, whereby Maguire was asked to teach art to the children in return for the group's participation in the administration of the project including the provision of translators (paid by the artist), establishing meetings, among other activities. It is important to underscore the importance of the negotiation undertaken with representatives of the families, given the centrality of this dimension to art within communities more generally (personal email communication with artist, 24 November 2017).

22 See also the exhibition catalogue (2012).

23 For Maguire, it was important to visit and re-visit the families with whom he had developed relationships (personal interview, March 2014). Other small details are worthy of note: his desire to keep the portraits 'together' and to sell them as a block; his consistent seeking out of spaces and places in which to display them and where he can engage with the wider public. His exhibition at the Fergus Gallery in New York in March–April 2015 featured a number of large-scale paintings about violence in northern Mexico. It was also accompanied by the supplementary material from the exhibition in VISUAL, Carlow, with an explicit activist/educator focus.

24 *Blood Rising* was made by the production company Bang Bang Teo on receipt of the Reel Art Award (worth €80,000). It was selected as the closing Gala event of the Dublin International Film Festival in 2013 and has been screened extensively since at over thirty universities across the UK, Ireland and the US including the University of Texas at El Paso. It has also been screened at arthouse cinemas internationally, including the Lighthouse Cinema in Dublin, the Curzon in London and the Loft in Tucson, Arizona. Shown at the European Parliament, it has been purchased by Sky Arts Television. *Blood Rising* was screened on 13 February 2018 at the Glucksman Gallery, University College Cork, as part of a series of events accompanying the exhibition, *Outposts: global borders and national boundaries* (30 November 2017–11 March 2018).

25 In a talk I gave on the Maguire project at the Universidad Autónoma de Ciudad Juárez (UACJ), there was initially great scepticism about yet another cultural practitioner visiting the city to undertake an art project and 'who doesn't even bother to learn Spanish' [*que ni se molesta en aprender español*]. However, the general reaction to the Maguire portraits at this workshop was overwhelmingly positive.

26 Maguire visited University College Cork to speak about the project in January 2013 and was the subject of a public interview (conducted by me) at the Glucksman Gallery in April 2014. He attended the display of the images in Liverpool, in the European parliament in Brussels and at the film festival in Cork to answer questions from viewers. He participated in another Q&A at the Glucksman Gallery in University College Cork, Ireland on 13 February 2018 where four of the portraits are displayed as part of the exhibition, *Outposts: global borders and national boundaries*.

27 The idea of the face as an image to lobby for justice is also key elsewhere in Latin America, particularly in Argentina and Uruguay since the dictatorship in the 1970s and 1980s and in the post-dictatorship period. The US artist Brian Carlson's project, *Aparecidos*, comprising more than 200 hand-painted portraits of victims of the dictatorship in Argentina, is a good case in point. I am indebted to Cara Levey for sharing her knowledge about similar projects in Argentina and elsewhere in the Southern Cone as well as her comments more generally on the chapter.

28 A selection of poetry from this project was later published, titled *I Love You: 65 International Poets United against Violence against Women* (2003).

29 Up to 180 murals have been painted throughout Ciudad Juárez by different artists and artistic collectives, including GH led by José Luis Alvarado and Maclovio Macías and the collective Rezizte. Most of the murals are portraits of the victims and they have elicited a mixed response from victims' families with some fervently supporting the initative and others, less convinced about their use as discursive strategy. This

    last point was noted by Alfredo Limas Hernández, in discussion at the Universidad Autónoma de Ciudad Juárez (UACJ) in February 2017).
30 This was displayed in Honey Space in Manhattan's Chelsea neighbourhood.
31 Dimensions varied throughout from larger scale, such as that of Ana Maria Gardea Villalobos (131 × 98) or Airis Estrella Enríquez Pando (145 × 120 cm) to the smallest portrait, that of Angel Octavio Atayde Arce (41 × 31 cm).
32 A *Través* [Across] (2011) and *Sonidos de la Muerte* [Sounds of death] (2012).
33 Spectators are asked to embroider the name *desconocida* in any language onto a piece of material that is available beside the exhibit. Lisa Bjørne Linnert participated in the symposium, 'Remember Them' organized by Professor Chris Harris at the University of Liverpool on 27 September 2013 where I had the opportunity to meet her.
34 Described as appliqué or embroidered designs on burlap, commonly referred to as patchwork or quilting: the *arpilleras* were a dominant form of feminized resistance to the regime of General Pinochet in Chile (1973–1990) and functioned as visible reminders of loss and pain as well as powerful testimonies to the disappeared.
35 'Remember Them' was the title of the exhibition in which Maguire's portraits were included and shown at the Victoria Gallery and Museum, University of Liverpool (27 September 2013–1 February 2014). Like the exhibition in Carlow, it included the *Desconocida* project, but unlike there, it also showed a series of hand-prints by Ciudad Juárez-based photographer, Julián Cardona and a film by Teresa Margolles titled *Irrigación*.
36 For the purposes of this discussion, I have used a number of sources: Levinas's discussion of the face in *Entre Nous: Essais sur le penser-à-l'autre* (1993) and its English translation, *Entre Nous: On Thinking-of-the-Other* (2000). I have also drawn on the helpful overview of Levinasian ethics provided by Bettina Bergo in the *Stanford Encyclopaedia of Philosophy* (2015). See also *The Levinas Reader* (Hand 1989). For critiques and discussions of Levinas, see, for example Zygmunt Bauman's *Postmodern Ethics* (1993) or Silvia Benso's *The Face of Things* (2000). For an excellent discussion of Levinasian ethics when applied to documentary cinema, see Sarah Cooper (2006). As can be seen, I have also relied extensively on Judith Butler's lengthy dialogues with Levinas's work (2004, 2009, 2011).
37 Controversy continues to surround Levinas's work including the relationship between ethics, ethnicity and politics. Butler maintains that Levinas's argument that ethical obligations were extended only to those bound by the Judeo-Christian traditions and, even more disturbing, that 'the Palestinian had no face' was deeply contradictory when considering his views on the 'other' (2011).
38 The 2011 quotations in the text are all taken from the Neale Wheeler Watson Lecture, delivered by Judith Butler, titled 'Precarious Life: The Obligations of Proximity', delivered at the Nobel Museum, Stockholm on 24 May 2011. This lecture is available at: https://www.youtube.com/user/NobelMuseum/videos [Accessed 20 June 2018].
39 Comment made during discussion of the Maguire project with students and staff from the Universidad Autónoma de Ciudad Juárez (UACJ) in February 2017. I am indebted to Ana Laura Ramírez Vásquez for the many helpful comments and observations she has shared with me on my work.
40 Adriana Cavarero's incisive reflections on violence explored in her book, *Horrorism: Naming Contemporary Violence*, offer further telling insights on the distinctions to be drawn between vulnerability and helplessness (2009: 29–32).
41 Elia Escobedo García was a guest of Frontline Defenders, a human rights organization based in Dublin, Ireland that focuses its fund-raising efforts on the activities of certain human rights activists, channelling their funds into ensuring their safety and security where possible and/or furthering the causes in which they are involved. For further information, see www.frontlinedefenders.org/ [Accessed 24 January 2018].

42 The publicity still for the documentary *Blood Rising* features Basil Al-Rawi's photograph of Elia looking at Erika's portrait. The photograph featured as part of the Photo Ireland exhibition at the Cervantes Institute, Dublin, Ireland, previously mentioned.
43 According to the dictionary of the Real Academia Española (RAE), '*Este vocabulario, etimológicamente procede del latín "alenitāre" o del sustantivo "aliento" y del sufijo flexivo "ar" infinitivo de los verbos. animar, infundir aliento o esfuerzo, dar vigour* [This word etymologically comes from the Latin '*alenitare*' or from the verb, 'breath' and the suffix, '*ar*' from the infinitive of the verbs, to animate, to impart breath or strength, to give strength].
44 It may be tempting on one level to dismiss something like this as trite affirmation of the so-called therapeutic value of art. However, if careful attention is paid to Elia's words, it is much more than this. She goes on to say in her interview that it is her children's '*logros*' or achievements, which are inspired by Erika, that are the most important elements in her life and constitute the source of pride which currently characterizes her work in the area of social justice (public interview, February 2013).
45 Statement uttered in *Blood Rising*, reiterated in personal interview, December 2012, Carlow.
46 Cara Levey argues that the didactic aspects of commemoration and cultural activity in Argentina in the post-dictatorship period have led to a potential perspective change amongst population, or at least sectors of population. The extent to which this shift in perspective has impacted the political sphere is less clear (2016).
47 This in no way should be read as though these were the only two female children to suffer violent death since the 1990s. Tragically, there have been many child victims of feminicide.

Works cited

Adam, Peggy, 2006. *Luchadoras*. Geneva: Atrabile.

Al-Rawi, Basil. 2017. *Regarding the Hispanic World* [Exhibition]. Photo Ireland Festival, Instituto Cervantes, Dublin. 2 May–29 June.

Arendt, Hannah, 1951. *The Origins of Totalitarianism*. New York: Schocken Books.

Banwell, Julia, 2015. *Teresa Margolles and the Aesthetics of Death*. Cardiff: University of Wales Press.

Baudelaire, Charles, 1974. *Selected Poems of Charles Baudelaire*. New York: Grove Press.

Bauman, Zygmunt, 1993. *Postmodern Ethics*. Oxford, Cambridge, MA: Wiley-Blackwell.

Bennett, Jill, 2005. *Empathic Vision: Affect, Trauma, and Contemporary Art*. Stanford: Stanford University Press.

Benso, Silvia, 2000. *The Face of Things: A Different Side of Ethics*. New York: SUNY Press.

Bergo, Bettina, 2015. "Emmanuel Levinas". *The Stanford Encyclopedia of Philosophy*. (Summer Edition). Edward N. Zalta, ed. [online]. Available at: https://plato.stanford.edu/archives/sum2015/entries/levinas/. [Accessed 16 January 2018].

Berlant, Laurent, 2008. *The Female Complaint: The Unfinished Business of Sentimentality in American Culture*. Durham, NC, London: Duke University Press.

Bjørne Linnert, Lise, 2006. *Desconocida, Unknown, Ukjent* [Collaborative art project]. Worldwide – present.

Blood Rising, 2013. [Film]. Directed by Mark McLoughlin. Bang Bang Teo.

Bolaño, Roberto, 2004. *2666*. Barcelona: Anagrama.

Butler, Judith, 2004. *Precarious Life*. London, New York: Verso.

———, 2009. *Frames of War: When Is Life Grievable?* London, New York: Verso.

———, 2011. *Precarious Life: The Obligations of Proximity*. The Neale Wheeler Watson Lecture. Location: Nobel Museum, Svenska Akademiens Börssal, 24 May. [online]. Available at: www.youtube.com/user/NobelMuseum/videos. [Accessed 20 June 2018].
Carson, Brian, 2012. *Aparecidos*. [Installation]. Locations worldwide – present.
Cavarero, Adriana, 2009. *Horrorism: Naming Contemporary Violence*. Trans. by William McCuaig. New York: Columbia University Press.
Challenger, Tamsyn. *400 Women (2010)* [Exhibition]. London 2010, Edinburgh 2011, Holland 2012.
Chauvet, Elina, 2009. *Zapatos rojos*. [Installation].
Chouliaraki, Lilie, 2010. Post-Humanitarianism: Humanitarian Communication Beyond a Politics of Pity. *International Journal of Cultural Studies*, 13 (2), 107–126.
Ciudad Juárez, 2015. Video [online]. Directed by Maya Goded. Available at: http://mayagoded.net/site/portfolios/ciudad-juarez/ [Accessed 24 January 2018].
Clifford, Emer, Forthcoming. *Otras Miradas: Representations of Gender Violence in Contemporary Mexican Visual Culture*. Thesis (Ph.D). University College Cork.
Cooper, Sarah, 2006. *Selfless Cinema? Ethics and French Documentary*. Oxford: Legenda.
D'Artali, Gino. *Facing Faces*, 2001. [Exhibition]. Museo de Arte e Historia, Mexico, 31 August–29 September.
———, 2003. *I Love You: 65 International Poets United Against Violence Against Women*. Fredericton, Canada, Ciudad Juárez, Mexico: Broken Jaw Press & Coalition of Artists United for Social Engagement.
Delgadillo, Victoria, and Maldonado, Rigo, 2003. Journey to the Land of the Dead: A Conversation with the Curators of the Hijas de Juárez Exhibition. *Aztlán*, 28 (2), 179–202 [online]. Available at: http://victoriadelgadillo.com/blog/wp-content/uploads/2013/03/Journey-to-the-Land-of-the-Dead1-1.pdf. [Accessed 20 June 2018].
Del Real, Yamina, 2011. *El cuerpo deshabitado* [Exhibition]. Museo Archivo de la Fotografía, Mexico. 16 June–28 August.
———, Lorenzano, Sandra, De Orellana, Margarita, and Ruy Sánchez, Alberto, 2013. *El silencio luminoso*. Mexico City: Artes de Mexico.
Driver, Alice, 2015. *More or Less Dead: Feminicide, Haunting, and the Ethics of Representation in Mexico*. Tucson: University of Arizona Press.
Espinosa Estrada, Guillermo, 2017. Las voces de Ayotzinapa. *Horizontal*, 26 July. [online]. Available at: https://horizontal.mx/las-voces-de-ayotzinapa/. [Accessed 17 January 2018].
Esposito, Scott, 2008. 2666 by Roberto Bolaño. *The Quarterly Conversation* [online]. Available at: http://quarterlyconversation.com/2666-by-roberto-bolano [Accessed 16 January 2018].
Ettinger, Bracha, 2006. *The Matrixial Borderspace*. Minneapolis, London: University of Minnesota Press.
Finnegan, Nuala, 2016. Staging Reconciliation: The Possibilities of Mourning in Rafael Bonilla's *La carta* (2010). *Bulletin of Spanish Studies*. [online]. Available at: https://doi.org/10.1080/14753820.2016.1248334 [Accessed 10 February 2018].
Franco, Jean, 2009. Questions for Bolaño. *Journal of Latin American Cultural Studies: Travesia*, 18 (2–3), 207–217.
Franco Migues, Darwin, 2013. Lucio Soria: "Las fotografías no deben mentir". *Nuestra aparente rendicion*. [online]. Available at: http://nuestraaparenterendicion.com/testigospresenciales/lucio-soria/ [Accessed 13 February 2018].

Franks, Mary Anne, 2005. An-Aesthetic Theory: Adorno, Sexuality, and Memory. *Feminist Interpretations of Theodor Adorno*. [online]. Available at SSRN: https://ssrn.com/abstract=2886644. [Accessed 16 January 2018].

Frontera 450+, 2006. [Exhibition]. Station Museum, Houston, TX. 21 October 2006–28 January 2007.

Gibler, John, 2016. *I Couldn't Even Imagine That They Would Kill Us. An Oral History of the Attacks Against the Students of Ayotzinapa*. San Francisco: City Lights.

Gloeckner, Phoebe, 2008. *La tristeza*. In Mia Kirshner et al., eds., *I Live Here*. New York: Pantheon Graphic Novels.

Hand, Sean, ed., 1989. *The Levinas Reader*. Oxford: Wiley-Blackwell, 289–297.

Hijas de Juárez, 2003. [Exhibition]. Social and Public Art Resource Centre (SPARC).

Hirsch, Marianne, 1997. *Family Frames: Photography, Narrative, and Postmemory*. Cambridge, MA: Harvard University Press.

If Images Could Fill Our Empty Spaces, 2013. [Film]. Directed by Alice Driver.

Kahlo, Diane. 2011. *Wall of Memories: The Disappeared Señoritas of Ciudad Juárez (2011)*. [Exhibition]. Tuska Center for Contemporary Art, University of Kentucky, Oct.

Keenan, Thomas, 2004. Mobilizing Shame. *South Atlantic Quarterly*, 103 (2/3), 435–449.

Kingsley, Anna, 2018. *Framing the Body: The Juárez Feminicides in Contemporary Mexican Visual Cultures (1993–2013)*. Thesis (Ph.D). Royal Holloway, University of London.

Kirshner, Mia, Simons, Michael, MacKinnon, J.B. and Shoebridge, Paul Shoebridge. 2008. *I Live Here*. New York: Pantheon Graphic Novels.

Kopf, Martina, 2010. Trauma, Narrative and the Art of Witnessing. In Birgit Haehnel and Melanie Utz, eds., *Slavery in Art and Literature: Approaches to Trauma, Memory and Visuality*. Berlin: Frank & Timme, 41–58.

Las mujeres de Juárez demandan justicia, 2002 [Poster Exhibition]. Mexico.

Levey, Cara, 2016. *Fragile Memory, Shifting Impunity: Commemoration and Contestation in Post-Dictatorship Argentina and Uruguay*. Oxford: Peter Lang.

Levinas, Emmanuel, 1989. *The Levinas Reader*. Sean Hand, ed. Oxford, Cambridge, MA: Wiley-Blackwell.

———, 1993. *Entre Nous: Essais sur le penser-à-l'autre*. Paris: Éditions Bernard Grasset.

———, 1999. *Alterity and Transcendence*. New York: Columbia University Press.

———, 2000. *Entre Nous: On Thinking-of-the-Other*. Trans. by Barbara Harshav and Michael B. Smith. New York: Columbia University Press.

Luckhurst, Roger, 2008. *The Trauma Question*. New York: Routledge.

Maguire, Brian, 2012–2013. *An Oasis of Horror in a Desert of Boredom*. [Exhibition]. VISUAL Centre for Contemporary Art, Carlow. 6 October–6 January.

Margolles, Teresa, 2009. *¿De qué otra cosa podríamos hablar?* [Installation]. 53rd Venice Biennial.

———, 2011. *A Través* [Across]. [Installation].

———, 2012. *Sonidos de la Muerte* [Sounds of death] [Installation].

Morillas, Maritza, 2006. *CaroDAtaVERnibus en Ciudad Juárez*. [Installation].

Ni Una Más, Not One More: The Juárez Murders, 2010. [Exhibition]. Leonard Pearlstein Gallery, Philadelphia. 15 May–16 July.

No nos cabe tanta muerte: Memorial a Ciudad Juárez, Mexico, 2013. [Exhibition]. Espai d'Arts de Roca Umbert, Barcelona. 7–30 November.

Norma, 2015. Video. [online]. Directed by Maya Goded. Available at: http://mayagoded.net/site/portfolios/ciudad-juarez/ [Accessed 24 January 2018].

Nyers, Peter, 2006. *Rethinking Refugees: Beyond States of Emergency*. New York, London: Routledge.

An Oasis of Horror in a Desert of Boredom, 2012. [Exhibition Catalogue]. Carlow, Ireland. Visual Centre for Contemporary Art and the George Bernard Shaw Theatre.

O'Hagan, Sean, 2015. Omar Victor Diop: 'I want to reinvent the heritage of African studio photography'. *The Guardian*, 11 July. [online]. Available at: www.theguardian.com/artanddesign/2015/jul/11/mar-ictor-ioi-want-to-reinvent-great-heritage-of-african-studio-photography [Accessed 13 February 2018].

Outposts: Global Borders and National Boundaries, 2017. [Exhibition]. Glucksman Gallery, University College Cork. 30 November 2017–11 March 2018.

Pollock, Griselda, 2010. Aesthetic Wit(h)nessing in the Era of Trauma. *EURAMERICA*, 40 (4), 829–886.

Primer Encuentro Internacional de Artes sobre el Femicidio en Ciudad Juárez, 2003. [Exhibition]. Museo de la Ciudad de Mexico. 28 November–10 December.

Project Diaspora, 2017. [Exhibition]. SCAD FASH Museum of Fashion + Film, Atlanta, GA. 17 February–18 August.

Rastros y Crónicas: Women of Juárez, 2009. [Exhibition]. National Museum of Mexican Art, Chicago. 16 October 2009–14 February 2010.

Saldívar, César, 2010. *Perder el Norte*. [Photographic Exhibition]. Palacio de Minería, Mexico City. 8 March–25 April.

Señorita Extraviada, 2001. [Film]. Directed by Lourdes Portillo.

Silva Londoño, Diana Alejandra, 2016. Street Art at the Border: Representations of Violence and Death in Ciudad Juárez. *Frontera Norte*, 28 (55), 33–52. [online]. Available at: www.scielo.org.mx/pdf/fn/v28n55/v28n55a2.pdf [Accessed 10 February 2018].

Staudt, Kathleen, 2008. *Violence and Activism at the U.S. Mexico Border: Gender, Fear and Everyday Life*. Austin: University of Texas Press.

Swanson Goldberg, Elizabeth and Schultheis Moore, Alexandra, 2011. Old Questions in New Boxes: Mia Kirshner's I Live Here and the Problematics of Transnational Witnessing. *Humanity: An International Journal of Human Rights, Humanitarianism, and Development*, 2 (2), 233–253.

Swoon. *Portrait of Silvia Elena*, 2008 [Installation]. Honey Space, Chelsea, NY. 30 May–5 July.

Volk, Steven S., and Schlotterbeck, Marian E., 2010. Gender, Order, and Femicide: Reading the Popular Culture of Murder in Ciudad Juárez. In Alicia Gaspar de Alba and Georgina Guzmán, eds., *Making a Killing: Femicide, Free Trade, and La Frontera*. Austin: University of Texas Press, 121–153.

4 Resilience and renewal in documentary film about *feminicidio* in Ciudad Juárez

Given the imagistic force of the feminicidal narrative, it is hardly surprising that the brutal murders of countless women in Ciudad Juárez have been harnessed as plot potential for commercial film-making. Indeed, the media narratives with their frequently sensational focus on serial killing, ensured that there was endless scope for the development of whodunit-style thrillers. As a result, there have been a number of feature films of varying quality, commitment and success; many with glamorous women at the centre. These include *Bordertown/Verdades que matan* with Jennifer López (Gregory Nava 2006), *The Virgin of Juárez* (Kevin James Dobson 2006) with Minnie Driver, and *El traspatio/Backyard* (Carlos Carrera 2009) featuring Ana de la Reguera.[1] The feature films in English have not enjoyed particular commercial or critical acclaim despite some interesting aspects and solid directing. *El traspatio*, based on a script by well-known playwright, Sabina Berman and directed by Carlos Carrera, famous for the box-office hit, *El crimen del padre amaro/The Crime of Father Amaro* (2002), resonated more with its cinema audiences and garnered solid reviews.[2] It was even selected as the Mexican contender for the Oscar nomination for best foreign language film in 2009, though it was not nominated. There have been short films too like, for example, the shocking *El otro sueño americano* [The Other American Dream] (Enrique Arroyo 2004), but it is in the realm of documentary production that the filmic responses to *feminicidio* in Ciudad Juárez can be best appreciated. Too numerous to list here, these films have been crafted by activists, photographers, academics and film-makers from Ciudad Juárez, other parts of Mexico and beyond.[3] Difficult to synthesize such a diverse body of work, the filmmakers involved in these projects embrace a wide range of techniques and utilize a rich register of poetic modes to forge visions of the crimes in Juárez that are mostly rooted in deep emotional attachment to the subject matter and a desire for justice, if not wider denunciation and political transformation.

This chapter scrutinizes two such examples of documentary production from both ends of the first decade of the twenty-first century, Lourdes Portillo's film, *Señorita Extraviada* [Missing Young Woman] (2001) and Rafael Bonilla's work, *La carta* [The Letter] from 2010. Arguing that the films are released at particularly pivotal moments in the recent history of feminicidal violence, I contend that distinct sets of tactics or representational modes are mobilized in response to those moments. The first documentary references the year 2001, the high point of the public focus on the association between the violence against women and the *maquilas* or the assembly plants that span the length of the US-Mexico border. This connection was intensified by the discovery of the bodies of eight women in the Campo Algodonero (Cotton Fields) and the ensuing media furore. In this regard, the film speaks back to dominant scripts about the crimes and the exceptionality of Ciudad Juárez and performs moments of wholeness, everyday life, and renewal, signified most poignantly by the frequent shots of shoes threaded throughout. The second documentary studied, *La carta*, captures the atmosphere of 2010 when Ciudad Juárez might properly be denominated an 'emergency zone' given the extreme levels of violence registered in the city with over 3,000 deaths recorded in that year alone. It looks at the use of the pre-modern communicative form of letter-writing as part of a project to build alliances between citizens in Ciudad Juárez and participants in a community project in Mexico City. Its portrayal of the primary protagonist, Paula Flores, long-term activist and mother of *feminicidio* victim Sagrario Gonzalez, charts new territory about mother-activism, and, unusually for a form so immersed in visual language, it presents the processes of reading and writing as possible vehicles for healing and regeneration from the wounds caused by *feminicidio*. These documentary films, thus, both provide innovative visual treatments of the pain of *feminicidio* and are a fitting showcase of the potential of documentary film to respond to its multiple complexities. I end my examination of the two films with a reflection on my viewing experiences of certain 'cinephiliac moments' (Keathley 2000, 2006) that had a particularly powerful impact. My reflection attests to the power of such moments to forge emotional linkages in the bodies of the films' spectators.

Señorita Extraviada: foundational text

Señorita Extraviada is one of the earliest on the subject of *feminicidio* in Ciudad Juárez and continues to be the focus of sustained scholarly interest.[4] It may be categorized as the best known and certainly among the most critically applauded of the many filmic responses to the violence against women in the border city.[5] Furthermore, as Laura Gillman affirms, this documentary, perhaps more than any other on the subject, 'helped raise consciousness of the crimes around the world' (2015: 140). The concern with violence evinced in the film forms part of Portillo's wider concern about issues of social justice and human rights evidenced in other documentaries she has directed including *Mothers: Las Madres de la Plaza de Mayo* (1986). Portillo's film output is diverse and includes documentaries on the Latina pop icon Selena, *Corpus: A Home Movie for Selena* (1999) as well as an intimate and rather chilling family portrait of her Uncle Oscar following his death and which raises questions about Mexico's treatment of homosexuality.[6] Concerned with the lives of the marginalized and those on the peripheries of society, she is, as Rosa Linda Fregoso points out, a 'practitioner of "vulnerable" film-making' (2001: n.p.). Born in Chihuahua but living in the US since she was thirteen,[7] Portillo oscillates very fluidly between outsider/insider perspectives on

116 *Resilience and renewal in documentary film*

the subjects she engages with to produce a body of work that has attracted much commercial and critical attention.

Señorita Extraviada showcases Portillo's aesthetic vision and exemplifies Bill Nichols's ideas around hybridity in documentary form, borrowing freely from what he defines as the performative, the observational and the poetic modes (Nichols 2001). In this way it splices conventional social realist documentary devices such as the expert interview, photographic images of victims; a contextualizing authorial voice-over alongside interviews with the victims' families (mostly but not exclusively their mothers). It also utilizes a dream-like structure which is a hallmark of her work, particularly some of the more recent productions. The approach adopted by Portillo sees a totalizing narrative structure, symbolized most potently by a conventional authoritative voice-over, undercut at various moments by instances of trauma that subliminally register the silenced agony of the victims. I would further suggest that in parallel with these instances of trauma, are moments of renewal that document or at least gesture towards the possibilities for resistance and resilience in the face of injustice and cruelty. Of particular interest within this process of renewal is the function of the iconography of shoes in the documentary and which will form the focus of the analysis. I argue that renewal constitutes a counter-narrative to both the unrepresentable nature of feminicidal violence more generally as well as to the hegemonic discourses surrounding the crimes at that time that circumscribed their interpretation within limiting constraints defined by globalization, organized crime and rapidly changing gender roles.

Released in 2001, *Señorita Extraviada* takes the spectator on a journey that starts with a map of Ciudad Juárez, thus ensuring clarity for its international audience. It then proceeds to introduce the backdrop to the murders, utilizing the familiar twin frameworks of drug-trafficking and organized crime on the one hand and the corrosive globalization emblematized so powerfully in the border region by the *maquila* industry, and accelerated (if not initiated) by the North American Free Trade Agreement or the Tratado de Libre Comercio (NAFTA/TLCAN), on the other. This analytical framework is carefully constructed from the outset through a series of establishing shots and thereafter sustained throughout the film, through the voice-over among other mechanisms. The opening visual sequence begins with a woman's face which fades to a shot of three individuals walking towards the camera and cuts to a shot of two women's shoes (not a pair) as they are arranged as part of a window display in a shoe shop. The next image is of school girls in uniform which moves to a bus making its way as though towards the viewer followed by a shot of a single girl dressed in a blue smock, reminiscent of a *maquila* or school uniform. This sequence fades to another image of a single child followed by the title screen introducing the film. Cutting to a shot of a man gesturing with his hand out towards the desert, the voice-over intrudes to start the process of formal narration. In this short establishing sequence, therefore, Portillo sets out the viewing but also the analytical parameters through which the subject matter will be assessed and presents certain key tropes that will recur throughout the visual treatment of the subject. One of these tropes involves shoes and this first image of them as part of a window display connotes the way in which women's purchasing power and their new-found identities as consumers has led to their demise. It also alludes to the wider significance of shoes and shoe-shops in the narratives of *feminicidio* in the city.[8] The second motif from this opening visual sequence involves the various shots of young women or girls in uniform and through which the emphasis on youth, innocence and vulnerability is established. The third image of significance involves the bus.[9] Connecting to shoes, it establishes mobility – access to and lack thereof – as a central trope of the feminicide narratives as well as a determining feature of the actual investigations. Indeed the murders generated a huge debate (and considerable change) about the inadequacy of public transport for workers more generally in Ciudad Juárez. In real terms, of course, women's newly acquired ability to travel freely and unaccompanied to work in the *maquilas* using public transport is a telling reminder of how urban life has been reconfigured. Moreover, the fact that the working women of Juárez lack the capacity to purchase private vehicles and thus depend exclusively on public infrastructure to support them means that the bus (and public transport more generally) as a signifier of mobility continues to be one of the great battlegrounds of the debate around the murders. The final shot, before the voice-over commences its narrative, is of the desert, the most famous topographical characteristic of the border region and now, so horrifyingly associated with the feminicides as a major dumping ground for many of the bodies. That the images – of shoes, of girls, of the bus – end with this over-riding shot of the desert ties them inextricably to this space, the border region, circumscribed by a hostile desert that conceals all truths. This viewing lens, so self-consciously established at the beginning, is complemented by a voice-over that structures the narrative that ensues, drawing the viewer/spectator always back to those 'lines of enquiry' that pinpoint Ciudad Juárez as the city of the future, the model of globalization that is, as the narrator suggests, 'spinning out of control'. Through this line of analysis, the murders are linked explicitly to the major quasi-legal superstructures of power in the region: the *maquila* industry ('*no hay quien lo toca*' [no one can touch them], says expert, Judith Galarza) and the *narco-tráfico* (the '*sub-mundo*' or underworld described so eloquently by Irene Blanco, defence lawyer of the most famous accused of feminicidal crimes, Abdel Latif Sharif Sharif). Of importance here is an understanding of how the multiple meanings of the film are sutured together through the sometimes arbitrary juxtaposition of different elements of 'ordinary' Ciudad Juárez life – buses, girls, shoe shops, Juárez citizens, the desert – into a totalizing narrative that tries to make sense of the murders as well as mourn the victims.

Traumatic instances

Within the logical narrative structure just described, however, are other voices, other stories and sets of visual sequences juxtaposed seemingly at random or interspersed between the voice-over and the voices of experts and activists. Frequently, they are the voices of the mothers and also the victims of violence:

subaltern discourses which document instances of traumatic encounter in ways that are deeply unsettling. These traumatic instances operate in parallel with the dominant narrative of a neoliberal violence unleashed against the women of the city and point seemingly to other explanations and other discourses at play. In this next section, I would like to explore briefly some of these traumatic instances to see how they are registered in the text in what are familiar methods within the body of trauma theory and which document in time-honoured fashion how trauma is displaced or disassociated as a way of 'working through' in the sense in which it is understood by Dominick LaCapra and others who follow his work (LaCapra 1994, 2001; Kaplan 2005).

The first example of these traumatic instances is revealed through the opening interview with one of the victims' mothers, Evangelina Arce. Seated with a child on her lap, Arce recounts the story of her own abduction when pregnant with Silvia, and the terror she endured during her ordeal. The story involves her being sold for fifteen pesos by a woman posing as her friend and being abused by her abductor who drove her around the city all night until releasing her the next day.[10] Given that this is the first interview of the documentary, it is tempting to read this as Amy Carroll does, as a staging of gender violence in Mexico as a process of 'uncanny repetition' (2006: 385) and in this way as a somewhat classic marker of trauma in the text. In addition, Gillman perceptively observes that:

> The testimony and images (of Arce) tell an inter-generational history of violence, kidnapping and murder. Portillo creates a visceral imaginary of the violence by showing how the violence visited upon the daughter has been part of the felt, embodied experience of the mother (and even the child in utero) and therefore is something that can be known through the materiality of the body.
>
> (2015: 150)

This emphasis on the inter-generational aspect is critical in understanding this sequence and the feminicidal violence more generally. As the testimony of Evangelina Arce so effectively illustrates, her daughter's experience is part of a cycle of historic violence against women in Ciudad Juárez. Indeed her recounting of his words to her bear testimony to both women's status as disposable. He tells her outright that, 'If I'd been someone else I'd have killed you and thrown you here and who would have realized?'[11] The emphasis on the cyclical, historically embedded nature of violence in this way counteracts dominant narratives that cast Ciudad Juárez in the role of aberrant exception. Foregrounded by frequently histrionic media coverage, the emphasis on exceptionality is further emphasized in scholarship on the murders by the reliance on Giorgio Agamben's work which takes exceptionality as a starting point for the understanding of border zones and their citizens' reduction to the status of bare life.[12] More importantly, however, this emphasis on multi-generational violence questions the narrative of urgency and immediacy suggested by the earlier rationalization of the murders that posit the dual frameworks of the recent drug wars and the *maquila* superstructure as direct causal explanations. This narrative of immediacy is problematic for the way in which it constructs Ciudad Juárez as an endless 'other', a place of extreme violence, the archetypal 'feral' city (Norton 2003), as discussed in Chapter 1.

Arce's quiet acknowledgement of the history of violence constitutes what might be seen as an uncanny instant of which there are several throughout the text including the description of the strange sensation felt by the mother of feminicide victim, Olga Carrillo, when hanging out the clothes on the morning of her daughter's abduction. Affirming that she felt odd that day ['*me sentía rara*'], her feelings gesture to the ways in which the lived trauma of *feminicidio* is felt in the bodies not only of the victims but of their families. A sense of uncanny, the idea of the strange sensation is encoded in many sequences throughout the early part of the film as the stories about the murders are dispersed as discrete fragments of horror. Nowhere is the strangeness better exemplified than through Paula Flores's account of the role played by her daughter's parakeets in the registering of her disappearance.[13] Paula's daughter, María Sagrario González Flores, was abducted in 1998 as she left her shift at Capcom, one of the many *maquilas* employing young women in Ciudad Juárez. Sagrario González's mother, Paula, interprets the behaviour of her daughter's pet parakeets, Luis and Clint, on the days surrounding González's disappearances as significant:

> I knew something was wrong. Her boyfriend Andres had given her two parakeets. When I went to put them out in the sun, my son told me that one of the parakeets was dead, the one called Clint. And so, the other parakeet called Luis only let her hold him, only her. I started to take him out and [. . .] I asked him about Sagrario. 'Luis, do you know where Sagrario is? Where is Mary?' And, he nodded. The parakeet seemed to understand, He shook his head as if he were saying, 'Yes'. The parakeet left on Tuesday and on Wednesday they found my daughter's body [. . .] I was always taken by the fact that the parakeets knew.[14]

Unlike the cyclical nature of violence emphasized in the earlier example, here we see an instance of the unexplained, a signal of yearning for the trace of the loved one in the natural world or in the environment around them so well-documented in trauma literatures. Furthermore, the centrality of the animal world to the understanding of life's patterns is deeply rooted in indigenous belief systems in Mexico but also recalls Paula's rural roots in Durango where, again, the prominence of animals as part of her everyday life was paramount. Lucy Bollington detects a tendency in narratives about violence more broadly to project the anxieties and trauma induced by violence onto non or post-human elements and subjects. In this way, dominant forms of representation (through language, for example) can be challenged and unsettled through the proliferation of the post-human as a category for processing violent death (Bollington 2018: 170).[15] Here then, the idea that the natural world including its non-human subjects, holds secrets about the killings not forthcoming from official sources is powerfully expressed and opens up a new way of seeing the violence done to Sagrario, an element which, we shall see in a later section of the chapter, is also reflected in *La carta*.

Other uncanny instances include the testimony of one of the central witnesses of the text, María, who narrates in great detail the story of her detention by police, as well as her rape and abuse at the hands of police officers. María's powerful account is relayed in multiple appearances; indeed she occupies more screen time than any of the other participants in the film. There are seven separate sections in which her story (ranging from under a minute to 3–4 minutes uninterrupted) is recounted with many sequences conspicuously and clunkily edited in ways that do not occur with the other women's testimonies. These cuts in the story function to communicate the gaps in the official narratives, the silences that have accumulated, the fragments of truth and untruth and the untold testimonies of the victims. The long pauses in her testimony may be read as aporia – those aporectic dislocations, so central to trauma studies – described by Roger Luckhurst in his interpretation of Derrida as a 'blocking of passage, a stalling or hesitation, a foot hovering on the threshold caught between advancing and falling back, between the possible and the impossible' (2008: 6). The gaps and silences then form another central recurring motif of the film, not just of the documentary diegesis where the voice-over tells us that 'I came to Juárez to witness the silence', but also of other feminicide narratives of which the grassroots organization founded by Guillermina González Flores (Sagrario's sister), *Voces sin eco*, is a prime example.[16] As we shall see also, the lengthy interventions by María serve to establish her as the most important source of authority in the film, a role that is critical to ensuring that her testimony about the feminicidal violence is received by the spectator as the horrifying truth. The way in which that happens is concretely linked to the use of the shoe motif, referred to earlier and which will be scrutinized in the next section.

So is it the shoes?[17]

Carroll observes, in a perceptive piece on the documentary, that *Señorita Extraviada* achieves a 'synesthetic, collage-like quality' (2006: 384). She writes that, 'it interrupts trajectories of documentation and bereavement, inserting into its diegesis both a series of questions and seemingly unrelated visual references' (2006: 384). In this section, I aim to chart the ways in which these visually unrelated references constitute alternative stories about Ciudad Juárez. I argue that, taken together, they signal coherence, a depth in the Jamesonian sense that seems to go beyond the reliance on globalization and organized crime as the primary drivers of death in Ciudad Juárez. Indeed, these visual contours would seem to envision a space in which both agency and resistance are possible. In particular, I would like to turn my attention to the multiple shots of shoes as a way of further exploring the ways in which Portillo visually questions the logic of the narratives around feminicide, patiently explained by the expert voices.

There are multiple ways of reading the images of shoes in the documentary, as Jean Franco notes.[18] On one level, they operate as narrative linking devices to the 'real' stories, one of which actually features in the documentary when the spectator is told that Olga Carrillo worked at the shoe shop, Tres Hermanos. Linked to this narrative of the 'real', there are the shots of shoes that signify destruction and death and that are diegetically linked to the murders being investigated. These feature images of the front cover of the magazine, *Proceso*, for example, and a shot of an investigator shoving a single dirtied white trainer into the face of the camera towards the end. In this way, they signal death and destruction and operate as 'signs of absence' as David MacDougall terms them, or metonymic signifiers of death (1998: 235).[19] Second, and as already mentioned in relation to the opening shot, the shoes function as signifiers of consumption and disposable income probably more than any other motifs in the film. Indeed, the gap between the image of pristine shoes as part of window displays (and therefore ripe for consumption) and their shabby, dilapidated appearance as crucial elements in crime scenes is striking. Functioning as signs of consumerism, they are devices that offer 'detours from the real' (Renov 1993: 7) into the symbolic terrains that are the battlegrounds of this debate. These include the radical shift in gender roles occasioned by the feminization of the labour force so marked from the 1980s onwards in Mexico and exacerbated under the terms of NAFTA.[20] Women's new purchasing capacity is aligned through the image of shoe consumption with ideas of mobility, also intimated by the frequent appearance of training shoes or sneakers – shoes that are, quite literally, used to run (away) and which, obviously, indicate failure in the cases of the victims documented on screen. Finally, there are different categories of shoes featuring frequent shots of working men's shoes positioned in somewhat random ways sometimes as part of a more complex mise-en-scène, or in others, occupying the full-screen frame. These shoes are fragments, objects from everyday life and they stand alongside other shots of working men's lives that proliferate in the film, a freeze-framed shot of a man selling *camarones* [shrimp] from a trolley and the shoe shiner, among other examples. Indeed, the juxtaposition of shoes of murdered girls with ordinary working men's shoes with shots of shoes in window displays further seems to reinforce this discourse of ordinariness operating in parallel with the narrative of violence and horror. The shoes, then, function as instances of everyday life, snapshots of a globalized, precarious existence.[21]

I read these images of shoes as reminiscent of Vincent Van Gogh's series of paintings of peasant shoes which were analyzed by Fredric Jameson in his much acclaimed work, *Postmodernism, or the Cultural Logic of Late Capitalism* (1984). According to Jameson's distinction between modernism and postmodernism, the Van Gogh peasant shoes, 'draw the absent world and earth into revelation around itself' (1991: 8).[22] Gesturing to a life beyond them, they stand, according to Chela Sandoval's illuminating analysis of them, 'on the side of life' (2000: 19). Jameson draws on Heidegger's original reading of the paintings whose analysis was 'organized around the idea that the work of art emerges within the gap between Earth and World' (1991: 7) and which is interpreted by Jameson as a Utopian gesture in the sense that there is a 'willed and violent transformation of a drab peasant object world into the most glorious materialization of pure colour in oil paint' (1991: 7). This gap between Earth and World taken in the context of the *feminicidios* is of interest, however, because cultural responses to the feminicides are frequently shot through with this same philosophical question. As already seen, the gap between the earth and the world is perfectly captured in earlier sequences in which it is affirmed that knowledge about the crimes rests – not with the authorities – but with Sagrario's parakeets or in the desert sand. I would argue that it is the metaphysical nature of the violence of the feminicides that continues to distinguish it utterly from the other two great axes of death ongoing in the border region – those caused by organized crime and migrant deaths related to border-crossing. In both of those cases, the frameworks of globalization, neoliberalism, multinational capitalism, border zones of exceptionality and linear cause/effect relations are presented as the rather obvious players that determine the death events. When we turn to the *feminicidios* on the other hand, while the neoliberal or structural nature of the violence is frequently invoked as a factor, we also see how the narratives are frequently couched in detectivesque terms, that is, 'who is killing the women of Juárez?' (as indeed it is in *Señorita Extraviada*).[23] In this way a teleological framework is invoked in which agents – family members, grassroots organizations – are always posited as questioning, seeking answers to the mysteries of the deaths. The deaths themselves, however, remain elusive, beyond grasp, the ultimate signifiers of an evil that is indefinable.

A final point of interest in Jameson's analysis concerns his argument around depth. We have seen already how the shoes differ widely in the text: sometimes they are single and abandoned, at other times they constitute part of a glossy window display. They are also shot whole and in pairs, pointing to the social totality beyond them, a depth that for Jameson is so at odds with what he sees as postmodernist art which, in his discussion, is exemplified by Andy Warhol's painting, *Diamond Dust Shoes*. This emphasis on depth and wholeness is striking: it is evident in the politicized nature of many narratives about the violence in seeing the feminicides themselves as an attack on the family and, by extension, on society. The strategic use of family photographs in the film with their emphasis on (frequently) patriarchal family wholeness and togetherness underlies this reading. It also functions as a heartrending counterpoint to the media characterizations of so many of the women as living so-called double lives as prostitutes and thus as belonging to broken family structures.

This emphasis on wholeness can also be seen in the final example of shoe shots that I would like to isolate for analysis. This involves a pair of white strappy sandal-like shoes that feature twice (Figures 4.1–4.2). The first shot of these shoes is of a woman's feet stepping out of them and it plays out against the aural testimony of María telling her story of incarceration by the police. In this moment, she relates how she was told to strip by the female police officer, prefiguring her account of rape at the hands of another police officer. In the classic manner then, the visual shot of stripping or removing accompanies in a logical fashion the diegetic narrative and 'makes sense'. The same shoes return in the closing stages of the documentary to show feet now getting back into the shoes played against a soundtrack of several isolated notes – not the recurring requiem music we have heard at length throughout – and which, I would like to suggest may be read as a

Resilience and renewal in documentary film   123

Figure 4.1 Woman stepping out of white shoes. *Señorita Extraviada,* directed by Lourdes Portillo, 2001

Figure 4.2 Woman stepping back into white shoes. *Señorita Extraviada,* directed by Lourdes Portillo, 2001

possible moment of restitution. While clearly bearing no physical resemblance to the Van Gogh series discussed by Jameson and others, in common with the men's shoes seen earlier, the act of stripping off and putting on again performs a moment of wholeness that emerges out of the brokenness and fragmentation elsewhere in the narratives. Indeed the voice-over explicitly underscores this emphasis on wholeness in introducing María back into the frame in her final decisive intervention in the film. As the narrator explains, 'When María first explained she was so afraid of the police she didn't reveal the *whole* story. With her husband's encouragement she is finally able to talk about the *entire* experience' (my emphasis). Wholeness thus is figured visually through the pairing together of shoes on feet about to take decisive steps. On the one hand, these steps are to be discerned figuratively in María's final explosive testimony and on the other more literally, in the sequences of images showing the citizens of Juárez walking (including several shots of their feet), marching and performing everyday instances of resilience and resistance. The return of the white shoes then – another uncanny moment in that they play no logical part in the diegetic narrative – functions as testimony to this resilience and perhaps silently marks a moment of renewal.

It should be emphasized that María's testimony is critical at this juncture in the documentary as it is in this sequence that she outlines her experience of seeing a portfolio of photographs shown to her by police officers during her incarceration that bear witness to feminicide and its knowledge (if not its execution) by members of the police. The reliance in the documentary on photographs is a really interesting feature of this testimony in the sense that the key witness here bears witness to photographs she has been shown of events, not to the events themselves. Notwithstanding the problematic ontological nature of photographic images in the digital era more generally, in Portillo's documentary, photographs are deployed as units of historical stability as when they are utilized throughout in the form of family photographs. This veracity and truth quality are wholly borne out by the authority of the narrative subject, the enunciator of the testimony – María. As historical subject, she is rendered reliable and authoritative by the amount of screen time in close-up accorded to her in the build-up to this moment and her reliability is corroborated formally in the film by other voices. Thus when María testifies to the truth of the torture, rape and gruesome murder of multiple victims as well as the complicity of the police (who have also raped her), she emerges as the voice of truth in the film.[24] Constituting probably the most chilling episode of the documentary, the traumatic irruption of the 'whole' story into the narrative at this point is signalled by the preceding image of shoes being put back on in preparation for walking. In broader terms, the mediated account of the atrocities using the vehicle of photographs not shown on screen speaks to the unrepresentability of the feminicides as when Bill Nichols writes about the challenge presented by the '"mortality of the body" and the way in which it ultimately eludes all strategies of representation' (1991: 236).[25]

As already noted, the image under scrutiny here shows shoes that are purposefully drawn together as though in preparation for movement. Following the dramatic revelations about the photographs, the documentary switches its focus to sequences of activism, energy and agency with Sagrario's sister, Guillermina, painting crosses purposefully and the criss-crossing images of daily life that testify to the resilience of Juárez citizens in the face of appalling violence. Returning the lens to the employees of the *maquila* who affirm that in spite of their fear they continue to go out with their friends, the documentary cuts to Guillermina and her spirited pledge not to be complicit nor to acquiesce in their silencing. Her quiet detailing of the many small ways in which Voces sin Eco, the grassroots movement she has founded, helps to alleviate the pain of *feminicidio* is also of note. The emphasis on verbs and action in her account is striking, pointing out the way the activists 'do' different things, including selling things or paying taxis to take girls home at night, among other activities. This sequence is interspersed with shots of people walking through the city as well as prolonged footage of the feet of people marching in protest against injustice and impunity. While the closing images feature shoes, a bus and the sexualized body of a female hanging as an ornament from a rear-view mirror inside a car, the final images are of a girl leaning on the railing inside a bus connoting life as usual. As Sergio de la Mora attests (2003), women here are shown as social actors intervening as subjects in their own narratives. In this way, the shoes share the common function of gesturing to a life beyond the narratives of destruction, narratives in which ideas of ordinariness and resilience feature prominently.

The rhythms and repetitions thus enacted within the text can be read as markers of the uncanny within the broad framework of understanding relating to trauma. Rather than fixing them, however, within a structure in which they might be seen as classic instances of repetition-compulsion and thus the traditional 'acting out' of trauma' in LaCapra's sense of the word and referred to earlier, perhaps we might also see these instances of the everyday in a more Lefebvrian sense as those rhythms and repetitions that offer the potential for radical renewal even while, according to him, they are still subject to processes of colonization. It could be argued that this instance of 'putting on again' returns us to Lefebvre's starting point, where the 'trivial details of quotidian experience showcase an existence colonized by the commodity, shadowed by inauthenticity, yet remaining the only source of resistance and change' (2014: n.p.). Perhaps this offers a more enabling reading of the text, as not simply locked within the conventional *maquila*/narco framework in a state of traumatized paralysis but rather offering glimpses of everyday ordinariness, gestures of wholeness and totality that signal a way through the evil which is nevertheless respectfully acknowledged and mourned throughout. In this way, as Avila notes, *Señorita Extraviada* draws our attention to the 'microphysics of power and the instantiations of resistance' (2012: 43).

Finally, it is important to note that the documentary is of a particular national moment. Released in 2001, it came out at a time when the horrors of the border/Juárez 'experiment' were becoming most apparent; the apex, perhaps, of the media's obsession with the assembly plants as the source of the victims and the same year as the discovery of eight bodies in Campo Algodonero. As the designated headquarters of the *maquila* industry in Juárez, the grim discovery cemented in the public imaginary the concrete link between that industry and the feminicidal violence. In this way, the documentary captures that moment when the *maquila*/murder paradigm was at its most politically and emotionally charged. So this moment, full of complexity, replete with the contradictions that are the hallmarks of traumatic representation, is somehow enacted by *Señorita Extraviada* through these sets of visual references that, following Lefebvre, critique the fixity of meaning and gesture to the possibility of renewal in line with his envisioning of a dynamic, empowering urban environment.[26] While this may seem a somewhat desperate interpretation of *Señorita Extraviada*, in so many ways a painstaking documentation of despair, it does at least shed some light on how we might go about approaching the problems of representing the atrocities in Ciudad Juárez in ways that go beyond the limiting frameworks that frequently circumscribe the victims and their families within this script of exceptionality, so eloquently described by Agamben but from which, it seems, there is rarely any form of dignified escape.

Resilience through writing: *La carta*'s homage to Paula Flores[27]

Similar strategies that emphasize ideas around activism, energy and resilience can be observed in other documentary films about the feminicidal wave in Ciudad Juárez. In the next section of this chapter, I would like to turn my attention to Mexican film-maker Rafael Bonilla's documentary film, *La carta* (2010). This film takes the well-known figure of Paula Flores Bonilla, already seen in *Señorita Extraviada*, and mother of *feminicidio* victim Sagrario González Flores, as its centrepoint, and traces her construction as victim/survivor as well as political activist across a range of causes including campaigns for environmental justice and against impunity. The narrative follows Paula as she charts an uneasy path through (at best) indifferent officialdom, and by paying consideration to her backstory as well as her multiple allegiances – to family, community and nation – a narrative of quiet heroism is forged. The documentary is of particular interest for the way in which it utilizes letter-writing as a vehicle or device through which redemption becomes possible and reconciliation can be achieved between the centre (Mexico City) and its troubled periphery (Ciudad Juárez). The documentary, as I shall show, enacts a decisive point in the narratives of violence in Mexico's recent history and stages an instance of national solidarity and mourning.

La carta is illuminating on a number of distinct levels, not least because of its careful construction of a case of heroism accomplished through the characterization of its protagonist. Paula Flores Bonilla is the mother of one of Ciudad Juárez's 'early' victims of *feminicidio*, in what is referred to in the documentary as '*el caso tan emblemático de Sagrario*' [the emblematic case of Sagrario]. This telling description signals the way in which Sagrario González Flores came to represent the quintessential victim of feminicidal violence of the 1990s. A worker in an assembly plant who disappeared mysteriously after her shift was changed without notice, young, poor, from the rural state of Durango, attractive with long, brown hair, Sagrario was the prototypical murder victim as defined by the media coverage and the police investigations. Sagrario's case, alongside the shoddy case notes, flawed investigation and botched conviction, features in many documentary films and artistic projects about Ciudad Juárez, and is included as part of a mural project of commemoration in the city.[28] As a result, her case came to occupy a prominent position in much of the public discourse concerning the 'muertas de Juárez', and Sagrario's mother Paula became a central figure in the mothers' activism that emerged as their response to the indifference shown by the state and federal authorities to the crimes.[29]

Motherhood as a vehicle for political activism (Bejarano 2002; Guzmán Bouvard 1994; Bosco 2004, 2006) is a familiar trope in the recent history of Latin America, embodied most powerfully perhaps by the Madres de la Plaza de Mayo in Argentina, but since then replicated in many forms and contexts across the continent.[30] Ciudad Juárez also boasts a sizeable panorama of relatives' organizations which, similar to mothers' groups elsewhere in the continent, protest about the atrocities and consistently agitate for appropriate legal redress for the crimes. Nuestras Hijas de Regreso a Casa, for example, while not exclusively a mothers' organization, is overwhelmingly dominated by mothers and other female relatives including grandmothers and sisters.[31] Melissa Wright has written extensively about the dynamics of grassroots organizing in Ciudad Juárez following the first wave of feminicidal violence. She points to two distinct phases: one that saw the coming together of previously active citizens in a broad coalition to 'talk back' to the authorities and to counter the victim-blaming discourse so excruciatingly apparent. The second phase saw a prolonged internationalization of activism around Juárez as well as tension over resources, representation and the rights of certain actors over others (Wright 2007; Rojas 2005). The tensions inherent in the 'activist mother' role in its broader sense have also been well documented. Sara Ruddick's writings about the creativity of 'maternal thinking' (1989), as well as the many other positive evaluations of maternal activism which have appeared, are balanced by academic concerns such as those articulated by Diana Taylor (1997, 2001) who argues persuasively that the performance of motherhood as exemplified by the Madres de Plaza de Mayo borrows heavily from the traditional nature of their role. Such tensions connect in turn to the idea of self-sacrifice or *abnegación* so strongly present in Mexican cultural discourses on femininity and so vividly evoked by Rosario Castellanos' archetype of the '*abnegada mujercita mexicana*'.[32]

In some ways, the figure of Paula is crafted from these same discourses of politicized femininity and specifically of motherhood found in Latin America (and elsewhere). Similar to the motivations underlying the activities of the Madres de Plaza de Mayo and discussed by Taylor, it is Paula's maternal responsibilities that drive her towards the pursuit of justice. As she tirelessly and selflessly searches for her daughter, her dedicated crusade is expressed as a kind of primaeval maternal urge. As another mother activist, Evangelina Arce, says in the film: 'All of us mothers feel that strong pain inside, no? Because our daughters were a little piece of us that became lost'. At the same time, the portrait of Paula stems from ideas about individual exceptionalism and heroism that privilege a different self-narrative, one that emphasizes political and sexual agency, as well as autonomy. Furthermore, Taylor's analysis identifies what she terms a 'disruptive space', which is a point of transition between the 'I' who is a mother and the 'I' who chooses to perform motherhood. Taylor's analysis of this space posits a distinction between the private motherly space, traditionally interpreted as socially restricted, and the public performance of motherhood, which brings with it collective action and the possibilities of political involvement and influence. There are clear differences in context here: the violence in Ciudad Juárez is perpetrated and enabled through a complex network of agents that includes the state but which is not committed directly by the state, unlike the situation in Argentina. However, Paula's narrative in Bonilla's documentary, while it speaks from the public space of collective motherhood, similar to that occupied by the Madres de Plaza de Mayo, it also inhabits a private space of identity. This space is disruptive, in Taylor's sense of the word, but not restrictive in the way she interprets it; rather it is determined by other elements, besides the maternal force, including kinship, love, sexual desire and agency. In *La carta* then, Paula's personal identity and sense of herself take centre stage as the documentary eschews the focus on a collective of women, choosing instead to privilege one single interlocutor. To go further, it could be argued that the focus on the power of collective political motherhood in the film is consciously sacrificed in favour of a kind of biopic approach to the mother figure. What is interesting about the portrait of Paula, then, is the way in which it juxtaposes two competing ideas around politicized motherhood based on a model of collective protest and solidarity (on the one hand) and the notion of the celebrity witness and proto-feminist heroine (on the other). This portrait of Paula is also modelled on ideas around individual exceptionalism and heroism that privilege a different self-narrative, one that energizes ideas around agency as well as autonomy. In the next section, I shall chart the way in which Bonilla constructs this narrative of heroism in *La carta*.

Heroism and celebrity

As already noted, the documentary constructs a multivalent portrayal of Paula as an exemplary, heroic mother activist in a biopic narrative that also provides a snapshot of a time of national crisis. The film focuses on Paula as a singular heroic figure, who, while her role is located within the wider struggle against impunity in Ciudad Juárez, is also valued for her personal story; her 'journey', as a mother, expressed in self-conscious ways, from innocence through the trauma of loss to a kind of sophisticated self-knowledge. Bonilla uses two different ways of framing Paula's story in order to underscore this conscious juxtaposition of the personal tragedy and the public persona. The first technique involves Paula's representation as the grieving witness, expressed through the sustained performance of a mother in mourning, conveyed by frequent crying with multiple close-ups of her tear-stained face, often when engaged in the act of reading. Paula repeats her anguished performance of mourning on many occasions in the documentary, often in a self-conscious manner, as when she states in a letter she has written to Sagrario and which she reads out on camera: '*nunca estuviste muerta para mí*' [for me, you were never dead].[33] This theatrically constructed portrait of victimhood and witness finds expression too in the filmic approach adopted when Paula tells the tale of her husband's suicide. Heart-broken by the murder of his daughter, Jesús Flores takes his own life; and Paula describes her despair amid tears, asking the painful question: '*¿Por qué me dejaste sola?*' [why did you leave me on my own?]. Paula's recounting of the suicide emphasizes not only her grief but her horror, as she reads his suicide note (another letter) left in the glove compartment of his car. As Paula reads out the letter, with its tender words of farewell, the camera intercuts with a screenshot of the newspaper account of her husband's suicide. In this account it is revealed that he has been found dead in the company of a woman in what is described as a case of homicide-suicide and an explicit reference to the fact that the dead woman found with him was his lover. In a moment of excruciating irony, the newspaper reports that this case is the thirteenth *feminicidio* in Ciudad Juárez that year (2006). As the film cuts away to a close-up of a grieving, weeping Paula, a song plays, the lyrics of which reinforce the storyline by making reference to a double love: '*Estoy queriendo a una rubia y a una morena tambien*' [I'm in love with a blonde and a brunette too] (Elizalde 2002).[34] The only diegetic reference to the parallel story of Jesús's betrayal of his wife which the press coverage has exposed, the song plays while Paula stares at the camera allowing the extra details about the circumstances of Jesús's death to be relayed to the audience. However, in terms of both screen time and mode of narration, the documentary privileges Paula's version of the story, putting the focus on Jesús's loving words of farewell to her as well as on her sense of solitude and paralyzing grief. The real-life events, then, are not allowed to interfere with the director's representation on film of the widow's grief and the audience's response to it as Paula mourns the loss of her husband and daughter.

In the second frame through which Paula is observed, she is portrayed as heroine: the film documents in detail the ways in which Paula becomes a role model and engages in activism within the community in order to keep the memory of her daughter alive. This image of Paula as stalwart survivor is expressed through various sequences including those that show, among other events, the community's participation in the making of *piñatas* and *tamales*, and in the traditional pre-Christmas celebration of the *posada*. The film soon turns its attention to other related projects and community causes, notably the fight for justice engaged in by the community of Lomas de Poleo. This vast area stretching from the outskirts of Ciudad Juárez to the Mexican border captured the headlines in 1996, when it became notorious as the site where multiple female bodies were discovered, thereafter being acknowledged to be one of the iconic sites of feminicidal violence.[35] The campaign in which Paula is involved in Lomas de Poleo was formed to protest against the unjust treatment of the communities occupying the higher part of Lomas, when these communities were fenced in, in 2005, in an illegal and arrogant act of power allegedly instigated by the Zaragoza brothers.[36] While the documentary references Paula's part in this wider struggle, including her imprisonment for public order offences during a protest in Lomas de Poleo in 2003, at all times, the case of Sagrario and Paula's role in the struggle for justice for her daughter are kept in mind, through being referenced visually and aurally, so that they are never far from the camera. An example is the scene in which she is refused entry into the cordoned-off area of Poleo: she responds to this refusal by stating purposefully: '*Ellos me conocen*' [They know me], an allusion to her public profile as an activist and as mother of a victim of *feminicidio*.

Numerous methods are employed, including slow motion shots and multiple close-ups, to frame Paula definitively as the grieving but stoic heroine. The high point of this process of characterization is illustrated by the performance of the song, 'Paula'. This song was composed specifically for the film and formed part of the wider goals of a project, led by a team at the Centro Cultural Casa Talavera at the Universidad Autónoma de la Ciudad de México to reach out to Paula and others affected by *feminicidio* in Ciudad Juárez. The song is first heard early in the film, and is sung, it may be assumed, by the same children who are to feature in the later footage; the song is repeated in full at the end, placing Paula at its epicentre:

Paula, mujer de amor,
mujer valiente,
mujer de lucha y dolor
Paula, tu voz es fuerza,
eres guerrera de corazón
Tu llanto triste y tu valor
Se conjugaron en mi canción
En tu mirada vemos la luz de la esperanza y la razón
Paula, Paula, Paula, Paula, Paula
Tu voz quiere fluir, abre caminos para seguir
Paula, tu voz escribo, ya no hay sueño para vivir.
Paula arde tu sangre, tienes coraje, tienes pasión
Tu llanto triste y tu valor se conjugaron en mi canción
En tu mirada vemos la luz de la esperanza y la razón
Paula, Paula, Paula, Paula, Paula.

[Paula, woman of love/Brave woman/Woman of struggle and pain. Paula, your voice is strength/You're a warrior of the heart/Your sad weeping and your bravery/ Have come together in my song/In your gaze we see the light of hope and the triumph of goodness./Paula, Paula, Paula, Paula, Paula./ Your voice wants to flow, to open paths to follow/Paula, I write your voice, there's no longer a dream we can live./Paula, your blood burns, you are angry, you are passionate. Your sad weeping and your bravery come together in my song./In your gaze, we see the light of hope and the triumph of goodness. Paula, Paula, Paula, Paula, Paula.][37]

The repeated mention of the heroine's name here is perhaps the most obvious marker of her prominent role and it functions to elevate her to the level of warrior. Sung by Illiana Hidalgo, the song identifies Paula as a dominant life-force in whom many historically established heroic characteristics – such as bravery, stoicism and the capacity for love – conjoin. The reference to her ability to open pathways signals clearly the way in which her 'work' as activist mother charts a path towards justice through creative dialogue and feminist coalition.

Resilience and renewal in documentary film 131

Figure 4.3 Paula Flores, from *La carta*, directed by Rafael Bonilla, 2010

We have seen then, how the portrait of Paula, as is clearly and rather hyperbolically shown in the song lyrics discussed, emphasizes her bravery and resilience. In this way the film, through the focus on one 'star' performer, contributes to a celebration of the politically active mother. In its depiction of Paula, however, the documentary also undercuts other more conventional representations of maternal activism. Departing from the notion of the 'good' mother, so central to the narrative of political motherhood elsewhere, the documentary goes on to foreground Paula's earlier life, filled with nostalgia and sweet memories, from growing up in Durango, then falling in love with Jesús, to the birth of her children, the move to Ciudad Juárez and the journey back to Durango.[38] Here, the spectator is allowed to observe Paula's journey from adolescence through love and sexual desire, when she recounts the time her mother first realized that (aged fourteen) she was wearing a bra; and when she recollected her growing sense of sexual attractiveness: '*Me gustaba verme bonita*' [I liked to look pretty]. Attention is also paid to her first date with Jesús and to the long walk to the ranch after their formal courtship is established. Their love story is punctuated by intimate, sometimes sexualized language as when she describes their final conversation saying that, 'he hugged me, he hugged me, he kissed me a lot, he said he wanted to take my breath away'. Here the more typical portraits of mother activists (particularly the Madres de Plaza de Mayo) as non-sexual, frequently religious women, focused solely and exclusively on the search for their lost children, is undercut in order to foreground Paula's active sexuality.[39] We can see, therefore, how the documentary, while it upholds certain traditional ideas of family, also undermines them not only through the sub-texts of betrayal, revealed most forcefully through the parallel yet non-narrated story of Jesús, but also through portraying the wider bonds of kinship and solidarity that exist or are formed both locally within Paula's community and beyond. Paula's story of loss in the most tragic of circumstances as well as her narrative of resilience and survival produce, then, a familiar script of bravery in the face of adversity.

Solidarity and coalition

This aspect of the portrayal of Paula, which foregrounds individual exceptionalism, is played off against a focus on her position within the wider community and features her participating in frequently politicized collective action. Images of community proliferate throughout the film, and are communicated through sequences showing a close-knit family unit, evidenced in particular during the interviews with Chuy, Paula's only son, and with Guillermina (Guille) her elder daughter, herself a prominent activist and one of the founder members of the organization Voces sin Eco. The initiative to preserve Sagrario's memory through the establishment of a kindergarten, which obtained local government support in 2002, demonstrates the power of collective action formed from shared familial trauma and loss. However, aside from her highly visible work as an activist against gender violence, Paula also inserts herself conspicuously into other, broader social struggles within the community. In showing her intervening in this way, the film makes links between different cycles of symbolic and structural violence in Mexico and illustrates the way in which they form part of a pattern of injustice. She demonstrates and expresses her solidarity with the widows and daughters of the Bracero programme, for example, those workers who participated in the government-funded worker programme during World War II and who have been battling the authorities for several decades in the interests of obtaining justice.[40] As already mentioned, Paula also becomes part of the activist circles of the *colonos* or dwellers of Lomas de Poleo who struggle against the impact of decades of land misappropriation and who end up effectively being imprisoned on their own land. Explanations given about the origins of the unrest and uproar in Lomas, interviews with the affected families, interventions by community activists and by participants in the *Poleo hablando* documentary film, all point to a self-conscious attempt by the director to portray Paula as an active citizen, effective beyond her personalized struggle for justice for her dead daughter. Paula's very public stay in jail following her arrest while participating in a rally for justice speaks to the way in which her private struggle has expanded to become a fight to help overcome other social injustices, other violences. The image of the pink cross in the interior of the car eloquently bears testimony to this distinction between the private pain of Sagrario's death and the public struggle for justice for Lomas in which Paula participates and which is taking place outside the car.

However, the power of the written word to sustain a community through atrocity and injustice provides the best example of how much strength of purpose and success can be derived from forging a community bound together by loyalty and solidarity. Set within the frames of her personal responses to the Sagrario narrative and of the wider narrative of community activism, Paula's theatrical performance of mourning is also to be understood within the context of letters which are read and written in the course of the documentary. Alongside Bonilla's portrayal of community activism, there is this other discourse which documents the network of exchanges and intercultural understanding which develops between Paula and her community in Ciudad Juárez and a group of women and children in Mexico City. Their network of exchanges depends on what might be seen as the rather old-fashioned method of communication through letter-writing. Its central importance underscored, of course, by the film's title, it performs many valuable functions in the documentary. In the first instance, Jesús's letter to his wife signifies letter-writing as a primary mode of communication through which he documents his safe arrival at Ciudad Juárez and indicates the possibilities that exist there for the wider family unit. In this case, the letter is used as the traditional material object sent from place A to place B, and as such demonstrates the marginalized status of the communities examined in the film, while identifying itself as a form of communication in places in which common technologies of communication (phones, television, computers) are still largely absent. Used in this way, then, the letter points towards a kind of pre-modern world in which the trappings of modernity are not yet in evidence and in which family celebrations, involving food, dancing, music and participation of the community, take centre stage.

In addition to fulfilling this important communicative function, the letter can also operate as a mode of expressing grief and a sense of loss, as when Paula writes letters to Sagrario following her daughter's disappearance, and when Jesús reads aloud a personal account of his grief at a press conference. The relationship between reading, writing and emotion is shown here as Jesús breaks down in tears, unable to finish reading his description to the end. It is glimpsed, too through the close-ups of Paula's tear-stained face as she reads Jesús's suicide note; in her demeanour as she reads her letter to Sagrario (mentioned earlier) and in the contents of the final letter she exchanges with the women and children in Mexico City. The wider network of kinship and support created by the writing of letters, which sustains Paula then, is showcased through the letter as a tangible and visible vehicle through which to communicate and exchange understanding and love.

The most important act of letter-writing in the film documents the links which are established between, on the one hand, Paula and her community of activists in Ciudad Juárez and, on the other, the children of the Centro Cultural Casa Talavera at the Universidad Autónoma de la Ciudad de México (UACM). The solidarity project in which these two groups are involved comprises a number of different participants including the Ollín Ahuilcuicatl choir from Casa Talavera, who sing the Paula anthem in the film. The project also forms part of a series of events publicized under the title 'Género, violencia y diversidad cultural en la frontera CJ-El Paso, Texas' with support from both the Universidad Autónoma de la Ciudad de México (UACM) and the Universidad Autónoma de México (UAM).[41] Paula's presentation of the letter to the assembled crowd, which had been written in response to the children's correspondence from Mexico City, comes in the scene following the preparation of the *tamales* and the scenes of celebration as part of the *posada*. This and the other letters referred to here, which form part of a cumulative process of network building, are placed into one large envelope for sending back to Mexico City; they attest to the bonds of solidarity that have been forged thanks to the initiative taken by the citizens in the capital city in reaching out to the community from Ciudad Juárez affected by violence. There are various interviews with people on camera speaking about the importance of the letters, the emotional support given to them through the letters and the friendships that have developed as a result. There is also the sense of an emerging solidarity articulated when an interviewee says that she felt a connection with one of her interlocutors through their shared view of the world asserting that what she said, 'connected with what I thought too'. This experience of exchange and dialogue shared through the letters, documents a cathartic process through which the overwhelming grief that characterizes the earlier letters shown in the film, is mitigated by smiles. In the film's final scenes, Paula is shown in Mexico City, giving thanks to the children for the letters of solidarity and support they have written, and presenting them with a portrait of Sagrario. Here a moment of mourning and commemoration is staged during which the image of the dead girl from Ciudad Juárez brought to Mexico City takes up her space on their walls and, it is inferred, in their hearts. As Paula says poignantly, '*mi hija está viva, se queda aquí con ustedes*' [my daughter is alive, she remains here with you].

If this filmed encounter between the centre (Mexico City) and the periphery (Ciudad Juárez) has lasting significance it is because this documentary production is filmed during one of the most highly charged periods of the current wave of violence affecting Mexico. The film documents this period in stark terms in its footage of the security operation, Operativo Chihuahua, in 2009, and by featuring on screen the famous pronouncement from the *Diario de Juárez* in July of that year: '*vivimos como en estado de sitio ciudándonos por un lado de los criminales y, por otro, de los soldados*' [we live as though in a state of siege looking out for the criminals on one side and for the soldiers on the other]. The year 2009 saw the massive deployment of state troops on to the streets of Ciudad Juárez to deal with the most murderous outbreaks of violence; indeed, during 2010, when the documentary was completed, there were in excess of 3,000 violent deaths in the city. Furthermore, the years 2009 (when the film was mostly shot) and 2010 (when it was released) represent the most brutal points of the violence in Ciudad Juárez as well as constituting the most aggressive phase of the Mexican state's interventions to control and contain the space of Ciudad Juárez, long conceptualized as the 'bad' border city in the Mexican national imaginary. In this context, amid widespread feelings of being under a state of siege and of being demonized by the metropolitan centres, quiet moments of commonly shared humanity like those experienced through the letter-writing project – however theatrical, or indeed 'old-fashioned' – acquire an ethical and affective charge.

The reading and the writing of letters, therefore, operate on multiple levels in this fascinating, polyvalent filmic portrait of the beleaguered figure of Paula. As modes of communication, bearing witness to poverty and to marginalization, these shared letters help us to understand the nature of the violence which the *feminicidios* have so tragically exposed. As vehicles for expressions of mourning and as modes of affective release, they record textually occasions of grief that can be played out in performance. Finally, as noted, the letter-writing, fostering a network of exchange, dialogue and friendship, contributes to the creation of a powerful catharsis and so to the reconciliation experienced by and between the metropolitan centre, Mexico City and the country's northern periphery, Ciudad Juárez. That this reconciliation is to be understood on a national level in its effects and implications, is vividly conveyed through the fact that, at the start of the documentary, the letters which make up the title *La carta*, are filmed shot through with the colours of the Mexican flag – a forceful way of communicating the idea of national mourning and collective grief. The political and affective power of *La carta* throws into sharp relief the multiple ambiguities inherent in the portrayal of Paula as political and community activist, as traumatized mother, and as agent of her own active, desiring sexuality. If Paula remains central in the final scenes, and if, through the song incorporated into the narrative, the film returns to the idea of Paula as fearless warrior or heroine, it is only after a painstakingly documented journey in which *La carta* has sought to demonstrate the possibilities for catharsis and reconciliation between different kinds of Mexican citizens including children from the urban neighbourhoods of Mexico City; as well as the traumatized relatives of the feminicidal victims from the rural regions of Durango. Viewed in the context of the violence in 2010, and amid growing concerns about Mexico's overall viability as a state, the potential of projects documented in films such as *La carta* to heal, transform and regenerate cannot be underestimated.

Uncanny encounters and affective shudders[42]

Exploring the recurrent tropes that help to craft the narratives in both documentary films studied in this chapter, it is clear that, while produced at very different moments in the history of feminicide in the region as well as speaking to very different audiences, both films defiantly mark their narratives with traces of ordinary and resilient life. It is clear too that both films – through different discursive strategies – stage emotional appeals to their audiences, often through sound. *La carta* does this through the repetition of the Paula anthem and, in *Señorita Extraviada*, the recurrent requiem music that accompanies the narrative throughout functions as a vehicle for commemorative and collective mourning. Indeed, the ability of cinema to collapse time into space means that (as other critics have noted), the documentary itself can be read as an eloquent requiem for all the deceased and disfigured female bodies from Juárez since 1993. I would argue that the emotional appeal of both films can also be located in distinct affective moments – punctum-like instances to use the language of Barthes's celebrated theorization of the functioning of the image – and that have a similar 'stinging' or 'piercing' affect.[43] I would like to close my analysis of both films with a brief examination of how my spectatorship of the films was impacted by two such moments. Taking my cue from Lesley Stern's essay on *Blade Runner*, I would like to consider how those piercing moments constructed an emotional linkage within the body of this spectator and how this in turn, might lead to the crystallization of a relationship of solidarity and recognition.

In *Señorita Extraviada*, this 'image-moment' (Keathley 2000) hinges around the closing seconds of María's testimony. As already examined, María's final appearances move her story away from her own ordeal at the hands of police officers at the notorious Cárcel de la piedra and into the stories (that are relayed to her via a series of graphic photographs) of the rape, murder and burning of other women victims. Following a brief sequence of images, her testimony concludes with an electrifying moment in which the whole trauma of feminicidal horror is collapsed into three words. With a voice that is unsteady with emotion, though her gaze rarely flickers, María describes how the women were set on fire following their sexual assault, finishing with the words, '*bien feo, pobrecitas*' [such ugliness, poor women]. I experienced this screen moment as a shudder (in the sense that art critic Barbara Bolt uses it),[44] but it might also be akin to the stomach-lurching as experienced by Lesley Stern in the revealing essay on her own reaction to a certain cinephiliac moment in *Blade Runner*:

> There is an extraordinary moment in Blade Runner when Pris, like a human missile, comes somersaulting straight toward us. One moment she is immobile (in a room full of mechanical and artificial toys she appears to be a wax doll); the next moment she is galvanized into life, her body moving at the speed of light. The force of her somersault charges the air; reconfiguring space and time, her bodily momentum is transmitted and experienced in the auditorium as bodily sensation. *My stomach lurches*. It is always surprising this moment, this movement, always and without fail it takes me aback. Yet what can it mean to yoke these incommensurate terms – always and surprising? Let me just say, at this point, that I am both surprised and haunted by this cinematic moment. I can't quite put my finger on the feeling it evokes, though there is a phrase of [Jean] Epstein's that resonates: 'On the line of communication the static of unexpected feelings interrupts us'.
>
> (1997: 350)

In the same way as Stern describes here, I too was both surprised and haunted by the impact this cinematic moment from *Señorita Extraviada* had on me and this surprise was felt bodily as though being pierced. In this regard, it may be likened to a punctum moment which, as Barthes describes, may be felt as a sting, a bruise, a poignant moment, a wound.[45] That a complex, multilayered, traumatizing tale of violence in multiple forms against women over a series of decades could possibly be condensed into a micro-testimony of three words is patently absurd, when analyzed rationally. And yet, as Noel King asserts, it is in the 'fetishizing of a particular moment, the isolating of a crystallisingly expressive detail' (cited in Keathley 2006: 30) that a more complete truth might be accessed and it may be recalled from the discussion earlier that this concept of wholeness was integral to the documentary diegesis receiving expression through the complex framing of shoes throughout.

The bodily sensation felt here by me, the lurching of my stomach, the stinging of my consciousness, however, might also be interpreted as yet another instance of the uncanny, a spectatorial feeling of strangeness, another bodily response that is echoed by Stern.[46] In the filmic analysis earlier, I isolated many examples of the uncanny throughout the film, exemplified most vividly by Evangelina's 'strange' sensation the morning of her daughter's disappearance as well as by the supernatural explanations favoured by Paula Flores in the narrative of her daughter's murder. This strangeness was further enhanced for me when I discussed the film in person with Paula Flores and during which she reiterated her belief in the power of the pet parakeets and their intervention in the search for Sagrario following her abduction. In this way, the sense of uncanny and strangeness felt in that moment signalled a sharing of my experience with the protagonist. This aligning of my emotional experience with hers – if only for a fleeting moment – enables, I would argue, the articulation of a relationship of continuity, a sense of a shared human experience that in turn can be harnessed for the construction of a relationship of global recognition and solidarity. Willemen describes the cinephiliac moment as full of 'a particular affective, emotional intensity [. . .] located not in the recognition of an artistic sensibility or intentionality beyond the screen, as it were, but in the particular relationship supported or constituted by the spectatorial look, between projected image and viewer' (1994: 126). It is in the articulation of this relationship then, during this momentary flash of recognition and shared unease that a common humanity is exposed and felt in the body.

In *La carta*, a similar moment occurs for this viewer, this time when the trauma of *feminicidio* is enunciated by Paula Flores Bonilla:

> Y yo no quería que llegara la noche. Y le gritaba con todos mis fuerzos [sic]. Y quería que ya me oyera que ya me escuchara aprovechaba la noche así. No hay ruido . . . yo decía en la noche está tranquila. Yo veo a las montañas tan enormes así están grandes, están muy lejos ¿dónde la hallo?
>
> [And I didn't want the night to come; I shouted at her with all my strength. And I wanted her to hear me, her to listen to me, I used the night like that. There's no noise, I said, the night is quiet. I see the mountains, so enormous, over there, so big, so far away. Where can I find her?]

During these emotionally charged words, the film cuts away to a lingering shot of the mountains as Paula asks the question about her daughter as though she were addressing the mountains directly. This appeal to the mountains and in particular the final three words, for me constitute another stomach-lurching moment, and I remain convinced that, of the multiple cultural responses generated by the feminicidal violence in Juárez, this particular outburst constitutes one of the most powerful articulations of the grief, pain and human anguish caused by the crimes.

When Paula says that she doesn't want the night to come, she reflects, on one level, the practical concern that it is only during the day that they can effectively search for Sagrario. On another level, though, this might be read as a desire for the halting of time itself, expressed through the compression of whole periods of trauma into intense expressive moments like the one described. It is difficult for me to watch this moment and separate it from my own personal experience of meeting and knowing Paula even though I had long experienced this stomach-lurching feeling when viewing this part of the documentary before coming to know her in person. In some ways, my knowing her didn't even 'matter' in terms of the emotional impact her testimony had. Perhaps this links to Stern's perceptive insights into the uncanny nature of these moments identified as 'a strange and unexpected meeting with yourself' (cited in Keathley 2006: 33). Viewing this moment for the first time shortly after losing my own mother and giving birth to my only daughter, I experienced Paula's expression of grief as one of anguish that I could participate in. In this regard, it became a moment in which the practice of viewing sutured my experience to Paula's and was revelatory in terms of how it illuminated the deep truth about *feminicidio* not available or accessible through other modes. I do not mean to collapse in any trite way the gulf of privilege that separates my lived experiences from those of Paula Flores. Nor is this the moment to digress about first world spectators as consumers of horror about the global South. This is more properly examined in Chapter 3. Rather, here, I am interested in how an emotionally piercing moment – that is mine to define and decide though it comes from somewhere outside of me – can help to construct a continuity, a binding relationship of solidarity and in this case, feminist recognition that is arguably where the contribution of film, as opposed to any of the other cultural practices studied in the book, might most effectively be located. If it is in these affective encounters that global solidarity can be constructed then surely it is testimony to cinema's power (the power of the moving image) to rupture the discontinuity between spectator and screen to access the pain of feminicidal violence. I need to emphasize, of course, that these are 'my' uncanny cinephiliac moments and mine alone: they demonstrate nevertheless, how emotional linkages in the bodies of film spectators are forged. How to sustain those moments of recognition when the 'feeling' has abated is, of course, the political challenge that such texts represent. Cinephiliac moments have been described as akin to the 'flashes of another history' (Keathley cited in Grant 2014: 49), and even if it is not possible to assert that these flashes correspond to resistant moments in the way imagined by Willemen (1994: 231), then they have, in this viewer at least, succeeded in the quiet communication of horrors that are feminicidal violence. It is perhaps in those quiet moments of recognition, that resistance begins.

Notes

1 Other feature-length films include *16 en la lista: Crimenes en Juarez* [16 on the list] (Rodolfo Rodobertti 1998); *Espejo retrovisor* [Rearview Mirror] (Lisa di Georgina 2002); *Las muertas de Juárez* [The Dead Women of Juárez] (Enrique Murillo 2001); and *Pasión y muerte en Juárez* [Passion and Death in Ciudad Juárez] (Javier Ulloa and Luis Estrada 2002). For discussion on Juárez film see Tabuenca Córdoba (2010). Short films of note include *Miércoles de ceniza* [Ash Wednesday] (Fernando Benítez 2005) and *El otro sueño americano* [The Other American Dream] (Enrique Arroyo 2004).

2 A selection of reviews suffices to demonstrate the positive reaction, del Razo (2009). See also the multiple reviews by spectators on *El séptimo arte* (2009). Available at www.elseptimoarte.net/foro/index.php?topic=11274.0. [Accessed 7 February 2018].

3 There are many documentary productions that take the feminicidal violence in Ciudad Juárez as their focus. They include *Performing the Border* (Ursula Biemann 1999); *Border*

Echoes/Ecos de una frontera (Lorena Méndez-Quiroga 2006); *Preguntas sin Respuesta: Los asesinatos y desapariciones de mujeres en Ciudad Juárez* (Rafael Montero 2004); *On the Edge: Femicide in Ciudad Juárez* (Steev Hise 2006); *La Batalla de las cruces: protesta social y acciones colectivas en torno de la violencia sexual en Ciudad Juárez* (Patricia Ravelo and Rafael Bonilla 2006); *Bajo Juárez: la ciudad devorando a sus hijas* (Antonio Cordero and Alejandra Sánchez 2006); *Silencio en Juárez* (Michela Giorelli 2009); *Desde que no estás* (Rosella M. Bergamaschi 2008); *Blood Rising* (Mark McLoughlin 2013); *Ciudad Juárez: La ciudad donde las mujeres son deshechables* (Alex Flores and Lorena Vassolo 2007); *Juárez: City of Dreams* (Bruno Sorrentino 2012); *If images could fill our empty spaces* (Alice Driver 2013); and *Mass Murder in Juárez* (Peadar King 2012), among many others. See Driver (2015) for a comprehensive filmography.
4 There is a considerable bibliography on the film, including work by Gillman (2015); Foster (2013); Sandell (2013); Carroll (2006); González (2003); de la Mora (2004); Mata (2011); Austin (2009); Franco (2013); Delgadillo (2011); Avila (2012); Driver (2015); Zavala (2016); Fregoso (2001, 2010). Baugh and Sorell devote a section of their recent work (2015) on resistance in chicano/a culture to *Señorita Extraviada* with essays and reflections from Mónica Torres, Claire Joysmith, Bienvenida Matías and Lourdes Portillo.
5 The documentary is much acclaimed and has won several prizes, including the special jury prize at Sundance in 2002. Perhaps its most obvious impact in the public arena was President Fox's establishment of La Comisión para Prevenir y Erradicar la Violencia contra las Mujeres en Ciudad Juárez following a film screening of the documentary to his wife, Marta Sahagún Fox. In this regard, it is as Jillian Sandell points out, 'one of the most important examples of cultural activism about the murdered and disappeared women in Juárez' (2013: 456).
6 *The Devil Never Sleeps/El diablo nunca duerme* (1994). For full details on filmography, see www.lourdesportillo.com [Accessed 10 February 2018].
7 Her website biography section describes her as 'Mexico-born and Chicana identified, Lourdes Portillo is a writer/ director/ producer of films focused on the search for Latino identity. She has worked in a richly varied range of forms, from television documentary to satirical video-film collage'. See www.lourdesportillo.com [Accessed 15 February 2018].
8 Shoes function as a unifying narrative and thematic thread throughout feminicidal discourse. The testimonial text, *El silencio que la voz de todas quiebra* [The silence that breaks the voice of all women] asks just why there are so many shoe shops along the main shopping area in Ciudad Juárez (1999: 82). Several of the victims of *feminicidio* were linked to shoe stores in Ciudad Juárez including Olga Carrillo, whose case is discussed in the film. Irene Mata writes that 'several other victims either worked or visited the shoe stores, Tres Hermanos and Zapatería Paris' (2011: 123). Dana A. Meredith and Luis Alberto Rodriguez Cortés write that shoes 'have become a symbol of feminicide' (2017: 250).
9 Buses continue to occupy a significant role in narratives of feminicide. A gang of bus drivers, *los choferes* (or '*los ruteros*'), was arrested in 1999 and implicated in the murders of eight women whose bodies were found at the Campo Algodonero. Bus drivers Victor García Uribe and Gustavo González Meza signed confessions to the murders claiming that these had been procured through torture. Meza died in prison in 2003 and García Uribe was released in 2005. In one of myriad twists in the feminicide narratives, a woman dubbed 'Diana, la cazadora de choferes' by the press, shot and killed two bus drivers in Ciudad Juárez in August 2013. For an interesting analysis of the phenomenon of Diana, la cazadora, see Baldrich (2014). As already mentioned in Chapter 3, in June 2017, in a case that attracted international headlines, an eleven-year-old girl, Valeria Teresa Gutiérrez Ortiz, was raped and strangled by a bus driver when travelling on his bus within the district of Nezahualcoyotl in the Estado de Mexico. For more information, see https://desinformemonos.org/valeria-me-maquille-hoy-quiero-justicia-las-ninas-este-pais-manifestacion-neza/ [Accessed 30 January 2018].

10 There is a recurring narrative throughout *Señorita Extraviada* about the role of women who contract girls for sinister purposes: this is seen in the case of the woman named Chatanel involved, it is alleged, in the disappearance of Olga Carrillo in 1995 and the involvement of another *'enganchadora de personas'* [trafficker] involved in the disappearance of María Isabel Nava Vásquez, according to her Father, one of the participants in the film. In this way, women's complicity within a system of endemic gender violence is eloquently exposed, as explored by Edward A. Avila (2012).

11 Throughout this chapter, for the purposes of clarity, I have translated original dialogue in Spanish in the films into English.

12 Giorgio Agamben's theories on 'bare life' (1998) and also Achille Mbembe's work on necropolitics (2003), both of which have informed extensively analyses of the violence in Ciudad Juárez (Schmidt Camacho 2006; Fregoso 2003; Driver 2015), are analyzed in Chapter 1.

13 In Gillman's illuminating reading of the haptic images in the film, she sees the parakeet as a 'recollection object', defined by Laura Marks as an object that encodes history and memory (2015: 154). For other interpretations of the presence of the parakeets, see Delgadillo (2011). Carroll also examines this episode in her article concluding that they might be seen as an example of the politicized spirituality discussed by Fregoso (Carroll 2006).

14 Paula has re-affirmed this story on many occasions and told me that she used to hold the parakeet in the days before the discovery of Sagrario's body and that he would peck her face to try and dry her tears (Personal communication, 25 November 2016).

15 In *La carta* (2010) which focuses exclusively on the figure of Paula Flores, there is an extended sequence following Paula's return to her home town in Durango. The emphasis on the contrast between the rural environment of Durango and the urban violence of Ciudad Juárez is striking. Furthermore, and central to the point made here, there are constant references to the environment and its non-human elements – the weather, the cold, the rain, the smell of the wood, and shots of Paula crossing through rivers, walking through fields, drinking fresh spring water ('which tastes of earth'), as well as shots and sounds of animals too.

16 The silence(s) that surround the question of *feminicidio* – culturally, politically, legally – remain key to an understanding of its emergence. Ileana Rodríguez develops the idea of silence as 'a metaphor for dissonance, a misspoken word, lies' (2009: 182) and she isolates the importance of the publication, *El silencio que la voz de todas quiebra* (examined in Chapter 5), as a mode of contesting the silence that 'speaks to the position of the government' (2009: 182).

17 Here, I am glossing a chapter title by Jeffrey T. Nealon, 'Is it the shoes: Otherness and exemplarity in Jameson, Heidegger and Derrida' in his book, *Alterity Politics* (1998).

18 A number of critics have isolated the images of shoes as worthy of examination. Carroll draws attention to the fact that the film is, 'especially attentive to images of shoes' (2006: 384) and Jean Franco writes that the shoes 'have multiple meanings – cowboy boots epitomize the regional culture, sneakers speak of the long walks home, and fashionable shoes in a store designate the consumer culture to which the girls aspired' (2013: 219–220). Avila develops a detailed and convincing reading of the shoes as an important 'filmic narrative interruption' that 'draws critical attention to the complex relationship between social reification, commodity fetishism and cultural myths of female disposability' (2012: 93). Ileana Rodríguez also talks about the fetishism of shoes that underlies many of the crimes and that 'can be read as signatures in a text' (2009: 184). See also Bienvenida Matías (2015) and Mónica Torres (2015). Kathleen Staudt reports a very high awareness of violence from research conducted in 2005 among Juarenses and points to the fact that the participants in the surveys identified tennis shoes as the 'optimal shoes for escape' (Staudt 2008: 64), an observation that makes the shots of tennis shoes from the documentary all the more poignant.

19 The importance of shoes as commemorative symbols of the Holocaust atrocities has been well documented. Oren Baruch Stier writes that 'Shoes, in the aggregate, are one of the most common symbols of the devastation and loss of the Holocaust. [. . .] As remnants of destruction on display, they are always evocative, especially of the absence the Shoah has left in its wake; they represent the Holocaust metonymically – they are part of whole as it were – because their existence as postmemorial artifacts is predicated upon the murders of those who wore them' (Stier n.p.). Jameson makes reference to shoes 'left over' from the Holocaust in his discussion of Warhol's *Diamond Dust Shoes* (1991: 8). See also Noah Shenker (2015). Shoes feature prominently in cultural representations of Holocaust atrocities, see, for example, the 4,000 shoes displayed at the US Holocaust Memorial Museum on loan from the State Museum of Majdanek in Lublin, Poland, and which represent a tiny fraction of those found at Majdanek in 1944. Other examples which also deploy the power of the shoe to evoke memories of the Holocaust include the installation known as the 'Shoes on the Danube Promenade' by sculptors Gyula Pauer and Can Togay, which comprised 60 pairs of rusted period shoes cast out of iron conceptualized as a memorial in front of the parliament building on the edge of the river.

20 The move from male- to female-headed households in Mexico from the 1980s onwards has been well documented. There is also excellent work on the role of women within the *maquila* industry on the US-Mexico border, noted already in Chapter 1, see especially Wright (1999, 2006).

21 It is hardly surprising that shoes are a prominent representative trope in cultural responses to the feminicides in Ciudad Juárez, particularly photography. Maya Goded's 2005–06 collection, *Desaparecidas*, Jaime Bailleres's image, '*En el desierto*' and Rigo Maldonado's image, '*Lo que quedó*' are examples as is the short film, *Ni una más*, directed by Alejandra Sánchez (2002). Antonio Zúñiga's play, *Estrellas enterradas* [Buried Stars] features the victims' search for their shoes as a central plot line. In the artistic sphere a particularly telling example is the Ciudad Juárez artist, Elina Chauvet's 2009 installation, '*Zapatos rojos*' [Red Shoes], in which multiple red shoes were displayed on the pavements of various streets and squares in Ciudad Juárez (and later other cities in Mexico and beyond). In a scene from Mario Bellatin and Marcela Rodríguez's project, *Bola negra: El musical de Ciudad Juárez*, shoes are included among the many human traces of life collected in an abandoned house. Lucy Bollington writes suggestively about the presence of the shoes here, saying that the writers' 'use of the shoe does not invoke the corpse or violence so much as it invokes flight and ruin – the film thus positions itself at a distance from visualizations of violence through the implicit re-encoding of a prominent symbol' (2018: 100). On a wider level, of course, it is important to signal the importance of philosophical discussions about feet, and the foot, as Sara Ahmed points out, 'stands apart' in a history of thought with reference to the work of both Merleau-Ponty and Descartes (2002: 17)

22 We should note that Van Gogh's shoes have been the subject of intense philosophical scrutiny as well as being analyzed by art historians. They were famously interpreted by Martin Heidegger who saw the painting on exhibition in Amsterdam in 1930; the experience came to play a focal role in an essay he was writing on the theory of art: *The Origin of the Work of Art* (1935). The art historian Meyer Schapiro (1998: 136–138) has taken issue with the hermeneutic approaches adopted by both Heidegger and Jameson and in particular, critiques Heidegger's gendering of the shoes (as belonging to a peasant woman). In a related context, Derrida was said (by Jameson) to make reference to the Van Gogh shoes as a 'heterosexual pair' though it seems generally acknowledged by Derrida scholars that there is no explicit reference to this as such in Derrida's examination of Van Gogh.

23 There is a proliferation of detective fiction about the feminicidal violence in Ciudad Juárez, some of which is the focus of discussion in Chapter 5.

142 *Resilience and renewal in documentary film*

24 Not everyone greeted María's testimony in the same way. Rosa Linda Fregoso relates how when the documentary was shown in Ciudad Juárez, local authorities publicly denounced her testimony (2012: 243). Long-term activist and scholar Kathleen Staudt also recalls a screening of the documentary in El Paso with Lourdes Portillo during which several audience members questioned the reliability of María as a witness (personal communication, 1 March 2017).
25 Mónica Torres also writes about this aspect in her analysis of the documentary (in Baugh and Sorell 2015).
26 Lefebvre writes that 'our towns will show us something quite different: the rebirth and reforming of community in factories and working-class neighbourhoods. There, other modes of everyday living, other needs, other requirements, are entering into conflict with the modalities of everyday life as imposed by the capitalist structure of society and life, and tending to re-establish a solidarity, an effective alliance between individuals and groups. How does this conflict manifest itself? Constantly beaten down, constantly born again, how is this solidarity expressed?' (2014: 233–234).
27 I am grateful for permission to reproduce this section of the argument from the article, 'Staging Reconciliation: The Possibilities of Mourning in Rafael Bonilla's *La carta* (2010). *Bulletin of Spanish Studies*, 84: 9–10 (2017) www.tandfonline.com/doi/abs/10.1080/14753820.2016.1248334.
28 As noted in Chapter 3, there are up to 180 murals painted throughout Ciudad Juárez in an initiative run by mothers and other relatives, which works with local artists to restore the faces of their missing and murdered daughters. Paula Flores told me that she no longer wanted the mural of her daughter, Sagrario, outside her home in Lomas de Poleo as it made her feel sad (personal communication 26 February 2017).
29 It should be noted that a man was convicted of Sagrario's murder, though her mother maintains that there remain multiple irregularities in the way in which the case was handled and tried and that many questions remain unanswered.
30 See, for example, the Comadres of El Salvador, the Conavigua Widows of Guatemala and the Damas de Blanco in Cuba. For more information and analysis, see Jennifer Schirmer, 'The Seeking of Truth and the Gendering of Consciousness: The Comadres of El Salvador and the Conavigua Widows of Guatemala' (1993), 30–64. See also www.damasdeblanco.com [Accessed 6 February 2018].
31 See http://nuestrashijasderegresoacasa.blogspot.ie/ [Accessed 1 June 2016].
32 See Rosario Castellanos's short story, '*Lección de cocina*' from the collection, *Álbum de familia* (1971). See also '*La abnegación: una virtud loca*' (1992). This article by Castellanos was based on the speech she delivered as part of the celebrations of International Women's Day in 1971.
33 The performative nature of motherhood in these contexts has been noted. See Diana Taylor (1997, 2001).
34 Lyrics by Mexican banda singer, Valentín Elizalde from the song, '*La rubia y la morena*', released in 2002. Elizalde was famously gunned down in 2006. It was widely believed that he was killed by Los Zetas for antagonizing them with one of his *corrido* songs. He was posthumously recognized with a Grammy Award in 2007.
35 As noted in Chapter 1, the killings of women in Ciudad Juárez have come to be associated with certain locations in the city and the discoveries of multiple bodies. These locations include Lomas de Poleo, as described, and Campo Algodonero, which featured as part of a case investigated by the Corte Interamericana de Derechos Humanos which found against the Mexican State in 2009. Other sites where victims were buried include Lote Bravo where three bodies were discovered in 1995 and the Valle de Juárez where the remains of multiple corpses were found in 2012.
36 The documentary *Poleo hablando* (León de la Rosa 2006), reveals how the actions of the Zaragoza brothers including the expulsion of families and the destruction of homes, would have been impossible without the complicity of the relevant local authorities. It thus highlights civil resistance to the culture of impunity in the region.

37 Lyrics and music are by Salia Evelyn Pérez Rodríguez, Elda Jéssica Martínez Mena and Beatriz Hernández Zamora. With grateful thanks to Beatriz Adelina Hernández Zamora at the Universidad Autónoma de la Ciudad de México (UACM), for permission to reproduce the lyrics in full.
38 Paula was forced out of Ciudad Juárez and back to Durango as a result of her prominence as an activist and in the face of growing violence against activists more generally. She subsequently returned to Lomas de Poleo.
39 As Diana Taylor writes: 'The women consciously modelled themselves on the Virgin Mary, the ultimate mother who transcends the public/private bind by carrying her privacy with her even in public' (2001: 102).
40 The scandal of the ex-Braceros has received much print and other media coverage. Broadly speaking it concerns the struggle of the former Braceros (or authorised guest workers in the US in the post-war period) and their families to extract the pension payments they are entitled to from the Mexican government. For further information, see: http://elnuevosol.net/2011/05/programa-bracero-la-lucha-por-los-derechos-de-los-trabajadores-del-campo/ [Accessed 6 Feb 2018]; and Jesús Aranda, 'Más de $5 billones, la cantidad que el gobierno deberá devolver a ex braceros', La Jornada, 10 de marzo 2016 www.jornada.unam.mx/2016/03/10/politica/013n1pol [Accessed 6 February 2018].
41 I am grateful to Beatriz Adelina Hernández Zamora for elucidating on the details of the project during a screening of the film with the director, Rafael Bonilla, and Paula Flores at the Cátedra Internacional Marcela Lagarde y de los Ríos, 24–25 November, 2016, Centro de Investigaciones y Estudios Superiores en Antropología Social (CIESAS), Tlalpan, Mexico City.
42 Much of the inspiration for this section of the chapter comes from Catherine Grant whose work in this area includes 'The Shudder of a Cinephiliac Idea? Videographic Film Studies Practice as Material Thinking' (2014) as well as a co-authored article with Christian Keathley (2014). I am profoundly grateful to Catherine Grant for her careful reading of this chapter and her enthusiasm for the project.
43 Keathley draws on Cardinal who, he says, 'reminds us that what is strongest in Barthes's response to the punctum is its "physical aspect. The recognition is an event which "stings" and engages his entire body"' (cited in Keathley 2006: 51).
44 Writing in a different context about art practice, Barbara Bolt writes, 'In the face of the seemingly limitless possibilities, practice cannot know or preconceive its outcome. Rather, the new emerges through process as a shudder of an idea' (Bolt, cited in Grant 2014).
45 We recall here, Barthes's description of the punctum as a 'sting, speck, cut, little hole – and also a cast of the dice. A photograph's punctum is that accident which pricks me (but also bruises me, is poignant to me)' (1980: 26–27).
46 Lesley Stern (1997) also draws a connection between the feelings produced by such cinephiliac encounters to the euphoric experience of the uncanny. See also Keathley, *Cinephilia and History* (2006).

Works cited

16 en la lista: Crimenes en Juarez, 1998. [Film]. Directed by Rodolfo Rodobertti. CPM Films.

Agamben, Giorgio, 1998. *Homo Sacer: Sovereign Power and Bare Life*. Trans. by Daniel Heller-Roazen. Stanford: Stanford University Press.

Ahmed, Sara, 2002. The Contingency of Pain. *Parallax*, 8 (1), 17–34.

Aranda, Jesús, 2016. Más de $5 billones, la cantidad que el gobierno deberá devolver a ex braceros. *La Jornada*, 10 March [online]. Available at: www.jornada.unam.mx/2016/03/10/politica/013n1pol [Accessed 7 Feb 2018].

Austin, Regina, 2009. Women's Unequal Citizenship at the Border: Lessons from three nonfiction films about the women of Juárez. In L.C. McClain and J.L. Grossman, eds., *Gender Equality: Dimensions of Women's Equal Citizenship*. New York: Cambridge University Press, 359–378.

Avila, Edward A., 2012. *Conditions of (Im)possibility: Necropolitics, Neoliberalism and the Cultural Politics of Death in Contemporary Chicano/a Film and Literature*. Thesis (Ph.D). University of San Diego. [online]. Available at: https://cloudfront.escholarship.org/dist/prd/content/qt7sh1f55b/qt7sh1f55b.pdf?t=ml5m0g [Accessed 15 February 2018].

Bajo Juárez: la ciudad devorando a sus hijas, 2006. [Film]. Directed by Antonio Cordero and Alejandra Sánchez.

Baldrich, Roxana, 2014. *Taking the Law into Our Own Hands: Female Vigilantism in India and Mexico*. Thesis (Master in Human Rights and Humanitarian Action). Paris: Paris School of International Affairs.

Barthes, Roland, 1980. *Camera Lucida: Reflections on Photography*. New York: Farrar, Strauss and Giroux.

Baugh, Scott L., and Sorell, Victor A., 2015. *Born of Resistance: Cara a Cara Encounters with Chicana/o Visual Culture*. Tucson: University of Arizona Press.

Bejarano, Cynthia, 2002. Las Super Madres de Latino America: Transforming Motherhood by Challenging Violence in Mexico, Argentina, and El Salvador. *Frontiers: A Journal of Women Studies*, 23 (1), 126–150.

Benítez, Rohry, et al., 1999. *El silencio que la voz de todas quiebra*. Chihuahua: Ediciones del Azar.

Blood Rising, 2013. [Film]. Directed by Mark McLoughlin.

Bola Negra: El musical de Ciudad Juárez, 2012. [Film]. Directed by Mario Bellatin and Marcela Rodríguez. Mexico: Instituto Nacional de Bellas Artes and En Chinga Films.

Bollington, Lucy, 2018. *Reframing Excess: Death and Power in Contemporary Mexican Literary and Visual Culture*. Thesis (Ph.D). University of Cambridge.

Border Echoes [Ecos de una frontera], 2006. [Film]. Directed by Lorena Méndez-Quiroga.

Bordertown, 2006. [Film]. Directed by Gregory Nava. Mobius Entertainment/El Norte Productions.

Bosco, Fernando J., 2004. Human Rights Politics and Scaled Performances of Memory: Conflicts Among the Madres de Plaza de Mayo in Argentina. *Social & Cultural Geography*, 5 (3), 381–402.

———, 2006. The Madres de Plaza de Mayo and Three Decades of Human Rights' Activism: Embeddedness, Emotions, and Social Movements. *Annals of the Association of American Geographers*, 96 (2), 342–365.

Carroll, Amy Sarah, 2006. "Accidental Allegories" Meet "The Performative Documentary": Boystown, Señorita Extraviada, and the Border-Brothel→Maquiladora Paradigm. *Signs*, 31 (2 Winter), 357–396.

Castellanos, Rosario, 1971. *Álbum de familia*. México: Fondo de Cultura Económica.

———, 1992. La abnegación: una virtud loca. *Debate Feminista*, 3 (6), 287–292.

Chauvet, Elina, 2009. *Zapatos rojos* [Installation].

Ciudad Juárez: La ciudad donde las mujeres son deshechables, 2007. [Film]. Directed by Alex Flores and Lorena Vassolo.

Corpus: A Home Movie for Selena, 1999. [Film]. Lourdes Portillo.

Delgadillo, Theresa, 2011. *Spiritual Mestizaje: Religion, Gender, Race, and Nation in Contemporary Chicano Narrative*. Durham, NC: Duke University Press.

Desde que no estás, 2008. [Film]. Directed by Rosella M. Bergamaschi.

DesInformémonos, 2017. "Por Valeria me maquillé hoy, quiero justicia para las niñas de este país": manifestación en Neza. 10 June. [online]. Available at: https://desinformemonos.org/valeria-me-maquille-hoy-quiero-justicia-las-ninas-este-pais-manifestacion-neza/ [Accessed 30 January 2018].

The Devil Never Sleeps/El diablo nunca duerme, 1994. [Film]. Directed by Lourdes Portillo.

Driver, Alice, 2012. Feminicide and the Disintegration of the Family Fabric in Ciudad Juárez: An Interview with Lourdes Portillo. *Studies in Latin American Popular Culture*, 30, 215–225.

———, 2015. *More or Less Dead: Feminicide, Haunting, and the Ethics of Representation in Mexico*. Tucson: University of Arizona Press.

El crimen del padre amaro [The Crime of Father Amaro], 2002. [Film]. Directed by Carlos Carrera.

El otro sueño americano [The Other American Dream], 2004. [Film]. Directed by Enrique Arroyo.

El traspatio [Backyard], 2009. [Film]. Directed by Carlos Carrera.

Espejo retrovisor [Rearview Mirror], 2002. [Film]. Directed by Lisa di Georgina.

Estoy queriendo a una rubia y a una morena tambien, 2002. [Song]. Lyrics by Valentín Elizalde, 2002.

Estrellas enterradas by Antonio Zúñiga, 2011. [Play].

Foster, D.W., 2013. *Latin American Documentary Filmmaking: Major Works*. Tucson: University of Arizona Press.

Franco, Jean, 2013. *Cruel Modernity*. Durham, NC: Duke University Press.

Fregoso, Rosa Linda, 2001. *The Devil Never Sleeps and Other Films*. Austin: University of Texas Press.

———, 2003. *MeXicana Encounters: The Making of Social Identities on the Borderlands*. Berkeley: University of California Press.

———, 2010. La transformación del terror: *Señorita Extraviada*, de Lourdes Portillo (2001). In Patricia Ravelo Blancas and Héctor Domínguez-Ruvalcava, coords., *Diálogos Interdisciplinarios sobre Violenica Sexual: Antología*. Ediciones Eón, Chicano Studies, The University of Texas at El Paso, 235–256.

Gillman, Laura, 2015. Haptic Visuality in Lourdes Portillo's *Señorita Extraviada*: Towards an Affective Activism. *FIAR Forum for Inter-American Research*, 8 (2), 139–159.

González, R., 2003. The Said and the Unsaid: Lourdes Portillo Tracks Down Ghosts in *Señorita Extraviada*. *Aztlán: A Journal of Chicano Studies*, 28 (2 Fall), 235–240.

Grant, Catherine, 2014. The Shudder of a Cinephiliac Idea? Videographic Film Studies Practice as Material Thinking. *Aniki*, 1 (1). [online]. Available at: http://aim.org.pt/ojs/index.php/revista/article/view/59/html [Accessed 7 Feb 2018].

———, and Keathley, Christian, 2014. The Use of Illusion: Childhood, cinephilia, object relations, and videographic film studies. *Cinea*, 19 June. [online]. Available at: https://cinea.be/the-use-an-illusion-childhood-cinephilia-object-relations-and-videographic-film-studies/ [Accessed 6 Feb 2016].

Guzmán Bouvard, Marguerite, 1994. *Revolutionizing Motherhood: The Mothers of the Plaza de Mayo*. Lanham: Rowan & Littlefield.

If Images Could Fill Our Empty Spaces, 2013. [Film]. Directed by Alice Driver.

Jameson, Fredric, 1984. Postmodernism, or the Cultural Logic of Late Capitalism. *New Left Review*, 146, 53–92.

———, 1991. *Postmodernism or, the Cultural Logic of Late Capitalism*. Durham, NC: Duke University Press.

Juárez: City of Dreams, 2012. [Film]. Directed by Bruno Sorrentino.
Kaplan, E. Ann, 2005. *Trauma Culture: The Politics of Terror and Loss in Media and Literature*. New Brunswick, NJ: Rutgers University Press.
Keathley, Christian, 2000. The Cinephiliac Moment. *Framework*, 42. [online]. Available at: www.frameworknow.com/vol-42 [Accessed 7 Feb 2018].
———, 2006. *Cinephilia and History, or The Wind in the Trees*. Bloomington, IN: Indiana University Press.
———, 2014. Letting the World Happen. *Aniki: Portuguese Journal of the Moving Image*, 1 (1), 63–72.
La Batalla de Las Cruces: protesta social y acciones colectivas en torno de la violencia sexual en Ciudad Juárez, 2006. [Film]. Directed by Patricia Ravelo and Rafael Bonilla.
LaCapra, Dominick, 1994. *Representing the Holocaust: History, Theory, Trauma*. Ithaca: Cornell University Press.
———, 2001. *Writing History, Writing Trauma*. Baltimore: Johns Hopkins University Press.
La carta [The Letter], 2010. [Film]. Directed by Rafael Bonilla.
Las muertas de Juárez [The Dead Women of Juárez], 2001. [Film]. Directed by Enrique Murillo 2001.
Lefebvre, Henri, 2014. *Critique of Everyday Life* (2nd Edition). London: Verso.
Luckhurst, Roger, 2008. *The Trauma Question*. New York: Routledge.
MacDougall, David, 1998. *Transcultural Cinema*. Princeton, NJ: Princeton University Press.
Mass Murder in Juárez, 2012. [Film]. Directed by Peadar King.
Mata, Irene, 2011. Documenting Feminicide: The importance of teaching Lourdes Portillo's *Señorita Extraviada*. *Chicana/Latina Studies*, 10 (2 Spring), 92–127.
Matías, Bienvenida, 2015. Between Anger and Love: The Presence of *Señorita Extraviada*. In Scott L. Baugh and Victor A. Sorell, eds., *Born of Resistance: Cara a Cara Encounters with Chicana/o Visual Culture*. Tucson: University of Arizona Press, 263–267.
Mbembe, Achille, 2003. Necropolitics. *Public Culture*, 15 (1), 11–40.
Meredith, Dana A., and Rodríguez Cortés, Luis Alberto, 2017. Feminicide: Expanding Outrage: Representations of Gendered Violence and Feminicide in Mexico. In Stuart A. Day, ed., *Modern Mexican Culture: Critical Foundations*. Tucson: University of Arizona Press, 237–258.
Miércoles de ceniza [Ash Wednesday], 2005. [Film]. Directed by Fernando Benítez.
Mora, Sergio de la, 2004. Terrorismo del Género en la Frontera de EUA-México: Asesinato, Mujeres y Justicia en *Señorita Extraviada* (Lourdes Portillo, 2001). *Cinema d'Amerique Latine*, 12 (1), 116–132.
Mothers: Las Madres de la Plaza de Mayo, 1986. [Film]. Lourdes Portillo.
Nealon, Jeffrey T., 1998. *Alterity Politics: Ethics and Performative Subjectivity*. Durham, NC, London: Duke University Press.
Nichols, Bill, 1991. *Representing Reality: Issues and Concepts in Documentary*. Bloomington, IN: Indiana University Press.
———, 2001. *Introduction to Documentary*. Bloomington, IN: Indiana University Press.
Ni Una Más, Not One More: The Juárez Murders, 2010. [Exhibition]. Leonard Pearlstein Gallery, Philadelphia. 15 May–16 July.
Norton, Richard J., 2003. Feral Cities. *Naval War College Review*, 56 (4), 97–106.
On the Edge: Femicide in Ciudad Juárez, 2006. [Film]. Directed by Steev Hise.
Pasión y muerte en Juáre [Passion and Death in Ciudad Juárez], 2002. [Film]. Directed by Javier Ulloa and Luis Estrada.
Performing the Border, 1999. [Film]. Directed by Ursula Biemann.
Poleo hablando, 2006. [Film]. Directed by León de la Rosa.

Preguntas sin Respuesta: Los asesinatos y desapariciones de mujeres en Ciudad Juárez, 2004. [Film]. Directed by Rafael Montero.
Razo, Fernando del, 2009. Sobre El traspatio de Carlos Carrera. *Nexos*, 1 Feb. [online]. Available at: www.nexos.com.mx/?p=12951 [Accessed 7 Feb 2018].
Renov, Michael, 1993. Toward a Poetics of Documentary. In Michael Renov, ed., *Theorizing Documentary*. New York: Routledge, 12–36.
Rodríguez, Ileana, 2009. *Liberalism at Its Limits: Crime and Terror in Latin American Cultural Text*. Pittsburg: University of Pittsburg Press.
Rojas, Clara, 2005. The V Day March in Mexico: Appropriate and (mis)use of Local Women's Activism. *National Women's Studies Association Journal*, 17, 217–228.
Ruddick, Sara, 1989. *Maternal Thinking: Toward a Politics of Peace*. Boston: Beacon Press.
Sandell, Jillian, 2013. The Proximity of the Here and the Urgency of the Now: Lourdes Portillo's *Señorita Extraviada*. *Social Identities*, 19 (3–4), 454–467.
Sandoval, Chela, 2000. *Methodology of the Oppressed*. London, Minneapolis: University of Minnesota Press.
Schapiro, Meyer, 1998. *Theory and Philosophy of Art: Style, Artist, and Society* (Selected Papers, Book 4) (4th Edition). New York: George Braziller.
Schirmer, Jennifer, 1993. The Seeking of Truth and the Gendering of Consciousness: The Comadres of El Salvador and the Conavigua Widows of Guatemala. In Sallie Westwood and Sarah A. Radcliffe, eds., *Viva: Women and Popular Protest in Latin America*. London: Routledge, 30–64.
———, 2006. Integral Bodies: Cuerpos Integros: Impunity and the Pursuit of Justice in the Chihuahuan Feminicidio. *e-misférica*, 3 (1). [online]. Available at: http://hemisphericinstitute.org/journal/3.1/eng/en31_pg_camacho.html [Accessed 10 February 2018].
Señorita Extraviada, 2001. [Film]. Directed by Lourdes Portillo.
Shenker, Noah, 2015. *Reframing Holocaust Testimony*. Bloomington, IN: Indiana University Press.
Shoes on the Danube Promenade, 2005 [Installation] by Gyula Pauer and Can Togay.
Silencio en Juárez, 2009. [Film]. Directed by Michela Giorelli.
Staudt, Kathleen, 2008. *Violence and Activism at the U.S. Mexico Border: Gender, Fear and Everyday Life*. Austin: University of Texas Press.
Stern, Lesley, 1997. I Think, Sebastian, Therefore . . . I Somersault: Film and the Uncanny. *Paradoxa*, 3 (3–4).
Stier, Oren Baruch, 2015. *Holocaust Icons: Symboliszing the Shoah in History and Memory*. New Brunswick: Rutgers University Press.
Tabuenca Córdoba, M.S., and Guzmán, G., 2010. Ghost dance in Ciudad Juárez at the end/beginning of the millennium. In Alicia Gaspar de Alba and Georgina Guzmán, eds., *Making a Killing: Femicide, Free Trade and La Frontera*. Austin: University of Texas Press, 95–119.
Taylor, Diana, 1997. Trapped in Bad Scripts: The Mothers of the Plaza de Mayo. In Diana Taylor, *Disappearing Acts: Spectacles of Gender and Nationalism in Argentina's Dirty War*. Durham, NC: Duke University Press, 183–222.
———, 2001. Making a Spectacle: The Mothers of the Plaza de Mayo. *Journal of the Association for Research on Mothering*, 3 (2), 97–109.
The Virgin of Juárez, 2006. [Film]. Directed by Kevin James Dobson.
Torres, Mónica F., 2015. Resisting the Violence of Values: Lourdes Portillo's *Señorita Extraviada* as Performative Utterance. In Scott L. Baugh and Victor A. Sorell, eds., *Born of Resistance: Cara a Cara Encounters with Chicana/o Visual Culture*. Tucson: University of Arizona Press, 282–287. See also, www.lourdesportillo.com/articles/articles_resisting.php [Accessed 10 February 2018].

Willemen, Paul, 1994. *Looks and Frictions: Essays in Cultural Studies and Film Theory*. London: BFI.

Wright, Melissa, 1999. The Dialectics of Still Life: Murder, Women, and Maquiladoras. *Public Culture*, 11 (3 Fall), 453–473.

———, 2006. *Disposable Women and Other Myths of Global Capitalism*. New York: Routledge.

———, 2007. Femicide, Mother-Activism and the Geography of Protest in Northern Mexico. *Urban Geography*, 8 (5), 401–425.

Zavala, Pablo M., 2016. La producción antifeminicidista mexicana: autoría, representación y feminismo en la frontera juarense. *Chasqui: Revista de literatura latinoamericana*, 45 (2), 57–69.

5 Toward an activist poetics: fiction responds to *feminicidio* in Ciudad Juárez

Two novels and a testimony

> I only know that I need to write, write and write in order to go on living. Or so that someone else can live through what I write.
>
> —Benítez et al. (1999: 89)[1]

So goes an extract from the diary of victim of *feminicidio*, Eréndira Ivonne Ponce Hernández, shortly before her body was found in Ciudad Juárez in August, 1998.[2] The sense of urgency in her words, as well as her enthusiasm for the project of writing is palpable. Moreover, she speaks to the generative power of the written word and her wish for someone to live through the words that she produces. The desire to act through writing the stories of pain, terror and death form the basis of the frequently heartbreaking testimonial text, *El silencio que la voz de todas quiebra* [The silence that breaks the voice of all women] published in 1999 and from which this quotation is taken. This chapter will probe the role played by a number of written texts in their attempts to excavate the multiple layers of meaning imbricated in the murders of women in Ciudad Juárez since the 1990s. It seeks to uncover the discursive strategies employed by these texts to mourn and memorialize the victims so cruelly erased by the feminicidal wave. Foregrounding possible discursive strategies and suggesting a blueprint for further action, Cristina Rivera Garza is one of the many prominent intellectuals in Mexico to engage with the searing societal anxiety produced by the violence of the current moment. Specifically she questions the role of writers, '*¿Qué tipo de retos enfrenta el ejercicio de la escritura en un medio donde la precariedad del trabajo y la muerte horrísona constituyen la material de todos los días?*' (2013: 19) [What kind of challenge confronts the practice of writing in an environment in which precarity with regard to work and the horrors of violent death are the stuff of everyday life?]. The link she isolates between precarity and violent death have been explored at length throughout the study; following her line of questioning, the chapter will interrogate the various ways that writing and storytelling more widely connect to human rights' consciousness-raising and towards building affective and political linkages. This final chapter in the journey through the cultural responses generated by feminicide in the city of Ciudad Juárez then, leads us to the responses recorded in written form; the poetry, the detective novels, the testimonial forms and the other ways in which the stories of feminicidal pain and horror have been encoded in writing.[3]

The chapter selects three case studies from the corpus of written texts available: the mystery novel *Desert Blood: The Juárez Murders* by Chicana writer Alicia Gaspar de Alba, which is examined alongside the much less known, but equally intriguing, *Ciudad final* [Final City] by Spanish author and academic Kama Gutier. I bookend the discussion of these two texts with an appraisal of the collaboratively assembled text, *El silencio que la voz de todas quiebra*, from which the chapter's opening extract is taken and one of the first written texts about the feminicidal crime wave that erupted in Ciudad Juárez in the early 1990s. All of the writers considered in the chapter are activists, in the sense that they seek out social and political change at the same time as they craft their creative responses to the crimes. Indeed, their texts shed light on the blurred boundaries between art and activism, exposing the limits of writing as well as its power. I will explore the texts' function of 'making visible' [*visibilizar*]; not just in terms of naming and re-humanizing the victims of the crimes but also in terms of their revelation of those structural layers that make the violence possible. The reliance on hybridity in the texts further showcases the need to go beyond traditional generic boundaries to identify more fluid ways of moving between these structural layers. In the texts' symbolic investment in making the crimes visible, they are located within a wider panorama of much current writing in Mexico about violence, including that of Rivera Garza, already referenced. In the final section, reading through Cristina Rivera Garza's reflections on writing as a response to pain and her innovative rethinking of the role of the Mexican writer working from a 'wounded place' (Rivera Garza 2015), the chapter considers the writerly interventions as an urgent call for societal change. Before commencing the detailed analysis of the chosen texts, however, a brief overview of writing about feminicide in Juárez is warranted.

Writing *feminicidio*

Marco Kunz (2016) provides a masterful overview of the range of prose fiction written either directly or touching on the subject of *feminicidio* in Ciudad Juárez in a tangential way. Of interest here is the way that the subject continues to attract the attention of writers globally, whether from the perspective of the genre of pulp fiction,[4] adolescent literature (Malpica 2006),[5] satire (Wimmer 2008) or mystery novel. Aside from writers in Mexico and the US, there is a body of work published in France and Spain, with isolated works also from writers in Italy, Poland, Germany and Ecuador.[6] The best known fictional treatment of feminicide in Ciudad Juárez is, of course, Roberto Bolaño's 2666, which was the subject of analysis in its theatrical interpretation in Chapter 2. Available in translation in multiple languages, it constitutes, as I point out in that chapter, something akin to a global literary talking point. Aside from this text, however, the most valuable written interventions on the subject of feminicide in Juárez have arguably been in the realm of the non-literary, including the groundbreaking *Huesos en el desierto* [Bones in the Desert] by Mexico city-based journalist Sergio González Rodríguez. This book comprises a series of rewritten articles about the murders that González Rodríguez published in the late 1990s in the Mexican newspaper, *Reforma*. The vicious attack perpetrated on the writer in Mexico City (and recorded in the book), signalled the very material dangers that faced journalists, researchers or activists who dared to question the power structures circumscribing meaningful investigation into the crimes.[7] Rodríguez's writing on Juárez and indeed on violence more widely,[8] has been of significant importance. *Huesos en el desierto* is primarily known as the book that gave rise to Bolaño's *2666* after the lengthy correspondence between the two authors and the forensic discourse of Bolaño's novel is taken directly from the police reports that form the basis of González Rodríguez's journalistic investigation. Labelled an 'anti-novel' by Bolaño (2011: 230–231), this classification signals the generic ambiguity of much of his writing and provides evidence of the ways in which the feminicidal crimes of Ciudad Juárez frequently find expression in non-traditional modes of writing that blend fiction and non-fiction elements in diverse and creative ways. Indeed, González Rodríguez's texts are curious hybrids that conjoin images, text and prose, the merging of traditional journalism with 'literary experimentation and academic analysis' (Jochum 2015: 105). Likewise, the influential text *Cosecha de mujeres: Safari en el desierto mexicano* (2005), published in English as *Harvest of Women: Safari in Mexico* (2006), by Diana Washington Valdez, constitutes another significant example of this non-literary excavation of the crimes. A journalist with the *El Paso Times*, Washington Valdez's interventions have been pivotal in terms of knowledge dissemination and her advocacy role – sustained over many years – means that her work is indispensable in any evaluation of *feminicidio* on the border. This text, while more conventional in form than *Huesos en el desierto*, goes beyond many journalistic accounts in its attention to rigorous contextualization, its reliance on academic research and its unequivocal concern for social justice. Other writers in this mould include Charles Bowden, whose work has already been mentioned in Chapter 2. Bowden exemplifies a writerly approach that combines journalistic appraisal with personal reflection, memoir or elements characteristic of the particularly Latin American written form of *crónica* or essay. Notwithstanding the problematic nature of Bowden's work in terms of how he frames both the city of Ciudad Juárez and the female victims, there is no denying the power of his prose nor his long engagement with the region and its people.[9]

Other non-literary and inventive approaches to *feminicidio* include testimonial forms, frequently interspersed in works of academic criticism or socio-political critique (Fregoso and Bejarano 2010; Benítez et al. 1999). An innovative example of intermedial approaches emerging from the written form is the opera-film *Bola Negra: El musical de Ciudad Juárez* (2012) by the acclaimed writer, Mario Bellatin working with composer, Marcela Rodríguez, based on a short story by Bellatin of the same name.[10] In common with many of the artistic responses surveyed in Chapter 3, there are also projects in which Ciudad Juárez is explored in a comparative framework with other global sites of atrocity and conflict. Mia

Kirshner's *I Live Here* (2008) is a good example of that kind of approach, one that is not without its ethical questions in terms of how its transnational dispersal may lead to troubling ellisions and erasures of both history and distinct subjectivities forged in radically different contexts.[11] Given the imagistic force of the narratives of feminicidal violence, seen so vividly in Chapters 3 and 4, it is perhaps not surprising that these narratives have also lent themselves to treatment as either graphic novel or in comic book form. Furthermore, the role of comic book cultures as a way of critiquing urban modernity (King and Page 2017: 137) means that this generic form was particularly suitable for the articulation of the horrors of feminicidal violence as a direct product of urban precarity. We have seen how spatiality and the way the urban environment is both (un)regulated and (dis) organized have contributed to the debates about how violence against women continues to reproduce itself in the border region. Many of the graphic novels grapple with this question including *El negocio de matar* [The Business of Killing] by Rocío Duque (2013) or *Luchadoras* by the French comic artist/writer Peggy Adam, published in 2009. The Canadian writer Phoebe Gloeckner contributes a section on Ciudad Juárez to the Kirshner project, just mentioned, and Edmond Baudoin-Troubs's *Viva la vida: Los sueños de Ciudad Juárez* (2011) was written as a form of travel diary. It can be seen, therefore, that the force of non-literary, frequently intermedial or multimedia interventions is notable as artists and writers struggle to assemble their ideas about social change and justice through an aesthetic practice that will resonate with multiple audiences.

Poetry provides another expressive terrain through which the horrors of feminicidal crime have been articulated. Poetry readings have been performed at the multiple gatherings, or *encuentros*, of writers, poets and social activists in the city of Ciudad Juárez and the wider region since the crimes began to be recorded in the early 1990s. These conversations and gatherings have served as energizing hubs for literary and other responses to the crimes (Rojas Joo 2016). There have been anthologies thematising gender violence in Ciudad Juárez, many of which also combine artistic responses to the crimes.[12] Chihuahan poet, Micaela Solís, wrote *Elegía en el desierto: In Memoriam* as a way of forging consciousness in lyric form and her refrain, 'ni perdón, ni olvido' (2004: 34) [no forgiving, no forgetting], resonates as a mode of contestation and *denuncia* (2004). Other poets from Chihuahua include the human rights activist Susana Chávez Castillo, who became a victim of *feminicidio* herself when she was brutally murdered in 2011, and Arminé Arjona (2004). Both of these writers highlight the inter-related dangers of precarity, gendered labour practices and the destructive patriarchal character of Juarense society as crucial interconnecting frameworks through which the crimes might be understood.[13] In this sense, they are consonant with Rivera Garza's position and their work may be seen as part of a wider wave of *necroescrituras* (2015), defined by her as a form of narrative production that formally critiques and defies the death, destruction and societal collapse evident in the current historical moment in Mexico.

Rosina Conde, born in Tijuana but currently based in Mexico City, is a writer, activist, performer and poet. A forceful presence among the many poetic voices to address the subject of violence in the northern border city, Conde is also a talented performer of her own poetry.[14] Reciting poems from her collection, *Poemas por Ciudad Juárez* in numerous locations nationally and internationally, Conde writes movingly of the need for a new language, for new words to name the cruelty of forced disappearance and death. Marjorie Agosín's bilingual collection of poetry, titled *Secrets in the Sand: The Young Women of Juárez* (2006), works to rupture settled narratives around the victims and eloquently inscribes their humanity. Evangelina Arce, the mother of a victim of *feminicidio*, published a book of poetry titled *Para mi hija, Silvia/For my daughter, Silvia* in memory of her daughter. Translated in collaboration with Alicia Partnoy and students at Loyola Marymount University, it constitutes another instance of the blurring of lines between poetic, academic and activist intervention. In this way, it can be appreciated how a certain poetics of gender violence has evolved in and about *feminicidio* in Ciudad Juárez. Indeed, in seeking to explore the particular affective and verbal appeal of the poetic form, poets have forged new ways of conceptualizing the horrors and remembering the victims.

Finally, in our trawl through the corpus of fictional texts to respond to violence in Ciudad Juárez, it is time to consider the ways in which the murders of women in the city have found expression in the mystery or the detective novel of which there are multiple examples in different languages. Some of these are based closely on the media narratives around feminicide in Juárez from the 1990s onwards with research gleaned from print media, TV and other forms. The novels focalize their fictional explorations in different ways but many of them utilize those same viewing parameters or frames examined in Chapter 1. In this way, they examine the links between globalization and the concomitant rise in violence against women; the prevailing mediatic portrayal of women as contaminated and in need of control; the rise in hyperviolent crime and related questions about masculinity, and the failure of the city's infrastructures to provide basic protections for its citizens. Worthy explorations of these dynamics in mystery or detective form include Stella Pope Duarte's *If I die in Juárez* (2008), which offers a particularly insightful account of the *maquila* and its place in Juárez life, and Maud Tabachnik's *He visto al diablo de frente: Los crímenes de Ciudad Juárez* [I've Seen the Devil Up Close: The Crimes of Ciudad Juárez] (2005). Patrick Bard's *La frontera: una novela de denuncia acerca de las muertas de Ciudad Juárez* [The Border: A Novel of Protest about the Murder of Women in Ciudad Juárez] (2004)[15] is a slightly more clichéd view but nonetheless gripping in its own way.[16] Other examples include Kama Gutier's *Ciudad final* [Final City] (2007) and Carmen Galán Benítez's *Tierra Marchita* [Wasteland] (2001). The mystery novel to have attracted by far the most commercial and critical acclaim, however, is Alicia Gaspar de Alba's *Desert Blood: The Murders of the Women of Juárez*, the subject of this chapter and also of numerous scholarly analyses.[17] As we will see, the teleological nature of detective fiction has proven to be attractive for many writers seeking answers to the crimes and justice for the victims. In this way, the genre of detective fiction often operates as a fulcrum from which competing, contradictory and sometimes complementary versions of feminicidal narratives collide and intersect.

This chapter will initially concentrate its analysis on two works of detective fiction in relation to the gender violence in Juárez, Alicia Gaspar de Alba's *Desert Blood: The Juárez Murders* (2005) and Kama Gutier's *Ciudad final* [Final City] (2007). In particular, I wish to focus on the central protagonists of each novel – both lesbian, Chicana academics employed at US universities, in precarious contractual situations – who take on the investigations into the murders prompted by a sense of horror at the cruelty of the crimes and incredulity at the official responses elicited by them. My focus is first to seek to understand how the construction of the protagonists as quintessential *mestiza* figures, as explored by Gloria Anzaldúa (1987), offers a way of unsettling the very polarized discourses that inflect debates about the murders. My enquiry also turns its attention to genre and the use of detective fiction as a model through which to explore real-life crimes. Located in a rich history of crime fiction by Chicano writers, the narrative grammar of both texts engages with the very limits of conventional detective fiction formulae. I consider how the generic frames of detective fiction work to enable metafictional narratives that integrate the acts of writing and activism thus going beyond the textual boundaries posed by the conventions of the genre. The following section of the chapter turns its attention to *El silencio que la voz de todas quiebra* [The silence that breaks the voice of all women] and the striking ways it commemorates and re-evaluates prevailing discourses around the crimes. In the final section of the chapter, I draw all three texts into a comparative reflection and explore the ways in which their rich confluence of voices forms part of a polyvocal community that destabilizes ideas about knowledge as rooted in the individual. Here, I turn to Rivera Garza's ideas around *comunalidad* as a form of collective action or labour, to see how they can help us assess the psychic processing of gender violence as articulated in the texts.

Literature, autobiography and activism in *Desert Blood* and *Ciudad final*[18]

In many ways, both books function as relatively conventional tales of detective fiction in which a series of murders are investigated by a detective-like figure. Both also constitute exemplary metanarratives in the sense that the interweaving of fact, fiction and autobiography within the detective 'plots', leads to an 'other' story in which the solutions are not so clear-cut and the murders remain unsolved. The texts negotiate the complex movement between these two sets of narratives and indeed the notion of movement and mobility are of paramount importance in the narratives themselves. Gaspar de Alba is a well-known academic and writer, and currently works as professor of Chicana/o studies, English, and women's studies at the University of California, Los Angeles (UCLA). *Desert Blood: The Juárez Murders* is by no means her only foray into fiction; she is the successful author of three novels, two books of poetry and two collections of short stories. The novel has been a commercial success and has been translated into Italian (2007), Spanish (2008) and French (2012).[19] The book forms part of an academic and personal interest in the murders on the part of Gaspar de Alba, who is a native of the El Paso/Juárez border. She has been involved in research on the crimes since 1998 and organized an international conference of major importance on the murders at UCLA in 2003.[20] Furthermore, she was heavily involved as an activist in terms of raising awareness about the murders in Juárez and continues to raise funds for various organizations, including Amigos de las Mujeres de Juárez, to which a portion of the royalties for the book is donated.[21] *Desert Blood* tells the story of Ivon Villa, an academic, married to a woman named Brigit and living in Los Angeles, who returns to El Paso, her place of birth, to formalize the adoption of a baby in Ciudad Juárez organized by her cousin, Ximena. While there, the mother of their soon-to-be-adopted baby is brutally murdered and this event precipitates Ivon's participation in the murder narrative in ways hitherto unimaginable. When her younger sister, Irene, disappears, the horror becomes personal as Ivon tries to track down the perpetrators. After a painstaking search, a snuff movie network, led by a corrupt Immigration and Naturalization Service (INS) agent, is discovered in a smelter plant and Ivon manages to find Irene alive, though suffering from horrific injuries, the result of repeated violent sexual assault. A series of dead bodies is also discovered at the site though the entire episode is blatantly covered up by the authorities. The novel ends as Ivon and Brigit plan their return to Los Angeles with their newly adopted son, Jorgito, the son of a *maquila* worker who is soon to die from cancer contracted through her work conditions.

Kama Gutier is a pseudonym for Josebe Martínez, a writer and academic with a similar profile to Gaspar de Alba as an author of both fiction about the border and a scholarly interest in border issues. A native of Navarra, Spain, Gutier graduated with a doctorate in Hispanic literatures from the University of California and has worked at the University of Miami, Colegio de México and the University of El País Vasco, where she is currently in the faculty of Hispanic literature. Based for more than fourteen years on the US-Mexico border, she was involved in a number of projects, including experimental film on or about the region. *Ciudad final* was published in Spanish in Barcelona in 2007 by the publishing house Montesinos and thus, while *Ciudad final* is not a Chicana novel in the sense that its author is from Spain, it is its use of a Chicana protagonist that is of such interest in this study. Gutier presented the book in Spain in Pamplona, at the VI *Muestra de Cine: El mundo y los derechos humanos*, organized by Amnesty International and the Navarra-based Instituto Promoción Estudios Sociales (IPES). There she spoke forcefully in terms of the social fabric underpinning the crimes as well as the culture of impunity embedded within the justice systems:

> In a global world, condemnation must also be global. The more people that become aware, know, see, listen and read about what's going on, the greater the international pressure.
>
> (2010)

Ciudad final narrates the story of the eponymous protagonist, Kama Gutier who, in common with Ivon Villa, is a native of the border region and travels to Ciudad Juárez at the invitation of the Corte del Estado (de Chihuahua) to cover the investigation into the Juárez feminicides. While there, she is plunged into an investigative maelstrom marred by errors at the level of policing, forensic examination, autopsies and legal processing. Piecing together the puzzle with help from a wide network of informants, Kama is finally able to unravel the mysteries behind the deaths of a number of the girls, and the book ends as she joins a number of protests against the apathy and corruption she has unveiled at the heart of the investigations. In defiance of the judge who has invited her to Juárez, she withholds some of the evidence she has collected and the novel ends on a rather open-ended note, with the final words, 'we had much to tell' (*Ciudad final*: 206), resonating clearly as a pledge to seek justice beyond the pages of the book.

The connections between both authors and their protagonists in terms of origins (*Desert Blood*), occupation, and name (*Ciudad final*), mean that readers are explicitly invited to draw autobiographical inferences and thus to read the books as part fact, part fiction. Both the main characters are US-based Chicana academics who are at the centre of novels about the Juárez cases in which both authors have been involved professionally. This is not in any way to start the relatively pointless quest of trying to establish autobiographical linkages[22] but rather to focus on the fact that both novels are unequivocally set up as texts that interweave fact, fiction and indeed activism into their folds from the outset in intriguing and innovative ways. The appeals to the readers to become part of a global 'denuncia' in *Desert Blood*; the convergence between fact and fiction at the end of *Ciudad final*; Gaspar de Alba's contribution to fund-raising for justice in Juárez; Gutier's involvement in human rights events all point to a marked ethical dimension present in the texts in which ideas about activism, protest and the search for justice are embedded both within the plots (where you might expect to find them) but also beyond the narrative frames in terms of how the books are presented, marketed and distributed.[23] Furthermore, the activist roles played by both authors and their other academic activities, such as publishing about the border (both authors have written extensively on the topic) point to the ways in which the 'literary apparatus' (Moreiras 2001: 2), incorporating the relationship between author-text-context, is imbricated within 'real' discourses of human rights, activism and protest.

Border voices: mobility and *mestizaje*

In this section, I would like to scrutinize the protagonists of both detective narratives who are of interest for the ways in which their construction as moving, fluid and unstable subjects serves to re-stage the settled dynamics of the narratives around *feminicidio*. Both protagonists are 'of' the border: Ivon in *Desert Blood* is from El Paso and in *Ciudad final*, the in-betweenness of the principal protagonist, Kama, is established as a geographical fact of birth:

> I was born in a stolen car (or borrowed, as my father used to say) on a bridge over the Rio Bravo, crossing the Mexican border from Juárez to El Paso, U.S. That night, I crossed the border for the first time.
>
> (*Ciudad final*: 7)

In establishing the narrator's links with movement from the very moment of childbirth, the novel establishes the travelling perspective as an epistemological standpoint that affords insight and knowledge. Aside from the links with the two central protagonists, references to travel permeate both books and cars, in particular, and their ability to move protagonists around and out of trouble, function as key signifiers in a textual space that is marked by frenetic movement. Movement is also central to the primary protagonist of *Desert Blood*, whose opening lines see her travel from Los Angeles where she is resident, to her city of birth, El Paso. In the novel, Ivon traverses the border countless times remaining an outsider in both spaces, a depiction that is illuminated in a series of dialogues with the 'local' informants, her cousin Ximena and Father Francis, a priest working for a local non-profit organization, Contra el Silencio:

> Look . . . I'm sorry I'm asking really dumb questions, okay? And I'm really sorry that I haven't lived here since 1989, and that I haven't been back since 1996, and that I don't know shit. Okay, that's been established.
> (*Desert Blood*: 39–40)

Many of these exchanges encompass Ivon's incredulity about life on the border and are framed through a series of questions posed in relation to the inhumane conditions in the *maquilas* about which she is becoming informed: 'She'll get fired if she's pregnant?' (*Desert Blood*: 12). When Ximena explains that this is routine ('Take your birth control if you want to keep your job'), Ivon replies, 'Are you shitting me?' (*Desert Blood*: 12). These exchanges posit Ivon as the dubious outsider, a classification she resists, certainly initially, as exemplified in the following conversation with Ximena when her insistence on being 'native' is showcased:

> Five minutes in Juárez and you're already pissing off the natives, huh?
> *I am a native*, said Ivon.
> You don't look like no native to me, homegirl, wearing shorts and leaning against the car looking all sexy in your California tan. *Te miras muy Hollywood.*
> (*Desert Blood*: 22, my emphasis)

These exchanges reinforce Ivon's position as ambivalent witness to the reality of life in both El Paso and Juárez and inscribe the context of the murders as definitively binational, an idea that is underscored through the textual demarcation of 'here' and 'there' throughout the text:

> Look, that's the way things work over *there*. I don't make the *pinche* rules.
> (*Desert Blood*: 16, my emphasis)

It is only when her little sister disappears that Ivon becomes an integral part of the unfolding mystery and it is after this point, that she immerses herself in trying to seriously solve the crimes from the 'inside' out.

The narrator in *Ciudad final* navigates a similarly ambiguous terrain to Ivon and references to her 'origins' are dispersed throughout the text. From her first dialogues with Sabina, the employee at the motel *El Fronterizo* with whom she strikes up an immediate friendship, she is marked ethnically and socially as a *gringa*. Responding to Kama's revelations about the recent demise of her relationship with a woman suffering from anorexia, Sabina states:

> I didn't like you telling me that. Why do gringos let everything out on the first day?
> Well, it's one's identity. . .
> (*Ciudad final*: 41)

Later, however, in her first encounter with the Judge, Catita Lombardi, she is accused of being a 'compatriot' in surprised and somewhat betrayed tones:

> Ah but aren't you North American? She didn't approve of my not-so-white appearance or my not so English language. – Your name deceived me, I thought you were an American blondie and instead you're one of us.
> (*Ciudad final*: 21)

Gutier's lack of direct response to this assertion cements this ambiguous notion of herself where on one occasion she refers to herself as half American (*Ciudad final*: 84), again underscoring the binational context of the murder environment in which she operates.

The sense of instability that surrounds the protagonists' origins and ethnicity is anchored in this here/there structuring trope that is further underlined by their insecure personal and professional positions in the US. The narrator at the start of *Desert Blood* states that, 'For the locals on each side of the river, the border is nothing more than a way to get home' (7). For both protagonists, however, the very notion of 'home' is problematic from the outset. We see this in their yearning for a certain kind of US dream of prosperity that resonates throughout their lives. In addition, they are presented as alienated from their supposed origins in Mexico and yet at more than first remove from attaining the goal of stability in the US. This is exemplified through their badly paid, untenured academic jobs in universities where their employers are either sceptical about their research (in the case of Saint Ignatius College's attitude towards Ivon's doctorate) or where they have been hired purely on the basis of tokenistic gestures of adherence to affirmative-action programmes (in the case of the University of Texas El Paso's hiring of Gutier):

> And that's how I came to be a Professor at the University of El Paso, for the good reason that I wasn't white and they needed to reach their quota for faculty of color.
> (*Ciudad final*: 17)

Ivon recalls her father's words, 'Dissertation, tenure, real estate – that was the order of things' (*Desert Blood*: 18), and the pressure to finish her dissertation in order to secure tenure forms a core part of the narrative. So while the protagonists are seen as frequently hankering towards the US as a topos of stability, it nevertheless remains elusive. This double-edged alienation, then, cements their positions as outsiders and locates them as subjects in constant flux, suspended somewhere between 'here' and 'there' in a space that is marked by intense movements back and forth.

The idea of subjects in flux is further explored through the sexual relationships highlighted in the novels and forged with women they meet (Kama) or re-connect with (Ivon) as the result of their attempts to untangle the mysteries of the Juárez femicides. The novels' frank exploration of lesbian desire is pronounced throughout and the importance of their sexual identity is casually introduced from the beginning, as in one of the first conversations between Sabina and Kama in *Ciudad final*:

> So you also go with women.
> Well, that's obvious. Surely you noticed that?
> Yes, and I liked it. That's why I told you about my girlfriend.
> (*Ciudad final*: 40–41)

In *Desert Blood*, Ivon mentions her marriage to Brigit in the opening pages and the references to her as *marimacha*, *manflora* and *sin vergüenza* all derogatory terms for lesbian and used by her mother, are interspersed throughout the narrative at frequent intervals. In *Ciudad final*, Kama divulges intimate details of her romantic life and engages in sex with a stranger during an unexpected meeting in the bathroom of a local bar:

> The girl continued to smile and [. . .] led me to one of the cubicles and closed the door. . . . I moved closed to her neck and hair to smell her and to forget the rest. She smelled soft and overpowering. She smiled and kissed me, as lost in the act as I was. She took off her dress. *Pure pleasure*. After a while I returned to the bar.
> (*Ciudad final*: 52–53, my emphasis)

Similarly, Ivon, in a state of extreme anxiety over Irene's disappearance, finally gives in to her desire for Raquel Montenegro, the first love from whom she has never recovered:

> She stroked the back of Ivon's neck. Ivon closed her eyes, absorbing the cool softness of Raquel's hand, the light scratch of her nails, the perfumed scent of her wrist. She turned her face toward Raquel's and kissed her, gently at first, then roughly, pulling her close, gnawing at her mouth with a hunger she didn't even realize she felt. Raquel did not resist.
> (*Desert Blood*: 264)

As is seen in this passage, Ivon's long-buried love for Raquel is re-ignited and it is later revealed that Raquel is having an affair with Ximena, Ivon's cousin and chief confidante. In *Ciudad final*, all the primary characters are lesbian: Kama,

Sabina (who becomes her closest friend throughout the investigations), as well as her cousin Bea. It would seem, therefore, that the integration of lesbian desire and sexual activity into the fabric of both plots draws attention to sexuality as a normative part of human experience and brings it into the mainstream in ways that are still very uncommon in conventional detective fiction, which from its inception was overwhelmingly dominated by central male detective figures frequently characterized as aggressive and domineering.

This notion of in-betweenness then – accentuated by both protagonists' links to the border and their sexuality – is centrally connected to the characters' mobility and their seamless movements between the US (Los Angeles and El Paso) and Mexico. Furthermore, as frequent border crossers, the protagonists are posited as nomadic subjects, so eloquently theorized by Rosa Braidotti and Caren Kaplan, who signal the nomadic subject as one of hybridity, mobility and flux (Braidotti 1994; Kaplan 1996: 92). Both texts are characterized by constant border crossing between El Paso and Juárez as the subjects go back and forth to collect evidence and talk to students (Kama) or to connect with family and conduct further investigations (Ivon). Indeed, movement and travel become key to the actual process of detection of the crimes. In *Ciudad final*, Kama decides to hide out on the *maquila* bus to travel the same route with El Chófer, the suspected killer, a risky strategy that finally pays dividends and sees him being apprehended. Similarly, it is while trying to cross the border in her sister's car that Ivon is detained by the corrupt border guard, Wilcox. This in turn, leads to her discovery of the snuff film network that is sadistically torturing and murdering girls in acts that are filmed and streamed live. In this way, the ritualistic crossings over and back form part of the rhythms of detection, as though the movement itself might contribute to the uncovering of the crimes. Furthermore, these mysteries remain inaccessible to other characters, including the El Paso-based investigating officer, Pete McCuts, in *Desert Blood*, and Escobar, the Juárez-based lawyer in *Ciudad final*, both subjects who remain static on either side of the border, unable to effect change.

This construction of female subjectivity in flux would seem to invite a reading of the characters as fluid, hybrid, quintessential borderlands subjects, as invoked by Gloria Anzaldúa's still-pivotal work, *Borderlands/La Frontera: The New Mestiza* (1987). Indeed *Desert Blood* seems to suggest this critical interpretation explicitly as Ivon – musing on her dissertation in the latter stages of the book – says, 'she was thinking about Anzaldúa's theories on border identity' (*Desert Blood*: 321).[24] Furthermore, Anzaldúa's famous definition of the border (where 'the Third World grates against the first and bleeds'; 1987: 335) features in the penultimate chapter of the book, which includes Ivon's reflections on the wider theoretical parameters framing the context of the murders in Juárez. *Ciudad final*, while not as obvious in its invocation of border theory around subjectivity, nevertheless weaves a sustained commentary about border life into the narrative thread through the frequent interventions of Sabina:

> It's fucked up Kama, the gringos come to take what they can and later they think that everything bad has come from here. Where does AIDS come from? The border. Disease, pollution, evil, poverty? From the border...
>
> (*Ciudad final*: 84)

According to Anzaldúa, the *mestiza* subject occupies multiple migratory speaking positions and certainly Kama and Ivon's freedom of movement enables them to enunciate from multiple positions, in both cases, allowing them to 'solve' the murder cases but also propelling them on emancipatory journeys of sexual self-discovery. Furthermore, Anzaldúa insists that the *mestiza* figure, 'not only sustains contradictions, she turns the ambivalence into something else' (1987: 79). This vital component of Anzaldúa's philosophy reads the *mestiza*'s fluid relationship with the spaces she inhabits as a creative act, one in this case which results in 'resolution' (of the crime) and also 'rupture' (with current ways of configuring the murders in cultural and political terms). It is to this notion of rupture that I will turn next to tease out the differing ways in which the murders have been focalized and represented.

In Chapter 1, we saw the various discourses that surrounded the narrativizing of the crimes, including what Fregoso denominates the 'moralizing discourse' or victim-blaming which posits the women as *maqui-locas* or 'sluts', in which the victims are held responsible for their own demise (2000: 138). In opposition to this, was a seam of analytical scholarship that held that globalization in which all the problems of Juárez, including the savage murders of the girls from the *maquilas*, are based on the impact of late capitalism.[25] As noted then, the first discourse has seen myriad pronouncements by the authorities as well as questionable promotional campaigns which detect moral differences between women who are safely ensconced at home (where they should be) and women (the 'working girls') who are out roaming the streets at night, by definition transgressing patriarchal norms and therefore punishable by society. On the opposite end of the spectrum, scholars have identified the aggressive model of globalization in operation in this part of the world and the misogynistic culture it nurtures as a major element in designating women as corporate garbage – disposable (in labour terms at any rate) and easily replaceable (Hu-Dehart 2007). Small wonder, then, that in viewing these women as the primary victims of a crime spree that sees the disposability of women's bodies on the global assembly line and the mutilation of women's bodies as part of the same singular process, the need to memorialize and commemorate is aligned with the desperate desire to foreground ideas around innocence and childhood. While the ideas around globalization as the foundational origin for gender violence have been critiqued, it is very much an over-arching structural framework for both novels. The detectives make repeated reference to the role of globalization and the social impact of the *maquilas* on gender roles in Juárez. In *Ciudad final*, Sabina is introduced as a former *maquila* worker and *Desert Blood* features the story of (among others), Elsa, the victim of scientific testing of contraceptives as part of routine pregnancy testing in the plants. Voices from the other end of the spectrum invested in victim-blaming include the Judge (*Ciudad final*) and Wilcox (*Desert Blood*), who articulate the widely accepted societal views about the women as 'bad girls'. In both of these polarized sets of imaging of the victims, neither is attributed agency and both are somehow frozen in a grotesque pastiche.

The characterization of Ivon and Kama as migrating, desiring, questioning subjects, therefore, undermines those static freeze-frames of the feminicide victims and unsettles the very dynamics surrounding how the murders are narrativized. The textual constructions of Kama and Ivon that foreground female sexuality, and indeed sexual pleasure, as central to feminine identity interrogate these very divergent viewpoints that continue to define the conceptualization and memorialization of the victims. One of the most evocative passages from Anzaldúa's work concerns the ways in which the *mestiza* subject can be a force for healing. In this sense, she becomes a vital source of restorative energy:

> *Soy un amasamiento*, I am an act of kneading, of uniting, and joining that not only has produced both a creature of darkness and a creature of light, but also a creature that questions the definitions of light and dark and gives them new meanings.
>
> (1987: 182)

By uniting information and intervening in the investigations, both Ivon and Kama participate as creatures that interrogate the definitions of light and dark in Juárez and help to move the focalization of the murders (and the murder victims) away from these polarized sets of extremes. When the image of the *maqui-loca* is thrust onto Ivon's radar in the form of a Barbie doll for sale by a young boy in a *colonia* (Desert Blood: 43), the reader is forced to contemplate the media-generated image of the 'bad' factory girls, drunk on their new-found disposable income. In a similar fashion, the powerful commemorations of the victims through images erected on crosses throughout Juárez and of which there are numerous examples in both novels, seek to remind the community of the children that have been so brutally erased. It is in this context, then, that the images of the border-crossing women who drink to excess, have sex with women and constantly get into trouble, challenge those fossilized perceptions and remind readers that identity is a complex, multi-faceted process.

This vision of the empowered, knowing, borderlands subject, therefore, serves to underscore notions of difference and indeed, the subjects' movement *per se* is conceptualized as a privilege or condition of the protagonists' in-betweenness and also their US citizenship. The books are careful to map the connections between movement and questions of class and ethnicity, staging the radically different consequences of border-crossing for different subjects. Indeed, the freedom to border-cross enjoyed by the principal protagonists in both novels stands in marked contrast to the experiences of the non-US citizens. The most obvious example of this is played out in *Ciudad final* in the scene where Sabina and Kama – both drunk after a night socializing – are apprehended at the border. While Kama is subject to arrest, as a US citizen the consequences are of little import and indeed are not mentioned again. Sabina, on the other hand, is denied indefinitely, the chance of attaining the papers needed to cross over to the other side. The novels are punctuated by continuous references to the freedom of movement enjoyed by the Chicana characters vis-à-vis the serious curtailment of movement of the Mexican characters. The Mexican characters in both texts appear as either murder victims (and therefore immobilized for ever); paralyzed by fear in their *colonias* (Marta and her mother after the attack in *Ciudad final*); dying from the ill-effects of *maquila* life (Elsa, who has contracted cancer in *Desert Blood*); or fleeing inland from fear (Rubí Reyna, the media reporter, in *Desert Blood*). The pleasures of 'interstitial subjectivity' (Kaplan 1996: 89) enjoyed by Ivon and Kama, therefore, are by no means available to all and here the glaring differences serve to illustrate the ethnic and class dimensions that are so fundamental in understanding the murders. This dimension is marked in the texts and references to race and ethnicity abound in both novels. Ivon ponders at length and throughout the novel about the significance of the disappearing brown bodies, 'What to do with all these fertile brown female bodies on the border?' (*Desert Blood*: 332) and Kama's musings about the dolls left in her motel room, 'I had never seen such white flesh around here' (*Ciudad final*: 11) point to the ways in which the nation state serves as the limits to this mobility in obvious and very brutal ways. It is on the complex interweaving of fact and fiction that the following section will centre, examining the effectiveness of the generic conventions of detective fiction to focalize these particular explorations of 'real' gender violence being perpetrated in Northern Mexico.

Narrative frames – *welcome to the real world of the border, baby girl*

It goes without saying that the use of a detective fiction structure places a frame on the narratives that is frustratingly and tragically absent from the real murder stories. On one level, the novels function as relatively conventional detective tales, employing a classic 'whodunit' narrative mode which features a resolution – albeit partial – in the closing pages. In *Desert Blood*, the resolution comes from the discovery of the snuff movie network (www.extremelylucky.com) led by Jeremy Wilcox, a corrupt border guard in collaboration with the so-called narco juniors or the obscenely spoilt rich offspring of drug lords. A series of clues are placed early in the narrative from the moment in Chapter 2 when the border guard is presented as Ivon's airplane companion through a long chain of other evidence that finally leads Ivon to the grim discovery in the ASARCO smelter plant. Reader satisfaction is gleaned from Ivon's ability to 'crack' the clues placed during this early conversation, including the roll of pennies produced by Wilcox during their conversation and which haunts her throughout the text. In a similar fashion, *Ciudad final* tracks a series of clues that finally leads Kama to reveal the complicity of Juárez's most powerful narco families in the murders of the *maquila* girls. It leads specifically to the exposure of the Judge's close family, whose recently constructed mansion, we later learn, is the graveyard of countless young victims who have been chosen from an online 'beauty' catalogue.

Notwithstanding this conventional approach to 'cracking' the crimes, the novels utilize this narrative framework as a way of asking bigger questions about the structures that uphold the abuses of power committed in Juárez. In this way, the protagonists don't function as 'normal' detectives in the sense that they try and apprehend the guilty and indeed when that happens it feels somewhat artificial given that the readers of both novels are aware, through the disclaimers and the extra-textual information provided, of the 'real' story with its history of impunity and incompetence. Instead the novels' force comes from the questions they pose in relation to the networks of power that conspire to conceal and that the texts attempt to overcome. In *Desert Blood*, Ivon devotes considerable time to trying to understand the wider configurations of knowledge that support the culture of impunity surrounding the crimes:

> This wasn't a case of 'whodunit', but rather of who was allowing these crimes to happen? Whose interests were being served? Who was covering it up? Who was profiting from the deaths of all these women?
> (*Desert Blood*: 333)

Similarly, *Ciudad final* uses the detective template as a way to critique the very fabric of border life that enables the crimes to occur: 'Unfortunately, the social decomposition of the border was to blame' (*Ciudad final*: 98). Furthermore, both texts employ the diverse range of voices that make up the detective community as a way of explaining and critiquing the social environment that perpetuates the crimes.

Gutier and Gaspar de Alba are by no means the first, of course, to use detective fiction as a means by which to critique 'real' societal and state corruption. The search for justice implicit in the very act of detection means that issues pertaining to social justice and the moral order *per se* are frequently embedded within detective narratives. Indeed, writers have traditionally used crime fiction – particularly that sub-genre referred to as hard-boiled or *novela negra* – as a vehicle for socio-political critique and politicized detective and crime fiction are commonplace in both the Anglophone and Hispanophone detective crime traditions. The political dimension of much Chicano crime narrative has already been noted and in the Mexican context, Paco Ignacio Taibo's *Belascoarán Shayne* series (1976–1993) perfectly exemplifies the potential of detective fiction to destabilize perceived notions about law, order and the state. Kama Gutier notes the attractiveness of the *novela negra* form for the examination of such real-life crimes in an interview:

> It has been difficult to conceptualize as a book, in the sense of adapting a theme that is so disturbing, so real, as well as being critical in such a way that would be attractive from a literary point of view. I think that's what noir fiction is all about. For me, this genre should raise those buried social issues and shine a light on what is really behind them. For her, this genre should raise those buried social issues and shine light on what is really behind them.
> (cited in Finnegan 2014: 102)

In this way, both authors employ the conventions of detective fiction as a way of framing the 'real' stories behind the crimes and their perpetrators. When Ximena says, 'Welcome to the real world of the border, baby girl' (*Desert Blood*: 16), she invites Ivon – and by extension, the reader – not only to enter the 'real' world of the crimes but also to confront the metafictional nature of the text with its complex interweaving of facts with the fictionalized elements. Both novels engage explicitly with established 'facts' about the murders in numerous ways with the use of a former FBI expert in profiling (mentioned in both novels)[26] and the inclusion of an Egyptian male character deemed responsible for some of the crimes, featuring in distinct sub-plots in both novels. The metafictional process is exploited to great effect in *Ciudad final*, whereby the 'fictional' plot – who is killing the girls of Juárez – is explained using one of the frequently cited 'real' theories. This involves Marcela Lagarde y de los Ríos's contention that the girls' photographs form part of an online catalogue created by the *maquilas* and 'given' to juniors to use and dispose of them as they will (cited in López-Lozano 2010: 139). In this way, the fictional and factual elements are seamlessly fused in the text. Indeed in *Ciudad final*, the gaps between the fictional plot of the novel and the factual framework begin to collapse at the end where the personal network of fictional characters (Sabina et al.) is aligned with an established list of 'real' participants including family associations. It is here, for example, that the novel makes reference to 'real' reportage on the murders in the form of the ground-breaking work of journalists Sergio González Rodríguez and Diana Washington Valdez, already discussed, and thus a potent dissolution between the novelistic and 'real' community is enacted.

Similarly, *Desert Blood* – while staging a resolution of its plot – is at its most powerful in chapter 45, when Ivon poses a series of blistering questions about the murders, the perpetrators and the frameworks of corruption that result in the slaughter of innocent brown women in the desert:

> Why were the bodies of one-hundred-thirty-nine *hijas de Juárez* rotting somewhere in the desert or the morgue?
>
> (331)
>
> What's the price of "free trade"?
>
> (332)
>
> Serial Killers or judiciales?
> Gangs or Border Patrol?
> All of the above?
> A factory of Killers?
>
> (333)

It was noted in the early stage of this chapter the way in which activism forms part of the textual fabric of the texts. It emerges again at the end of *Ciudad final* in the image of the enchained protestors – Kama among them – determined to continue investigating with the promise of telling more echoing long after the protests have abated. The narrator says:

> I thought that it didn't matter if they took me out of the country, because the next day I would return to be *there* because all of us should be *there*
> (*Ciudad final*: 206, my emphasis)

In this passage, she establishes the need to be in Juárez as an ethical act, to turn away from an indifferent US and to actively take up the cause *for* Juárez, *in* Juárez. *Desert Blood* ends on a similarly resolute note, with a long section of acknowledgements that culminates in an appeal for readers to sign an online petition to end the violence against girls and women in Juárez (www.petitiononline.com/NiUnaMas). Gaspar de Alba writes:

> I hope this book inspires its readers to join the friends and families of the dead and the disappeared women of Juárez. Only in solidarity can we help bring an end to this pandemic of femicides on the border. Ni Una más!
> (*Desert Blood*: 346)

What is perhaps more interesting in these cases, then, is not that the novels are employed in time-honoured fashion to provide a thinly veiled critique of the murders and the structures of power that sustain them. Rather, it is in the interstices between fact, fiction and, crucially, the link to activism through their use of borderlands subjects, that their political charge might ultimately be located.

Postscript: breaking the silence

It seems fitting that I should turn, or rather return, in this final section of the chapter, to a text that was produced in Ciudad Juárez by writers immersed in that environment and especially so, considering it is one of the earliest written texts in circulation about the feminicidal crime wave. While not privileging Ciudad Juárez as the only place from which legitimate insights about Ciudad Juárez can be enunciated; twenty-five years of scholarship and activism later, it is important to be conscious of how Ciudad Juárez represents an intense contact zone through which discourses, theories and narratives about feminicidal violence have been tested, recycled and rehearsed endlessly. In this regard, we might note the extent to which *El silencio que la voz de todas quiebra* still generates affection and esteem among the community in Ciudad Juárez. As has been well-documented elsewhere (Báez Ayala 2006), *El silencio* may be defined as a collective shout of despair against the injustice of the crimes committed against 137 women between the years of 1993–1998 exhaustively chronicled with forensic detail by the writers involved: Rohry Benítez, Adriana Candia, Patricia Cabrera, Guadalupe de la Mora, Josefina Martínez, Isabel Velázquez and Ramona Ortiz.

Like many of the written texts about feminicide in Ciudad Juárez, highlighted earlier, *El silencio* is a hybrid mix of different narrative forms and modes, including image, text and figurative materials (maps, charts). Juxtaposing analysis of the different events that characterized the narrative arc of feminicide in the city during those years, including the theories about serial killers; the widely derided campaigns to make the city and its women safer; and the roundly dismissed involvement of outside 'experts', including Robert Ressler, from the FBI, and the Spanish criminologist, José Antonio Parra Molina. These form a thread around a series of tributes to seven of the victims – Silvia Elena Rivera Hernández, Elizabeth Castro García, Olga Alicia Carrillo Pérez, Sagrario González Flores, Argelia Irene Salazar Crispín, Adriana Torres Márquez and Eréndira Ivonne Ponce Hernández – that form the written records of extinguished life in the city. On explaining the rationale in terms of the selection of victims' voices to feature, Adriana Candía asserts that it was precisely because all seven also wrote, either in diaries or in other forms and thus the function of writing to inscribe agency and apportion life is paramount. Drawing from interviews with family members of the victims, these sections function partly as lament, partly as testimonial, and partly as denunciation. Interspersed with the testimonial section are what might be termed reflections, or *crónicas*, including the final, 'Croquis para llegar a Lomas de poleo' [Sketch to Get to Lomas de Poleo], which seeks to capture the ontological essence of a city associated with the cruel abandonment of its more vulnerable citizens. The text includes a folded map marked with the locations where the women's bodies were found and charts giving known details of the victims.

Written collaboratively, *El silencio* forms part of a long Mexican literary tradition of *talleres*, or workshops of creative writing that seek to bring communities of writers together. The importance of these *talleres* in forging communal safe spaces for creativity, particularly, if not exclusively for women writers, cannot be underestimated (Finnegan 2007: 311). Indeed, the form of the workshop and the expressed wish of the authors to write collectively of their impotence and frustration (Benítez et al. 1999: 1) demonstrates the extent to which these *talleres* contribute towards the creation of a feminist solidarity and coalition, a concept to which we will return in the closing pages. Finally, it should be noted that *El silencio* forms an inter-text with the best known theatrical response to the crimes, *Mujeres de arena* [Women of Sand] by Humberto Robles, which borrows extensively from both the narrative format and the content in its refashioning of the narrative as performance. The trajectory of the book's production, publication and afterlife is also of interest. Struggling to find a publisher for their work, it was published by Ediciones del Azar in Chihuahua and was an immediate success. Interviews with the authors followed, nationally and in the US, and the project was endorsed in a review by no less a powerful figure than Elena Poniatowska, an emblem of feminist progressive politics.[27] It formed part of wider controversy when in the same year, Victor Ronquillo published the tome, *Las muertas de Juárez* with the publishing house Planeta. Accused of stealing much of his material and reframing it within a piece of junk pseudo-journalism (Gaspar de Alba 2014: 178),[28] there remains a residual bitterness felt by the collective at this appropriation of the narrative of violence against women in Ciudad Juárez by people unconnected with that city and seemingly determined to exoticize, sexualize and commodify the stories of pain and anguish emerging from it.

The stories present in *El silencio* evoke many of the hallmarks that have been presented and represented in other cultural responses, including the sense of the uncanny that permeates discovery and reactions to the crimes as they are revealed.[29] For instance, Bertha Alicia, the sister of victim, Adriana Torres Márquez says, 'I knew from the day she disappeared that my sister was not coming back, I knew it or I had a feeling' (1999: 73). In another segment, we read that, 'Gloria had a bad feeling the same day that my sister disappeared: she dreamed that Eréndira was crying. She even felt her in the bed next to her, like she used to do, but this time she was desperate as though she wanted to tell her something' (1999: 91).[30] This rupturing of conventional epistemologies whereby answers to questions are felt in the body or revealed in dreams throws the limitations of any detectivesque approach, with its investment in rationality and order, into sharp relief. Here, the feelings and sentiments held by the bodies and unconscious of the families are as accurate, and in most cases, more accurate, than any police-reporting or attempts at crime-solving. We can appreciate too the way in which texts like *El silencio*, which privilege other forms of knowing and seeing, force us to look at and read the crimes in different ways.

In addition, we find again echoes of the post and non-human elements that play such a critical role in the unfolding narratives around the disappearances and deaths of women in the city. For example, in reference to Adriana Torres Márquez, we are told that she disappeared, 'As though the earth had swallowed her up' (1999: 74) gesturing to the role played by natural forces and the natural world in the extermination of the women and that was so vividly explored in the documentary films examined in Chapter 4. The desert is, of course, central to this topography of horror and the connection between the evils of feminicidal violence and elemental forces that are beyond our understanding is crucial to the narrativizing of the crime and strongly present in testimonies by family members. This is unsurprising on lots of levels; it is common in trauma narratives for appeals to the natural world to supplant those more rational explanations for experiences of emotional pain. Moreover, it is only logical that the families would seek alternative explanations for their loved ones' demise, particularly in the presence of such acute institutional neglect (by the police, by the state authorities, by society more widely). We recall Bollington's helpful identification of the post-human as a critical element in narratives of violence in Mexico more widely (2018: 165–185). In this regard, the metaphysical dimension of the evil that subtends feminicidal violence is present only through instances of uncanny or through unnatural or, indeed, supernatural occurrences and entities. *El silencio* is thus part of a broader set of cultural responses – even though it precedes most of them – that seeks answers to the existential origins of feminicidal violence and its ramifications in the borderlands. In this next section, through memories rooted in the body and the senses, I trace how the text moves back in time to re-create and re-imagine the victims' early lives and motivations.

The problems posed by temporality have been central to the narrative paradigms of feminicide, a narrative that is, as we have noted, frequently marked by its investment in linearity and its dependence on an ending that is brutal, chaotic and final. It is this, of course, that has led to a proliferation of detectivesque formats both in writing and in film and of which the earlier texts studied in this chapter are effective examples. If the foundational impulse in mystery novels is the discovery of a body, then it follows that their plots conventionally move backwards in time to tease through the events leading up to the body's discovery in an inverted temporality that is the hallmark of the detective genre in its multiple cross-cultural manifestations. *El silencio* attempts to provide a middle section to this storyline involving a detailed, meticulous and sensitive contextualization of Ciudad Juárez in the 1990s, in order to provide a base level of understanding from which the crimes might be comprehended. Indeed, this 'middle' is embedded within a finely tuned and frequently biting critique of the failures and limitations of the various attempts by civil and state authorities to actually address the feminicidal crime wave. And then there is the question of the beginning. Here we can see how *El silencio* attends, often in very sensitive ways, to the backstories of the women selected as case studies. It is at pains to provide the readers with a portrait of the female victims; their past, often their childhood, sometimes idealized in the rural settings from which many of the women victims featured had originally come. It does not, however, fall into the trap of sanitizing the victims or their families. Indeed, it is surprisingly frank about the conflicts frequently observed between the victims and their families and has no qualms about presenting the victims as sometimes happy, sometimes studious, sometimes frivolous, sometimes careless, selfish or self-obsessed. In this way, it inscribes a narrative of normative and universal adolescent identity marked by trips to the cinema or outings to concerts. Moreover, the narrative highlights the common, shared range of emotions experienced by youth on this spectrum, including joy, happiness, frustration and anger.

These emotions frequently receive sensual expression through an emphasis on the things the women liked to eat, the music they liked to listen to, or the way many of them loved to dance. For example, we learn of Sagrario's love of watermelon, 'sweet watermelon, red watermelon, juicy watermelon . . . how Sagrario loved fruit' (*El silencio*: 57) and how Olga Alicia, loved, 'a brilliant gel nail-colour, a dessert of carrots with honey, a Sunday at the matinee' (*El silencio*: 43). The shared love of music and dancing is notable in many of the segments devoted to the victims, including Silvia, who loved the pop culture icon Selena (*El silencio*: 15); Sagrario, who would spend the afternoons copying down songs so she could later sing them (*El silencio*: 53); and Argelia, whose passion for the music of the group, *Límite*, is vividly evoked: 'Of all things, she loved music, it was her passion; her favourite song was Sentimientos/Feelings, from the group, Límite; when she heard it she would start to sway, it made her crazy' (*El silencio*: 67). Argelia's sister, Claudia, talks about how she would dance to the death on Saturdays (*El silencio*: 67), a tragic turn of phrase in the circumstances. Similarly, the reader learns of how her feet would always move without her even realizing, as if they were following some kind of rhythm from deep inside her and that only she could hear (*El silencio*: 89), an account that conveys a sense of rebellious youthful energy and exuberance.

This return to the body has multiple resonances; on one level it functions to re-humanize those victims who have been so cruelly discarded. This, we have seen too, is a function of many other cultural products about feminicidal violence committed in Ciudad Juárez. To revivify or to breathe life into static, often wholly inaccurate, mediatic portraits of women serves a vital restorative function, providing a counter-narrative that corrects the record, quite literally, in the case of the written texts. It also provides a space through which families may be able to start a process of mourning, or even healing. That the question of healing is fraught with a myriad political questions about truth and forgetting in the face of unanswered questions and justice so clearly denied has been amply rehearsed and its parameters are beyond the scope of this discussion.[31] As Sara Ahmed asks, in her reflections on the emotionality of texts, 'How does pain enter politics?' (2004: 20) and this central dilemma is articulated formally by the text as the personal testimonies of loss wend their way through and insert themselves into the sections of explicit political denunciation. However, the recourse to the body – to the senses, to movement, to taste, smell and sound – returns the storytelling function to the body, but this time the story is not of desecration, rape and murder, but one of desire and love. Sagrario attests to 'love' being her most frequent emotion (*El silencio*: 57) and we have already noted the emphasis on dance as a particularly gratifying form of self-expression. Elsewhere, the victims' portraits speak of kindness (Silvia) or dreams and ambition (Olga Alicia). In this way, the memories of life before death, evoked through sensual experience, are what remain.

To affect and be affected[32]

As I re-read this text at the end of a long period of immersion in the tales of tragedy, poverty, pain and of suffering that constitute the stories of feminicide in Ciudad Juárez since the early 1990s, I am overwhelmed by feelings of sadness and melancholy. The melancholy is present because of a secondary temporal displacement and the knowledge – not available, of course to the writers of the text in the late 1990s – that nothing much would change; that feminicide would continue unabated; and that during the period of writing this piece the bodies of three women would be found on the same day in Ciudad Juárez (4 January 2018). Obscured from view at that time also was the knowledge that the strategies of dehumanization and the parallel narratives of impunity and corruption would continue, both accelerated and intensified in the run-up to the presidential elections in 2018 in a country fractured both politically and socially. In this regard, I turn to the idea of the archive of feeling explored by Ann Cvetcovich when she talks 'of cultural texts as repositories of feelings and emotion' (cited in Ahmed 2004: 14). If this draws us to a re-imagining of activism on the grounds of grief along similar lines to Candice Amich's illuminating reading of the Guatemalan performance artist, Regina Galindo (2017), then it may constitute a call to arms, even when that call is made from within a framework of sadness. On this level, then, you can read *El silencio* as a narrative inscription of grievability, echoing Butler (2009), through its complex layering of context, accompanied by a profound commitment to rehumanization. Moreover, it evokes a certain ethics of writing that is remarkably absent in so many of the approaches to the crimes. Taking the definition of affect derived from Baruch Spinoza as the capacity 'to affect and be affected' (Leys 2011: 442), then perhaps that is where *El silencio*'s power lies.[33] That I end in sadness, therefore, seems fitting. And yet, taking this text with the two detective novels studied in tandem, we can see too that they are also texts of hope, of energy, of movement and agency. From the dancing, the dressing up, the love-making and the eating with friends and family, they offer a vision of a differently configured life, one that we might argue operates within a vision of communality. It is on the process of coming together and the sense of communality – directly linked with polyvocality and agency – that I would like to conclude my analysis.

Conclusions: community, polyvocality, agency

Central to Anzaldúa's imagining of the borderlands is the notion of polyvocality articulated in a space of plurality and ambiguity in which multiple speaking voices can perforate established modes of categorization. Anzaldúa's insistence on polyvocality as a cornerstone of borderlands subjectivity receives explicit treatment in the three texts studied in this chapter, both through the construction of the protagonists in the case of the detective novels and with *El silencio*, through its formal constitution as a text of many voices. In this sense, the texts, through their ability to narrate from and through different speaking positions, embody the very essence of *mestizaje* theorized at length by Gloria Anzaldúa and explored earlier. The texts also suggest, however, that they form part of a confluence of voices, a community of knowledge, that functions as a circuit of knowledge transfer. Indeed, all three examples posit the notion of community as absolutely critical to the detection and revelation of the crimes through the establishment of a panorama of characters and writers/investigators who serve to assist, explain, translate and help the 'outsiders' to piece together the complex puzzle of the murders under investigation. In this way, it would seem to point to the marked importance of *comunidad* as a way of confronting and understanding the unfolding realities. Furthermore, this emphasis on the coming together of multiple voices shows how the texts studied serve to deconstruct the existing understanding of the murders through an unsettling of the dominant frames used to frame the crimes and their victims. Cristina Rivera Garza's work is critical here in helping us to understand the complex dynamics of community construction and the way in which it enables writing to be part of a generative, healing aesthetic practice.

In the case of *Ciudad final*, the articulation of the community view involves an emphasis on multiple peripheral characters including, most importantly, Sabina, the local cipher of knowledge, and the Judge, Catita Lombardi, who, while frequently hostile, provides vital clues into the authorities' attitudes towards the perpetrators of the crimes and their victims. There are also Kama's students from El Paso, who intervene in specific ways to assist the investigation; her cousin, Bea; the mother of the victim, Ana Amalia; the survivor, Marta, whom she interviews; the lawyer, Escóbar (who is gunned down in the latter stages) and her uncle Segundo. Forming a diverse *vox populi*, it is through her interaction with these characters that Kama ultimately makes sense of the framework of mystery surrounding the feminicides. Similarly, in *Desert Blood*, Ivon utilizes a wide network of cross-border knowledge bases, including her cousin Ximena; the policeman, Pete McCuts; the priest, Father Francis; as well as her former lover, Raquel Montenegro. Indeed, the puzzle is finally solved for Ivon following the painstaking collation of data from this broad range of sources. Many of the voices function to explain and 'translate' the murders for their disbelieving detectives: 'They're called *muchachas del sur* because so many of them come from small towns and villages in the south. Their families never even find out they're missing. Or worse: dead' (*Desert Blood*: 24). In the same way, Sabina informs Kama about the circulating theories on the feminicides as well as sharing her own personal views at length and in detail: 'Sure everybody knows, it's the juniors. Little rich kids that have money and can do what they like' (*Ciudad final*: 14).

This emphasis on community view is located within a rich tradition of Chicano detective fiction in which a *Raza* or ethno-political perspective frequently pervades. Departing from classical models of hard-boiled detectives who represent 'solitary, existential perspectives', according to Francisco Lomelí, Teresa Márquez and María Herrera-Sobek, *Raza* detectives represent 'a community view' (2000: 301). According to their formulation, many Chicano detectives have a collective viewpoint and Chicano detective novels generally are inflected by a political commitment and awareness of social injustice. They go so far as to suggest that 'the Raza detective promises to become a vigorous agent for social and cultural change' (2000: 302). The idea of community-based resistance finds its strongest echo in the final lines of *Ciudad final* when the community comes together to mourn but also to protest. It is perhaps at this moment that the potential for the *Raza* detective to become an agent of cultural change, as imagined by Lomelí, Márquez and Herrera-Sobek is most clearly realized:

> We spent the night entwined with each other, facing these enormous mountains. My students, many mothers, people from the community, the associations, the *maquilas*, accompanied us in the vigil.
>
> (*Ciudad final*: 205)

Here, the singular voice of Kama becomes sutured into a united voice of community and the realization that it is only through this mode of resistance that any justice can be envisaged. *Desert Blood* ends on a similarly optimistic note as Ivon's family unite to support Ivon's sister, Irene, to come to terms with the devastating impact of her rape and enforced imprisonment. The words, '*qué familia*' (341) [what a family] bear testimony to the ideological import of the trope of 'family' and reveal a process of healing, which, while not quite complete, points to a quiet note of redemption and hope. This powerful image of a committed force against impunity resonates insistently at the end of the novel, where the fictional and the metafictional narrative modes begin to converge.

Community is a similarly charged notion in *El silencio que la voz de todas quiebra*. In its most obvious form, it manifests itself through the collaborative act of writing undertaken by the authors from whose work in the *talleres* the text is derived. Beyond this act of formal collaboration, however, we can see how the testimonial sections illuminate the centrality of community and family to the preservation of counter-narratives about the victims but also to the process of justice-seeking and mourning. Many of the victims speak of their need for togetherness and closeness with their family members and friends. Of Silvia, her mother says, 'she didn't want to stay on her own' (*El silencio*: 15) and Olga Alicia's mother talks of how a long hug before going to sleep or a kiss in the morning were some of her favourite things (*El silencio*: 43). Elisabeth would escape to visit friends after school and Sagrario speaks of her desire to have many friends (*El silencio*: 57). Later she says that her favourite things of all are to sing, to talk with friends, to have fun, to share, to be with her family and dedicate her time to them (*El silencio*: 57). Furthermore, the stories of the victims as part of wider relations with family and community reverse the tropes of isolation and aloneness that permeate the tales of abduction, rape and murder. While there was sustained speculation in the years leading up to the publication of *El silencio* about girls being chosen from catalogues to be brutalized at parties or to be sacrificed as part of gruesome satanic rituals, the vast majority of feminicidal deaths are of single bodies, found alone. In this way, the loneliness of the violent experiences by the death visited upon their bodies is in sharp contrast to the visions evoked in *El silencio* that show them dancing, eating and arguing with family members and friends (70). From this we can see that what lives on is the relational – the connectedness to mothers, extended families and the wider community.

The desire for communion with others here resonates directly with Cristina Rivera Garza's reflections on *comunalidad*. Indeed, we can read the visions of community articulated in all three of the texts studied here through the widely cited writing of Cristina Rivera Garza[34] who contends that certain forms of writing perform a social function. These forms, she explains, are rooted in Barthes's notion of the death of the Author and foreground community approaches, that see language as a common social tool, and whereby collectivity and sharing form the basis of a new aesthetics, frequently articulated through intermedial interplay and playful exchange. We can see how this perfectly encapsulates the kind of play present in the two detective texts, whereby subject, protagonist, identity are all in continual flux. Furthermore, collectivity is embedded in the very texture and form of *El silencio* and echoes through the text in its haunting testimonial sections from disparate community voices, through its quiet reflections on cruelty, and through the detailed exposure of police failure and corruption. In this sense, the texts are rooted in what Rivera Garza calls 'the practices of communality' (2013: 270). As might be expected, this is an active reading process in which readers collaborate with writers to piece together the puzzle (in the case of the detective fiction, this is self-evident). Indeed, *El silencio* directly interpellates its reader from the opening line, 'IF YOU HAVEN'T BEEN IN THE DESERT, you don't know the meaning of the word, "nothing"' (*El silencio*: 2). No stranger to detective fiction herself, Rivera Garza's *La muerte me da* (2007), shares much with the approaches of both Kama Gutier and Gaspar de Alba through its emphasis on intertextual play. However, it is in Rivera Garza's finely developed notion of communality that the texts most closely approximate her vision of a generative aesthetics.[35] Focusing on a notion of *comunalidad* rooted in a Mesoamerican historical understanding of the term, Rivera Garza isolates the concept as a form of collective labour and at its most basic, '*un estar-con-otros*' [a being with others] (2013: 281). Thus she perceives writing in this manner as a fundamental conduit whereby 'shared vulnerability' (to invoke Butler again) can be realized. We can see the extent to which this relational connectedness is embedded both within the narratives and beyond in the activist metanarrative frameworks that sustain them. In this way, the texts inscribe Rivera Garza's sense of being together, a sense of being there for the other and constituted by the other (2013: 274–275). It is from this site, then, that micropolitical resistance might commence.

Much of the written work produced in response to the feminicidal violence in Juárez would seem to be an attempt to uncover the cultural logic that shapes the gendered intersections of economics, culture and politics and which has resulted in the systematic killing of women there since the early 1990s. The elliptical ending of *Ciudad final* – evidence of Anzaludúa's polyvocality – suggests that a *Borderlands* approach rooted in Rivera Garza's idea of *comunalidad* might pave the way for an activist response to injustice and impunity. In this sense, all three texts seek to tell a coherent fictional story about the murders, one that is not possible in 'real' life, where the murders are mired in chaotic, fragmented disputes about globalization and the role of women located on a borderline writ large as a space of violent death. While these fictional narratives do not, of course, 'solve' any of these disputes, they do offer another way of 'looking' that goes beyond the static frameworks that currently circumscribe the debate – and more importantly the victims – in an endless cycle of impunity and despair. Following this, we might interpret the constellation of multilayered voices in all of the texts studied as evoking a communal sense of being *with* others, of being *among* others and being there *for* others. This, then, is the starting point.

Notes

1 Translations from the primary texts (Benítez et al.; Gutier) in this chapter are my own. Page references are to the original Spanish and appear following the translations in parenthesis.
2 In 2012, fourteen years after the crime was committed, José Luis Franco Almaraz was arrested for the murder of Eréndira Ivonne Ponce Hernández. He was subsequently released without charge and the case remains unsolved.
3 For the purposes of this chapter, I do not include theatre as part of the "written" responses to feminicide even when many of them clearly also constitute written texts. However, this is because they are the subject of analysis in Chapter 2 which contains an overview of many of the most important interventions in theatre and performance. See Appendix.
4 There is a wide range of what might be termed pulp fiction involving generic, standard plotting, poorly developed characterization, little contextualization or historical knowledge. These texts contribute little to any serious exploration of gender violence

in this part of the world. See Kunz (2008, 2016). Authors that might be cited in these terms include Pendleton (2012); Villiers (2011); Pitarch Clark (2007) and Hawken (2011).

5 Malpica's book, *Hasta el viento puede cambiar de piel*, is dedicated to the hundreds of disappeared in the northern region of Mexico and represents a sensitive exploration of the painful and complex dynamics of disappearance.

6 Kunz lists a number of these titles including *Finis Terrae* by Danis Arona (2007); *Las vírgenes del desierto* by José Vicente Pascual (2009); *Las muchachas de la lluvia* by Edna Iturralde (2013); *Llorona on the Rocks* by Charlotte Bousquet (2010); *Balada de perros muertos* by Gregorio León (2009) among others. In addition, he draws our attention to a novel in Polish, *Ciotka matych dziewczynek* by Izabela Szolc (2007). Unable to read this novel, I note that its cover features a photograph of a dark-skinned Mexican woman in a pink vest, a clear alignment with some of the visual paradigms that characterize the narrativization of *feminicidio* in Ciudad Juárez.

7 Mexico remains one of the most dangerous places in the world to be a journalist and is located on a list of countries regarded as 'not free' by the organization Freedom House which collates data in relation to a number of categories worldwide. Andrea Noble (2015: 402) makes reference to this in her discussion of the representation of death and atrocity in the press and other media. See www.freedomhouse.org/report/freedom-world/2017/mexico [Accessed 9 February 2018].

8 Other writing by Sergio González Rodríguez on the violence of the contemporary moment include *El hombre sin cabeza* [The man without a head] (2009), *Campo de Guerra* [Battlefield] (2014) and *Los 43 de Iguala* [The Iguala 43] (2015).

9 Tobias Jochum provides a balanced and insightful discussion of Bowden's work (2015).

10 This intermedial project was published as a graphic novel in collaboration with the Argentine artist Liniers in 2017.

11 Swanson Goldberg and Schultheis Moore (2011) offer a good analysis of the pitfalls of such transnational approaches.

12 See, for example, *Jirones y arena* (2010), an anthology of poetry and painting, produced by the Instituto Nacional de las Mujeres. See also *Sangre mía: Poetry of Border, Violence, Gender and Identity in Ciudad Juárez* (Rathbun and Rojas Joo 2013) and by the same authors, *Canto a una ciudad en el desierto: Encuentro de Poetas en Ciudad Juárez* (2004). See also Carmen Amato (2004), *Encuentro Internacional de Poetas en Ciudad Juárez: Poesía y derechos humanos*. There have been numerous international interventions in the area of poetry including the web-based collective in Spain, Escritores por Ciudad Juárez and the publications of their work which can be found online. For further information, see http://escritoresporciudadjuarez.blogspot.ie/ [Accessed 9 February 2018].

13 See Rojas Joo (2016) for an overview of the work of these poets.

14 Many of Conde's performances are available online. See, for example the recording for Monociclo, Revista Literaria: www.youtube.com/watch?v=8LFvtQaY5_c. I was privileged to hear her perform her celebrated piece, *Those were the Days* (ensayo autobiográfico) at the Centro de Investigaciones y Estudios Superiores en Antropología Social (CIESAS), 25 November 2016, Tlalpan, Mexico City.

15 Originally published in 2002 in French, titled *La frontière: Thriller*.

16 Other titles include Malú Huacuja del Toro's *La lágrima, la gota y el artificie* (2006). For a discussion of these and other texts, see López-Lozano (2010).

17 See, for example, Mata (2010); López-Lozano (2010); Zavala (2016); Avila (2012).

18 This section of the analysis on *Desert Blood* and *Ciudad final* is largely derived from a chapter I wrote titled 'Moving Subjects: The Politics of Death in Narratives of the Juárez Murders' (2014). I am grateful to Routledge for their permission to reproduce this work.

19 The book was published in Italian by La Nuovo Frontiera press titled, *il deserto delle morti silenziose: Femincidi di Juárez* and has also been published in French, *Le sang du desert*, translated by Santiago Artozqui. (www.desertblood.net/) [Accessed 9 February 2018].

20 'The Maquiladora Murders, Or, Who is Killing the Women of Juárez?' was organized by the Chicano Studies Research Center at UCLA in co-sponsorship with Amnesty International. For more information, see www.chicano.ucla.edu/research/maquiladora-murders-project [Accessed 10 February 2018].
21 *Desert Blood* (345). Gaspar de Alba also informs in her blog on the book tour that she donated 50% of all honoraria to the same organization. See www.desertblood.net/8.html [Accessed 15 February 2018]. The conference featured multiple fund-raising opportunities including a silent auction of artwork and a donations section on the website.
22 These linkages are in some ways very explicit as in Ivon's discovery of the murders in the opening pages through an article in *Ms.* magazine written by a male author (not named) titled 'The Maquiladora Murders' (*Desert Blood* 3). In the introduction to the edited collection of essays, *Making a Killing*, Gaspar de Alba writes that she first came across the murders (like Ivon) through reading Sam Quiñones's article, "The Maquiladora Murders" in *Ms.* magazine in 1998. These and other obvious details make it difficult to read against the grain of the 'reality' or 'facts' and in any event, contribute to the enjoyment of the work. In the disclaimer to *Desert Blood*, Gaspar de Alba states that some of the suspects and public figures that appear in this book are taken from periodical and television reports. (Gaspar de Alba 2005: v–vi).
23 Helena María Viramontes, in her review of the book, crystallises this link explicitly: 'Let me say something loud and clear: *Desert Blood: The Juárez Murders* deserves the widest readership possible. In fact, copies of the novel should be delivered to the El Paso Police Department, La Migra, and the FBI with a post-it saying: "mandatory reading"' (Gaspar de Alba 2010).
24 Melissa Wright also explores the connections between Anzaldúa's conceptualization of the *mestiza* and the female subjectivities that are produced by the *maquila* industries (1998).
25 See Miguel López-Lozano's excellent discussion of Juárez detective fiction (2010: 128–153) in which he makes reference to Fregoso's analysis (134). Fregoso has returned to the subject in subsequent publications (2003, 2006). See also Irene Mata (2010: 15–40).
26 Rob Ressler of the FBI was drafted to Juárez to evaluate the investigative processes and his official report generally exonerated the investigation amid a storm of protest. (Washington Valdez 2006). This character appears as Bob Russell in *Desert Blood* and in other fictional explorations of the phenomenon, most notably, as Albert Kessler in Roberto Bolaño's 2666.
27 For further information on Poniatowska's involvement see: www.jornada.unam.mx/2001/10/01/aborto_poni/poni_juarez2.htm [Accessed 14 February 2018].
28 For further information on this controversy, see Palacios Goya (1999).
29 In Chapter 4, we saw how these episodes of the 'uncanny' make up a series of traumatic instants throughout the documentary film, *Señorita Extraviada*.
30 Other examples include, 'Irma felt a strange sensation. Something heavy like a stone in her chest that came over her all of a sudden' (1999: 40).
31 See, for example, Candice Amich's revealing discussion of performance, affect and feminism in the work of Regina Galindo which also focuses on sexual violence and the Truth Commission in Guatemala (2017: 91–104).
32 I am drawing here on Baruch Spinoza's concept of affectus. See Eric Shouse (2005).
33 The literature on affect and the so-called 'affective turn' is wide-ranging. Ruth Leys offers a helpful overview and critique (2011). See also Ticineto Clough and Halley (2007).
34 These texts include the essays, *Los muertos indóciles: necroescrituras y desapropiación* (2013), the detective novel, *La muerte me da* (2007) and *Dolerse: textos desde un país herido* (2015), another example of the kind of hybrid text discussed in this chapter, combining testimony, personal reflection and essay.
35 For an excellent discussion of the implications of Rivera Garza's theory of aesthetics in the face of the current violence, see Bollington (2018: 75–87).

Works cited

Adam, Peggy, 2006. *Luchadoras*. Geneva: Atrabile.
Agosín, Marjorie, 2006. *Secrets in the Sand: The Young Women of Juárez*. Buffalo: White Pine Press.
Ahmed, Sara, 2004. *The Cultural Politics of Emotion*. New York: Routledge.
Amato, Carmen, ed., 2004. *Memoria del VII Encuentro Internacional de Poetas en Ciudad Juárez: Poesía y derechos humanos*. Ciudad Delicias: Chihuahua Arde Editoras.
Amich, Candice, 2017. The Limits of Witness: Regina José Galindo and Neoliberalism's Gendered Economies of Violence. In Elin Diamond, Denise Varney and Candice Amich, eds., *Performance, Feminism and Affect in Neoliberal Times*. New York: Springer, 91–104.
Anzaldúa, Gloria, 1987. *Borderlands/La Frontera: The New Mestiza*. San Francisco: Aunt Lute Books.
Arce, Evangelina, 2011. *Para mi hija, Silvia/For my daughter, Silvia*. London: Blank Slate Books.
Arona, Danila, 2007. *Finis terrae*. Milan: Mondadori.
Avila, Edward A., 2012. *Conditions of (Im)possibility: Necropolitics, Neoliberalism and the Cultural Politics of Death in Contemporary Chicano/a Film and Literature*. Thesis (Ph.D). University of San Diego. [online]. Available at: https://cloudfront.escholarship.org/dist/prd/content/qt7sh1f55b/qt7sh1f55b.pdf?t=ml5m0g [Accessed 15 February 2018].
Báez Ayala, Susana, 2006. De la impotencia a la creación testimonial y la denuncia social: *El silencio que la voz de todas quiebra*. In Domínguez-Ruvalcaba, Héctor and Ravelo Blancas, Patricia, eds., *Entre las duras aristas de las armas: Violencia y victimización en Ciudad Juárez*. Mexico: Casa Chata (Centro de Investigaciones y Estudios Superiores en Antropología Social (CIESAS), 185–219.
Bard, Patrick, 2002. *La frontiere: Thriller*. Paris: Seuil.
———, 2004. *La frontera*. Barcelona: Grijalbo.
Baudoin-Troubs, Edmond, 2011. *Viva la vida: Los sueños de Ciudad Juárez*. Bilbao: Astiberri Ediciones.
Bellatin, Mario, and Liniers, 2017. *Bola Negra*. Mexico: Sexto Pisto.
Benítez, Rohry, et al., 1999. *El silencio que la voz de todas quiebra*. Chihuahua: Ediciones del Azar.
Bola Negra: El musical de Ciudad Juárez, 2012. [Film]. Directed by Mario Bellatin and Marcela Rodríguez. Mexico: Instituto Nacional de Bellas Artes; En Chinga Films.
Bolaño, Roberto, 2004. *2666*. Barcelona: Anagrama.
———, 2011. *Between Parentheses: Essays, Articles, and Speeches, 1998–2003*. Trans. by Natasha Wimmer. New York: New Directions.
Bollington, Lucy, 2018. *Reframing Excess: Death and Power in Contemorary Mexican Literary and Visual Culture*. Thesis (Ph.D). University of Cambridge.
Bousquet, Charlotte, 2010. *Llorona on the Rocks*. Argemmios: Saussay la Campagne.
Braidotti, Rosa, 1994. *Nomadic Subjects: Embodiment and Sexual Difference in Contemporary Feminist Theory*. New York: Columbia University Press.
Butler, Judith, 2009. *Frames of War: When Is Life Grievable?* London: Verso.
Diez, Rolo, 2005. *Hurensohne [Matamujeres]*. Trans. by Horst Rosenberger. Heilbronn: Distel Literaturverlag.
Duque, Rocío, 2013. *El negocio de matar. Cuadernos feministas*. Available at: http://rociosart.blogspot.ie/p/el-negocio-de-matar-capitulo-1.html [Accessed 10 February 2018].
Escritores por Ciudad Juárez, 2017. [online]. Available at: http://escritoresporciudadjuarez.blogspot.ie/ [Accessed 9 February 2018].

Finnegan, Nuala, 2007. *Ambivalence, Modernity, Power: Women and Writing in Mexico Since 1980.* Oxford: Peter Lang.

———, 2014. Moving Subjects: The Politics of Death in Narratives of the Juárez Murders. In Catherine Leen and Niamh Thornton, eds., *International Perspectives on Chicano/a Studies: "This World is my Place".* New York: Routledge, 88–108.

Freedom in the World: Mexico Profile, 2017. Freedom House. [online]. Available at: www.freedomhouse.org/report/freedom-world/2017/mexico [Accessed 9 Feb 2018].

Fregoso, Rosa Linda, 2000. Voices Without Echo: The Global Gendered Apartheid. *Emergence Journal for the Study of Media and Composite Cultures,* 10 (1), 137–155.

———, 2003. *MeXicana Encounters: The Making of Social Identities on the Borderlands.* Berkeley: University of California Press.

———, 2006. We Want Them Alive! The Politics and Culture of Human Rights. *Social Identities,* 12 (2), 109–138.

———, and Bejarano, Cynthia, eds., 2010. *Terrorizing Women: Feminicide in the Américas.* Durham, NC: Duke University Press.

Galán Benítez, Carmen, 2001. *Tierra Marchita.* Mexico: Fondo Editorial Tierra Adentro.

Gaspar de Alba, Alicia, 2005. *Desert Blood: The Juárez Murders.* Houston: Arte Público Press.

———, 2010. *DesertBlood.net.* [online]. Available at: www.desertblood.net/ [Accessed 9 Feb 2018].

———, 2014. *[Un]Framing the "Bad Woman": Sor Juana, Malinche, Coyolxauhqui and Other Rebels with a Cause.* Austin: University of Texas Press.

———, and Guzmán, Georgina, 2010. *Making a Killing: Femicide, Free Trade, and La Frontera.* Austin: University of Texas Press.

González Rodríguez, Sergio, 2002. *Huesos en el desierto.* Barcelona: Anagrama.

———, 2009. *El hombre sin cabeza.* Barcelona: Anagrama.

———, 2014. *Campo de Guerra.* Barcelona: Anagrama.

———, 2015. *Los 43 de Iguala.* Barcelona: Anagrama.

González, Yeana, ed., 2016. *El silencio de los cuerpos: relatos sobre feminicidio.* Mexico: Ediciones B.

Gutier, Kama, 2007. *Ciudad final.* Barcelona: Montesinos.

Hawken, Sam. 2011. *The Dead Women of Juarez.* London: Serpent's Tail.

Huacuja del Toro, Malú, 2006. *La lágrima, la gota y el artificio.* Córdoba: Editorial Ariadna.

Hu-Dehart, Evelyn, 2007. Globalization and Its Discontents: Exposing the Underside. In Antonia Castañeda, Susan H. Armitage, Patricia Hart and Karen Weathermon, eds., *Gender on the Borderlands: The Frontiers Reader.* Omaha: University of Nebraska Press, 244–260.

Instituto Nacional de las Mujeres, 2010. *Jirones y arena.* Mexico: Instituto Nacional de las Mujeres.

Iturralde, Edna, 2013. *Las muchachas de la lluvia.* Madrid: Alfaguara Juvenil.

Jochum, Tobias, 2015. "The Weight of Words, the Shock of Photos": Poetic Testimony and Elliptical Imagery in Sergio González Rodríguez' *The Femicide Machine.* FIAR – *Forum for Interamerican Research,* 8 (2) (Sep), 92–119. [online]. Available at: http://interamerica.de/volume-8-2/jochum/ [Accessed 24 January 2018].

Kaplan, Caren, 1996. *Questions of Travel: Postmodern Discourses of Displacement.* Durham, NC: Duke University Press.

King, Edward, and Page, Joanna, 2017. *Posthumanism and the Graphic Novel in Latin America.* London: UCL Press.

Kirshner, Mia, et al., 2008. *I Live Here.* New York: Pantheon Graphic Novels.

Kunz, Marco, 2008. Femicidio y ficción: los asesinatos de mujeres de Ciudad Juárez y su productividad cultural. *conNotas,* 6 (11), 117–153.

———, 2016. Las 'muertas de Ciudad Juárez': construcción e impacto cultural de un acontecimiento serial. In Marco Kunz et al., eds., *Acontecimientos históricos y su productividad cultural en el mundo hispánico*. Germany: Lit-Verlag, 137–156.
León, Gregorio, 2009. *Balada de perros muertos*. Madrid: Nowtilus.
Leys, Ruth, 2011. The Turn to Affect: A Critique. *Critical Inquiry*, 37 (Spring), 434–472.
Lomelí, Francisco, Márquez, Teresa, and Herrera-Sobek, María, 2000. Trends and Themes in Chicana/o Writings in Postmodern Times. In David R. Maciel, Isidro D. Ortiz and María Herrera Sobek, eds., *Chicano Renaissance: Contemporary Cultural Trends*. Tucson: University of Arizona Press, 285–305.
López-Lozano, Miguel, 2010. Women in the Global Machine: Patrick Bard's *La frontera*, Carmen Galán Benítez's *Tierra marchita*, and Alicia Gaspar de Alba's *Desert Blood: The Juárez Murders*. In Héctor Domínguez-Ruvalcaba and Ignacio Corona, eds., *Gender Violence at the U.S.-Mexico Border: Media Representation and Public Response*. Tucson: University of Arizon Press, 128–151.
Malpica, Javier, 2006. *Hasta el viento puede cambiar de piel*. Mexico: SM de Ediciones.
Mata, Irene, 2010. Writing on the Walls: Deciphering Violence and Industrialization in Alicia Gaspar de Alba's *Desert Blood*. *Melus*, 35 (3), 15–40.
Monociclo Revista Literaria, 2017. *Rosinda Conde – Poemas por Ciudad Juárez*. Video. [online]. Available at: www.youtube.com/watch?v=8LFvtQaY5_c [Accessed 9 Feb 2018].
Moreiras, Alberto, 2001. *The Exhaustion of Difference: The Politics of Latin American Cultural Studies*. Durham, NC: Duke University Press.
Mujeres de arena by Humberto Robles, 2002. [Play].
Noble, Andrea, 2015. History, Modernity and Atrocity in Mexican Visual Culture. *Bulletin of Spanish Studies*, 92 (3), 391–421.
Palacios Goya, Cynthia, 1999. ¿Públicó Víctor Ronquillo *Las muertas de Juárez*? *El Universal*, 30 October [online]. Available at: http://archivo.eluniversal.com.mx/cultura/1884.html [Accessed 9 February 2018].
Pascual, José Vicente, 2009. *Las vírgenes del desierto*. Granada: Traspiés.
Pendleton, Don, 2012. *Massacre à Ciudad Juárez*. Paris: Gerard de Villiers.
Pitarch Clark, Ricardo, 2007. *KRTM Snuff Movie*. Zaragoza: Maghenta.
Poniatowska, Elena, 2001. La ciudades fronterizadas son hoteles de paso. *Jornada*, 1 Oct. [online]. Available at: www.jornada.unam.mx/2001/10/01/aborto_poni/poni_juarez2.htm [Accessed 9 Feb 2018].
Pope Duarte, Stella, 2008. *If I die in Juárez*. Tucson: University of Arizona Press.
Rathbun, Jennifer, Joo, Rojas, and Armando, Juan, eds., 2004. *Canto a una ciudad en el desierto: Encuentro de Poetas en Ciudad Juárez*. Mexico: Ediciones La Cuadrilla de la Langosta.
———, 2013. Sangre mía. Poesía de la frontera: violencia, género e identidad/Blood of Mine. In *Poetry of Border: Violence, Gender and Identity in Ciudad Juárez*. Las Cruces: Center for Latin American and Border Studies, Publicaciones de Arenas Blancas, New Mexico State University.
Rivera Garza, Cristina, 2007. *La muerte me da*. Mexico: Tusquets Editores.
———, 2013. *Los muertos indóciles: necroescrituras y desapropiación*. Mexico: Tusquets Editores.
———, 2015. *Dolerse: textos desde un país herido*. Mexico: Surplus Ediciones.
Rojas Joo, Juan Armando, 2016. Género e identidad, elementos en la poesía comprometida de tres poetas chihuahuenses: Arminé Arjona, Susana Chávez y Micaela Solís. *iMex Revista*, 16 March. Ediciones IX, Frontera Norte II. [online]. Available at: www.imex-revista.com/genero-e-identidad/ [Accessed 8 February 2018].

Ronquillo, Víctor, 1999. *Las muertas de Juárez: crónica de una larga pesadilla*. Mexico City: Planeta Mexicana.
Shouse, Eric, 2005. Feeling, Emotion, Affect. *M/C Journal*, 8 (6) (Dec). [online]. Available at: http://journal.media-culture.org.au/0512/03-shouse.php. [Accessed 14 February 2018].
Solís, Micaela, 2004. *Elegía en el desierto*. Ciudad Juárez: Universidad Autónoma de Ciudad Juárez.
Swanson Goldberg, Elizabeth and Schultheis Moore, Alexandra, 2011. Old Questions in New Boxes: Mia Kirshner's *I Live Here* and the Problematics of Transnational Witnessing. *Humanity*, (Fall), 233–253.
Szolc, Izabela, 2007. *Ciotka matych dziewezynek*. Warsaw: Nowy Świat.
Tabachnik, Maud, 2005. *He visto al diablo de frente: Los crímenes de Ciudad Juárez*. Spain: Artime Ediciones.
Taibo, Paco Ignacio II, 2010. *Todo Belascoarán: La serie completa de Héctor Belascoarán Shayne*. Mexico: Planeta.
Ticineto Clough, Patricia, and Halley, Jean, 2007. *The Affective Turn: Theorizing the Social*. Durham, NC: Duke University Press.
Villiers, Gérard de, 2011. *Ciudad Juárez*. Paris: Gérard de Villiers (S.A.S. 190).
Washington Valdez, Diana, 2005. *La cosecha de mujeres: Safari en el desierto mexicano*. Mexico: Océano.
———, 2006. *Harvest of Women: Safari in Mexico*. Burbank: Peace at the Border.
Wimmer, Stefan, 2008. *Der König von Mexiko*. Frankfurt am Main: Eichborn.
Wright, Melissa, 1998. Maquiladora Mestizas and a Feminist Border Politics: Revisiting Anzaldúa. *Hypatia*, 13 (5), 114–131.
Zavala, Pablo M., 2016. La producción antifeminicidista mexicana: autoría, representación y feminismo en la frontera juarense. *Chasqui: Revista de literatura latinoamericana*, 45 (2), 57–69.

Conclusion
Notes towards the possible

While conducting research for my Ph.D in Austin, Texas in 1994, I began to hear reports about the disappearance and murder of young women in the US-Mexico border town of Ciudad Juárez. Indeed, as we have learned from our journey through the feminicidal narrative, from the early 1990s onwards, stories about women who had been mutilated, raped, murdered and abandoned in the desert surrounding the city started to insinuate themselves into local, national and international public consciousness. Since then, a light has been shone on the crime of *feminicidio* and the murders of women from Ciudad Juárez, as we have seen, have become something of a global cause célèbre. Its continued proliferation throughout the Americas most especially in Guatemala and other parts of Mexico have ensured that the horrors of *feminicidio* and what is frequently its very public, excessive nature, remain internationally visible. However, as mentioned in the introduction, there was also something about the murders in Ciudad Juárez that pierced public consciousness both within and beyond Mexico for reasons that are difficult to quantify. Perhaps it is because of this indefinable quality that the city has come to represent a kind of 'ground zero' or global reference point (Melgar 2014) for the crime of *feminicidio* constituting the paradigmatic case study for a phenomenon that is now demanding global recognition and action.

Cultural Representations of Feminicidio at the US-Mexico Border has examined a selection of key texts that form part of a wide-ranging corpus of work in film, music, literature, theatre, art, sculpture, multimedia among many other forms that respond to the crimes committed against women in the northern city. Here I return to the words of Steven S. Volk and Marian E. Schlotterbeck, who contend that 'it is precisely because the state has failed so abjectly in stopping these murders that "fictional" narratives have become both the site where victims are mourned and the means by which justice can be restored.' (2010: 121–122). Taking this as a starting point, I have argued that the cultural expressions about Juárez present us with a suggestive lens through which structural, systemic and historic patterns of violence can be best comprehended and challenged. These cultural products are multi-directional, often hybrid texts, they foreclose fixed readings and many of them fundamentally challenge hegemonic narratives about the crimes. Guided by a set of questions that include how the cultural products are received by those that witness and consume them, the book has probed the conditions that shape local, national and transnational acts of witnessing. In this regard, I have queried the extent to which the modes of representation and mediatization employed by the different cultural practitioners have demarcated their interpretation and reception. Furthermore, I have considered how the affective responses generated by such texts can intervene in human rights' discourses and craft the potential for transitional justice. There are no easy answers to these complex questions and they in turn open up new interpretive avenues and reveal the ways in which the cultural responses to feminicidal violence can record, reflect and mediate emotional experience in the broader sense. Attentive to cultural products from both within and outside Mexico, the study has demonstrated the ways in which responses to the trauma of *feminicidio* are negotiated and framed in different linguistic, social and political contexts.

In seeking to elucidate the potency of cultural texts produced in response to feminicide in Ciudad Juarez since the early 1990s, the book has considered different genres and expressive modes – theatre, art, film and writing – and filtered the analysis through distinct theoretical prisms. Chapter 1 offered a framing of the nature of feminicidal violence as it has evolved since the early 1990s in Ciudad Juárez. In doing this, it strives to carve out a pathway for researchers through the bewildering and frequently competing ideas and discourses about gender violence that probe multiple theoretical, ethical and ideological avenues of thought. These include contested ideas around globalization and paradigms of neoliberalism as well as ideas around the powerful framework of necropolitics, increasingly omnipresent in analyses of the contemporary violent moment in Mexico. It also delved into those criss-crossing and contradictory narratives about women's roles as they negotiate the globalized regimes of neoliberal labour that insert them explicitly as essential components and experience the concomitant resistance from a society invested in strict dichotomies between public and private womanhood. It deliberates on the question of masculinity and its multiple iterations, both toxic and destructive when viewed in the context of feminicidal perpetration.

This concern with masculinity is taken up again in Chapter 2, where we saw how long-standing performative histories of a certain kind of masculine dominance pervade the Catalan theatre stage and how these erupt through the interpretation of 2666 by Àlex Rigola at the Teatre Lliure. Examining the performance of Alba Pujol in the role of Rosita Méndez through the lenses of hysteria and sacrifice, allowed for a reading that while it acknowledges the troubled histories of representation that subtend it, also allows space for agency and contestation. Chapter 3 immersed itself in the varied and discrepant art practices that make up the body of artistic work responding to feminicidal horror. Focusing on the portrait project of Brian Maguire, in particular, it explored the possibilities for transnational witnessing – rooted in a Levinasian ethical practice – to then problematize that positioning. Following this, it asks further questions about the aesthetics of immediacy that renders Juárez a site of humanitarian emergency as well as an aesthetics of portraiture that freezes their subjects within a Western classical tradition.

Chapter 4 explored the potential of documentary film about Ciudad Juárez engaging with one of the best known cultural responses to the crimes, *Señorita Extraviada* by Lourdes Portillo. Reading the iconography of shoes, so central to that film, through a lens informed by Jameson and Sandoval allows us to see how the film stages moments of resilience at the same time as it mourns the victims of feminicide in the city. I then turn my attention to Rafael Bonilla's *La carta* investigating the ways it juxtaposes traditional characterization of mother activists alongside a construction that privileges agency as well as energy. Placing both films in dialogue in the final section, I investigate the way that distinct cinephiliac moments (Keathley 2006) might prompt moments of resistance. Chapter 5 turns its attention to literature or writing, interpreted in its broadest sense. Focusing on the well-known text, *Desert Blood* by Chicana academic and writer, Alicia Gaspar de Alba, I compare this approach to that adopted by Basque author Kama Gutier in the lesser studied novel, *Ciudad final*. Drawing these works into conversation with one of the earliest written responses to feminicide in Juárez – *El silencio que la voz de todas quiebra* [The silence that breaks the voice of all women] – a response that is collaborative and emphatically rooted in the local; I ask how these texts might form part of a wider project of *comunalidad*, as envisioned by Rivera Garza (2015).

The book evaluates those cultural products crafted from within Mexico and is attuned to the ethical, political and symbolic resonance of those cultural interventions that are forged from outside of Mexico – in the US, in Europe – and that are frequently the primary mode of public access to the topic internationally. It is particularly attentive to those spheres of distribution in which the cultural products circulate as well as the contexts of their reception. Many of the cultural expressions studied have received little critical attention: examples include the European exhibition of Irish artist Brian Maguire's portraits of victims of *feminicidio* and the transposition of Roberto Bolaño's novel, *2666*, to stage by Àlex Rigola at the Teatre Lliure in Barcelona in 2007. Ultimately, the book has sought to uncover the cultural significance of these products in the global artistic circuits in which they circulate through the observation of the dynamics of proximity/distance that define the conditions of witnessing and shape relations of empathy and solidarity.

Rooted in work from a number of disciplinary areas, it is important to underline that the scope of the textual corpus and the generic samples provided for close study have demanded a similarly variegated theoretical engagement. Thus the book has drawn on work from scholars including Rosa Linda Fregoso, Rita Laura Segato, Ileana Rodríguez, Julia Estela Monárrez Fragoso, Alicia Gaspar de Alba, Alicia Schmidt Camacho, Héctor Domínguez-Ruvalcaba, Patricia Ravelo Blancas, María Socorro Tabuenca Córdoba and Sergio González Rodríguez among many others. It also engages with a wide body of philosophy and critical theory, frequently deployed in discussions about ethics and cultural representation including the work of Jacques Rancière, Emanuel Levinas, Georges Bataille, Judith Butler and Cristina Rivera Garza among others. This interdisciplinary approach to the horrors of feminicidal violence is paramount if we are to illuminate and tease through the ethical predicaments raised by the heterogenous nature of the corpus under study. In this way, the book speaks directly to the need for debates around gender violence to take account of cultural production, the ethics of representation and the politics of emotion and affect in shaping local, national and transnational responses.

By accepting that 'systems of representation bear directly on historical change by establishing habits of thought crucial to rationalizing particular actions' (Gullace 2002: 10), the aesthetic works produced in response to the horrors of *feminicidio* in Ciudad Juárez signal possibility, an opening, a refusal to fix meaning. But they also trouble the official narratives or beliefs about the crimes and have the power to unsettle fixed and persistent paradigms that lock the victims of *feminicidio* within a political and cultural battleground where they have no control and are utterly silenced. Ultimately I have argued that the cultural texts about *feminicidio* in Juárez and what they mean, matter. There is much at stake here: it is acknowledged that there is a 'politico-ethical urgency and analytical complexity posed by atrocities such as the Juárez feminicides' (Jochum 2015: 92) and that cultural producers struggle in different ways for the 'best' way of telling these stories of brutality, cruelty and death. Questions of ethics, of positionality, of representation and of the affective power of such texts to transform and transfix their audiences, therefore, acquire political importance as the murders remain largely unsolved and forgotten. In this regard, it is imperative to examine this body of work in order to uncover the ways in which it participates in the work of mourning, re-humanization and commemoration. As Cynthia Bejarano points out,

> There is a continuing need to remember in order to never forget, since feminicides are now archived from public memory even as new carnage unfolds . . . witness-survivors, and by extension witness-observers, have a responsibility to always remember in order to maintain their struggle for resolution, justice and secure communities.
>
> (in Paterson 2015: n.p.)

An aesthetics of murder

Itari Marta, the actor who plays the character of Bety in Zuñiga's play *Estrellas enterradas* is forthright in her articulation of the social function of art in these contexts of urgency and pain, 'to inform in order to educate; to inform in order to disconform, to inform in order to transform' (cited in Báez Ayala 2006: 267). These words in turn take us down the pathways examined in the introduction whereby art can reveal in order to transform. Linked to this, of course is the all-important relationship between art – interpreted in its widest sense – and beauty and aesthetics. Indeed, hovering around discussions about ethics, empathy, trauma and activism is the notion of beauty as some form of almost spectral presence, a floating signifier daring us to question its existence and its relevance. It is imperative to return to these questions of beauty and aesthetics; they are not divorced from the debates around ethics, empathy, trauma and activism, rather they are the constitutive modalities of those very frameworks. Elaine Scarry elaborates with passion on beauty's function as part of a wider Humanities agenda of forging a better world:

> The objects residing at the center of inquiry – the visual arts, the verbal arts, great philosophic treatises – are objects of beauty. Like objects of beauty in the natural world, they increase our capacity for fairness by decentering us, enabling us to step outside ourselves and stand on the margins.
>
> (cited in Evans 2017)

Taking inspiration from her envisioning of beauty as a mode of social justice through its capacity for decentering, troubling and reconfiguring, we have seen how the cultural texts studied effortlessly navigate the boundaries between art, politics, justice and beauty to forge what Lucy Bollington eloquently terms a 'poetics of pain' (2018: 77). Here her words chime with those of Cristina Rivera Garza when she writes about the challenges of writing in a wounded country, constituting the epitome of what she calls, 'these texts in pain, these painful texts'. In doing so, they make up a repertoire of cultural remembrance that can endure. Not only that, in the re-reading of books, the re-screening of films, the re-installation of art pieces and the repeated performances of theatre, they will continue to inscribe these stories of unimaginable loss in the public imaginaries that have access to them in a cycle of repetition and renewal.

Secretive repetitions

This idea of repetition brings me finally to the closing thoughts. I have written elsewhere in this book about the way in which repetition functions as perhaps *the* defining logic of feminicidal crime in the sense that one is never far from the next instance of barbarity. Repetition, as scholars Butler (1993) and Berlant (1997) have shown is the operational mode through which the institutions that circumscribe and give meaning to our lives – family, nation, heterosexuality, to name but a few – are inscribed in our collective through repetitive gestures that seem largely invisible, and hence all-powerful. It is here that we encounter the many paradoxes of feminicide seen first through its utter and overwhelming visibility as social narrative in Mexico, including the familiarity with which the term appears in the print media and is spoken by schoolchildren, lawyers, students and the general population. Linked to this, we have to recognize its reiterative capacity, its neverending 'thereness' and the seeming inability of the state including its legal institutions and its structures of governance to end it. In concert or, rather, disconcert with this, there is the recurring trope of secrecy, also omnipresent in narratives about feminicide. A seeming paradox therefore presents itself; how can something that is hypervisible and constantly repeating itself remain secretive and disclosed from view? We have seen time and again how the cultural texts express the tension between these seemingly contradictory positions, and indeed how the notion of the secret – in which all the knowledge about the crimes is contained – is frequently assigned to the natural or non-human dimensions of the stories. In this regard, we think of Paula Flores's agonizing appeal to the mountains for help in finding her daughter in Bonilla's film, *La carta*, or the many assertions that the secrets of *feminicidio* in Ciudad Juarez lie buried in its desert sands. Bolaño, of course, is credited with the most famous pronouncement about the secretive dimension to the killings, encapsulated in 2666 when he says, '*Nadie presta atención a estos asesinatos, pero en ellos se esconde el secreto del mundo*' (Bolaño 2004: 439) [No one pays attention to these killings but the secret of the world is hidden in them]. Here we should recall – returning for an instant to a world in which the struggle for legal, moral and social accountability is enacted over and over by non-governmental organizations (NGOs), grassroots organizations, activists and victims' families – that, as Schmidt Camacho incisively points out, the answers to the narratives lie with the perpetrators (2004: 46). Indeed it is the perpetrators who remain most invisible, most secretive in narratives about feminicidal crimes. Theories about who *could* or who *might* have committed these crimes ranged from the most sadistic extreme (makers of snuff movies or the crazed offspring of narco leaders, the so-called juniors) to those boyfriends and husbands, who seemingly just lost control for a moment of 'madness', a moment that led to yet another body of a dead woman. Hiding behind labels such as '*monstruo*' [monster] or '*diablo*' [devil], such pathologizing of perpetrators has led to (yet another) cycle of repetition. And as has often been articulated, until mainstream discourse shifts from considerations of pathology and passion to more sustained, intelligent and systematic appraisals of the structures of power that undergird the systems of social relations in the borderlands, then, it would seem, we are going nowhere.

I would like to end with words taken from the diary of *feminicidio* victim, Eréndira Ivonne Ponce Hernández, murdered in 1998, and reproduced in the compelling testimonial collage, *El silencio que la voz de todas quiebra* [The silence that breaks the voice of all women], studied in the final chapter. Pre-figuring Bolaño's words, she writes:

> I don't know what's wrong with me. I'm scared.
> Thinking about it more, it's not fear that I'm feeling. It's a premonition. A premonition that I'm going to discover something. A secret. The biggest secret in the world.
> (Cabrera in Benítez 1999: 94)

My journey through the painful secrets of feminicidal violence has taken me to this moment and the fear felt by Eréndira in what we know to be her final months. Pausing to imagine the ordeal experienced by her before her body was found – twelve days following her disappearance with her hands tied, face down – leads us to the abyss in which the secret of *feminicidio* lies; in full view and yet forever unknown. Perhaps studies like this one, following Rivera Garza's piercing exploration of the role of culture during the current moment of extreme inhumanity in Mexico, might lead us to a place of 'being with others' (2013: 274); or towards a sense of *comunalidad*, still open, still waiting to be fully articulated. However ephemeral or imperfect this may seem, perhaps, for now, it is the best that can be done.

Works cited

Báez Ayala, Susana, 2006. Los colores del amanecer: La dramaturgia social en Ciudad Juárez. In Víctor Orozco, ed., *Chihuahua hoy, 2006: Visiones de su economía, política y cultura*. Vol. 4, Chihuahua: Instituto Chihuahuense de la Cultura and Universidad Autónoma de Ciudad Juárez, 255–284.

Benítez, Rohry, et al., 1999. *El silencio que la voz de todas quiebra*. Chihuahua: Ediciones del Azar.

Berlant, Lauren, 1997. *The Queen of America Goes to Washington City: Essays on Sex and Citizenship*. Durham, NC: Duke University Press.

Bollington, Lucy, 2018. *Reframing Excess: Death and Power in Contemporary Mexican Literary and Visual Culture*. Thesis (Ph.D). University of Cambridge.

Bolaño, Roberto, 2004. *2666*. Barcelona: Anagrama.

Butler, Judith, 1993. *Bodies that Matter: On the Discursive Limits of 'Sex'*. New York: Routledge.

Evans, Brad, 2017. The Intimate Life of Violence: Brad Evans interviews Elaine Scarry. *Los Angeles Review of Books*, 4 Dec. [online]. Available at: https://lareviewofbooks.org/article/histories-of-violence-the-intimate-life-of-violence# [Accessed 12 February 2018].

Gullace, Nicoletta, 2002. *The Blood of our Sons: Men, Women and the Renegotiation of British Citizenship During the Great War*. Basingstoke: Palgrave Macmillan.

Jochum, Tobias, 2015. "The Weight of Words, the Shock of Photos": Poetic Testimony and Elliptical Imagery in Sergio González Rodríguez' *The Femicide Machine*. FIAR – Forum for Interamerican Research, 8 (2) (Sep), 92–119. [online]. Available at: http://interamerica.de/volume-8-2/jochum/ [Accessed 24 January 2018].

Keathley, Christian, 2006. *Cinephilia and History or, The Wind in the Trees*. Bloomington, IN: Indiana University Press.

Melgar, Lucía, 2014. Nuestra violencia, nuestra impunidad. *Nexos*, 1 December [online]. Available at: www.nexos.com.mx/?p=23503 [Accessed 14 February 2018].

Paterson, Kent, 2015. Women Never Forgotten: The Murals and Memorials of Ciudad Juárez. *fronteranortesur*, 3 August. Available at: https://fnsnews.nmsu.edu/women-never-forgotten-the-murals-and-memorials-of-ciudad-juarez/ [Accessed 12 February 2018].

Rivera Garza, Cristina, 2015. *Dolerse: Textos desde un país herido*. Mexico: Surplus Ediciones.

Schmidt Camacho, Alicia, 2004. Body Counts on the Mexico-U.S. Border: *Feminicidio*, Reification, and the Theft of Mexicana Subjectivity. *Chicana/Latina Studies: The Journal of MALCS*, 4 (1 Fall), 22–60.

Appendix

This Appendix contains a list of key texts in different generic areas that pertain to *feminicidio* in Ciudad Juárez.

Artworks (including photography) and exhibitions

This list seeks to capture some of the biggest exhibitions of art wholly or partly devoted to *feminicidio* in Ciudad Juárez.

Bjørne Linnert, Lise, 2006. *Desconocida, Unknown, Ukjent* [Collaborative art project]. Worldwide – present.

Challenger, Tamsyn, 2010. *400 Women*. [Exhibition]. London 2010, Edinburgh 2011, Holland 2012. Various artists.

Chauvet, Elina, 2009. *Zapatos rojos*. [Installation].

Ciudad Juárez, 2015. Video. [online]. Directed by Maya Goded. Available at: http://mayagoded.net/site/portfolios/ciudad-juarez/ [Accessed 24 January 2018].

d'Artali, Gino, 2001. *Facing Faces*. [Exhibition]. Museo de Arte e Historia, Mexico. 31 August–29 September.

Del Real, Yamina. 2011. *El cuerpo deshabitado*. [Exhibition of Photography]. Museo Archivo de la Fotografía, Mexico. 16 June–28 August.

Feminicidio en México: Ya Basta, 2017. [Exhibition]. Museo de Memoria y Tolerancia, Mexico. January–May.

Frontera 450+, 2006. [Exhibition]. Station Museum, Houston, TX. 21 October 2006–28 January 2007. Participating artists included Susan Plum, David Krueger, Celia Álvarez Muñoz, Carmen Montoya, Margarita Cabrera, Arturo Rivera, Teresa Serrano, Maya Goded, Coco Fusco, Teresa Margolles, Kaneem Smith, Sara Maniero, Elia Arce, Luis Jiménez, Lise Bjørne Hannert, Angela Dillon, Kaneem Smith.

Goded, Maya, *Desaparecidas*, 2005–2006 [Photography].

Hijas de Juárez, 2003 [Exhibition]. Social and Public Art Resource Centre (SPARC). Artists included Adriana Alba-Sanchez, Yolanda Amescua, Judith F. Baca, Raul P. Baltazar, Yreina Cervántez, Victoria Delgadillo, Ofelia and Elena Esparza, Consuelo Flores, Ester Hernández, Jenina, Alma Lopez, Jose Lozano, Azul Luna, Rigoberto Maldonado, Francisco 'Chisco' Ramirez, Martha Ramirez, Victor Rosas, T. Pilar, and Martin Sorrondeguy.

Kahlo, Diane, 2011. *Wall of Memories: The Disappeared Señoritas of Ciudad Juárez*. [Exhibition]. Tuska Center for Contemporary Art, University of Kentucky, October.

Las mujeres de Juárez demandan justicia, 2002. [Poster Exhibition]. Mexico.

Maguire, Brian, 2012–13. *An Oasis of Horror in a Desert of Boredom*. [Exhibition]. VISUAL Centre for Contemporary Art, Carlow. 6 October 2012–6 January 2013.

Morillas, Maritza, 2006. *CaroDAtaVERnibus en Ciudad Juárez*. [Painting & Installation].

Ni Una Más, Not One More: The Juárez Murders, 2010. [Exhibition]. Leonard Pearlstein Gallery, Philadelphia. 15 May–16 July. Participating artists included Kiki Smith, Nancy Spero, Andrea Marshall, Teresa Serrano, Celia Álvarez Muñoz, Alice Leora Briggs, Lise Bjørne Linnert, Tim Rollins & KOS and Arlene Love and Jen Blazina, Yoko Ono, Brian Maguire.

No nos cabe tanta muerte: Memorial a Ciudad Juárez, Mexico, 2013. [Exhibition]. Espai d'Arts de Roca Umbert, Barcelona. 7–30 November. Participating artists included Montse Roure, Amilcar Rivera, Mina Hamada, Hanamaro Chaki, Paula Laverde, Poncho Martínez, Elisabeth Siefer, María Romero, Mónica Lozano, Mayra Martell, Mónica Ruiz, Silvia Antolin, Ximena Pérez Grobet, Reme Domingo, Rodolfo Green, José Andrés Peraza, Fernanda Álvarez, María Rivera, Diana Espinal. Guadalupe Cano y Lucía Escobar.

Norma, 2015. [Video]. [online]. Directed by Maya Goded. Available at: http://mayagoded.net/site/portfolios/ciudad-juarez/ [Accessed 24 January 2018].

Rastros y Crónicas: Women of Juárez, 2009. [Exhibition]. National Museum of Mexican Art, Chicago. 16 October 2009–14 February 2010. Participating artists included Adrianna Yadira Gallego, Ana Teresa Hernández, Amalia Benavides, Ambra Polidori, Azul Luna, Carla Rippey, Cecilia Álvarez Muñoz, Consuelo Jiménez Underwood, Ester Hernández, Esperanza Gama, Eva Soliz, Favianna Rodríguez, Judithe Hernández, Karen Musgrave, Linda Vallejo, Monica Huitron Flores, Patricia Acosta, Pilar Acevedo, Rocío Caballero, Rosario Guajardo, Sandra Vista, Stephanie Manríquez. Susan Plum, Veronica Cardoso Nagel and Victoria Delgadillo.

Saldívar, César, 2010. *Perder el Norte*. [Photographic Exhibition]. Palacio de Minería, Mexico City, 6 March–25 April.

Swoon, 2008. *Portrait of Silvia Elena*. [Installation]. Yerba Buena Center for the Arts, San Francisco and Honey Space, Chelsea, NY. 30 May–5 July.

Film

16 en la lista: Crimenes en Juarez, 1998. [Film]. Directed by Rodolfo Rodobertti. CPM Films.

Bajo Juárez: la ciudad devorando a sus hijas [Beneath Juárez: a city devouring its daughters], 2006. [Film]. Directed by Antonio Cordero and Alejandra Sánchez.

Bola Negra: El musical de Ciudad Juárez, 2012. [Film]. Directed by Mario Bellatin and Marcela Rodríguez. Mexico: Instituto Nacional de Bellas Artes; En Chinga Films.

Blood Rising, 2013. [Film]. Directed by Mark McLoughlin. Bang Bang Teo.

Border Echoes [Ecos de una frontera], 2006. [Film]. Directed by Lorena Méndez-Quiroga.

Bordertown, 2006. [Film]. Directed by Gregory Nava. Mobius Entertainment/El Norte Productions.

Ciudad Juárez: La ciudad donde las mujeres son deshechables [Ciudad Juárez: The city where women are disposable], 2007. [Film]. Directed by Alex Flores and Lorena Vassolo.

Ciudad Juárez: Tan infinito como el desierto [Ciudad Juárez: as infinite as the desert], 2004. [Film]. Directed by Alejandro Macías and Tony Castro.

Desde que no estás [Since you've been gone] 2008. [Film]. Directed by Rosella M. Bergamaschi.

El otro sueño americano [*The Other American Dream*], 2004. [Film]. Directed by Enrique Arroyo.

El traspatio [Backyard], 2009. [Film]. Directed by Carlos Carrera.

Espejo retrovisor [*Rearview Mirror*], 2002. [Film]. Directed by Lisa di Georgina. Cine Producciones Molinar.

Femicidio, hecho en México [Femicide: Made in Mexico], 2003. [Film]. Directed by Vanessa Bauche.

Hecho en Juárez [Made in Juárez], 2003. [Film]. Directed by Arturo Chacon.
If Images Could Fill Our Empty Spaces, 2013. [Film]. Directed by Alice Driver.
Juárez: City of Dreams, 2012. [Film]. Directed by Bruno Sorrentino.
Juárez, desierto de esperanza [Juárez, desert of hope], 2002. [Film]. Directed by Cristina Michaus.
La Batalla de Las Cruces: protesta social y acciones colectivas en torno de la violencia sexual en Ciudad Juárez [The battle of the crosses: social protest and collective action against sexual violence in Ciudad Juárez]2006. [Film]. Directed by Patricia Ravelo and Rafael Bonilla.
La carta [The Letter], 2010. [Film]. Directed by Rafael Bonilla.
Las muertas de Juárez [The Dead Women of Juárez], 2001. [Film]. Directed by Enrique Murillo.
Mass Murder in Juárez, 2012. [Film]. Directed by Peadar King.
Miércoles de ceniza [Ash Wednesday], 2005. [Film]. Directed by Fernando Benítez.
Ni una más, 2002. [Film]. Directed by Alejandra Sánchez.
On the Edge: Femicide in Ciudad Juárez, 2006. [Film]. Directed by Steev Hise.
Pasión y muerte en Juáre [Passion and Death in Ciudad Juárez], 2002. [Film]. Directed by Javier Ulloa and Luis Estrada.
Performing the Border, 1999. [Film]. Directed by Ursula Biemann.
Preguntas sin Respuesta: Los asesinatos y desapariciones de mujeres en Ciudad Juárez [Unanswered questions: The murder and disappearance of women in Ciudad Juárez],2004. [Film]. Directed by Rafael Montero.
Señorita Extraviada [Disappeared young woman], 2001. [Film]. Directed by Lourdes Portillo.
Tierra prometida [Promised land], 2003. [Film]. Directed by Ángel Estrada Soto.
The Virgin of Juárez, 2006. [Film]. Directed by Kevin James Dobson.

Theatre

2666 by Àlex Rigola, 2007. [Play].
The Acts – Vigia by Jill Greenhalgh and Michael Brookes, 2006–2008. [Performance].
Among the Sand and the Smog by J. Jiménez-Smith, 2006. [Play].
Antígona: las voces que incendian el desierto, 2005 by Perla de la Rosa. [Play]. In Guadalupe de la Mora, ed., *Cinco dramaturgos chihuahuenses*. Ciudad Juárez: Fondo Municipal Edito Revolvente, 186–228.
Deserere (El desierto) [Desert] by Cruz Robles, 2007. [Play]. In Enrique Mijares, ed., 2008. *Hotel Juárez: dramaturgia de feminicidios*. Durango, Mexico: Universidad Juárez del Estado de Durango/Union College/Editorial Espacio Vacío.
Dramaturgias y feminicidios. Project conceived by Alejandra G. Rebelo. Theatre texts by Avila, Galindo, Aguilar and Hernández available for download in pdf. [online]. Available at: www.dramaturgiasyfeminicidios.com/textos [Accessed 10 February 2018].
Estrellas enterradas by Antonio Zúñiga, 2011. [Play]. In Enrique Mijares, ed., 2008. *Hotel Juárez: dramaturgia de feminicidios*. Durango, Mexico: Universidad Juárez del Estado de Durango/ Union College/ Editorial Espacio Vacío.
The Ghosts of Lote Bravo by Hilary Bettis, 2015. [Play].
Gritos de Justicia [Cries of Justice] by Leopoldo Ibarra Saucedo, 2008. [Play]. In Enrique Mijares, ed., 2008. *Hotel Juárez: dramaturgia de feminicidios*. Durango, Mexico: Universidad Juárez del Estado de Durango/ Union College/ Editorial Espacio Vacío.
The Incredible Disappearing Woman by Coco Fusco, 2003. [Play].
Iphigenia Crash Land Falls on the Neon Shell That Was Once Her Heart by Caridad Svich, 2004. [Play].

Jauría [Pack of Dogs] by Enrique Mijares, 2008. [Play]. In Enrique Mijares, ed., 2008. *Hotel Juárez: dramaturgia de feminicidios*. Durango, Mexico: Universidad Juárez del Estado de Durango/ Union College/Editorial Espacio Vacío.

Justicia Light by Ernesto García, 2008. [Play]. In Enrique Mijares, ed., 2008. *Hotel Juárez: dramaturgia de feminicidios*. Durango, Mexico: Universidad Juárez del Estado de Durango/ Union College/Editorial Espacio Vacío.

Justicia Negada [Justice Denied] by Perla de la Rosa, 2013. [Play].

La ciudad de las moscas [City of Flies] by Virginia Hernández, 2008. [Play]. In Enrique Mijares, ed., 2008. *Hotel Juárez: dramaturgia de feminicidios*. Durango, Mexico: Universidad Juárez del Estado de Durango/Union College/Editorial Espacio Vacío.

Las muertas de Juárez by Grupo Sinergía, 2004. [Play].

Lomas de Poleo by Edeberto "Pilo" Galindo, 2003. [Play]. In Enrique Mijares, ed., 2008. *Hotel Juárez: dramaturgia de feminicidios*. Durango, Mexico: Universidad Juárez del Estado de Durango/ Union College/Editorial Espacio Vacío.

Los Trazos del Viento [Traces of the Wind] by Alan Aguilar, 2008. [Play]. In Enrique Mijares, ed., 2008. *Hotel Juárez: dramaturgia de feminicidios*. Durango, Mexico: Universidad Juárez del Estado de Durango/Union College/Editorial Espacio Vacío.

Mientras dormíamos: el caso Juárez [While we slept: The case of Juárez] by Lorena Wolffer, 2001. [Play].

Mujeres de arena [Women of sand] by Humberto Robles, 2002. [Play]. [online]. Available at: https://mujeresdearenateatro.blogspot.ie/p/texto-en-espanol.html [Accessed 15 February 2018].

Mujeres de Ciudad Juárez by Cristina Michaus, 2001. [Play].

Murmullos en el Páramo [Whispers in the wasteland] by Mercedes Hernández, 2011. [Play].

Ni una más by Rossana Filomarino, 2014. [Dance]. Available at: www.youtube.com/watch?v=xPcMQTYLmQg [Accessed 10 February 2018].

River of Tears/Río de lágrimas by Las Meganenas, 2012. [Play].

Rumor de Viento [Murmur of the Wind] by Norma Barroso, 2004. [Play]. In Enrique Mijares, ed., 2008. *Hotel Juárez: dramaturgia de feminicidios*. Durango, Mexico: Universidad Juárez del Estado de Durango/Union College/Editorial Espacio Vacío.

Sirenas del Río [Mermaids of the River] by Demetrio Avila, 2008. [Play]. In Enrique Mijares, ed., 2008. *Hotel Juárez: dramaturgia de feminicidios*. Durango, Mexico: Universidad Juárez del Estado de Durango/Union College/Editorial Espacio Vacío.

Tlatoani: las muertas de Suárez by Juan Tovar, 2006. [Play]. In Enrique Mijares, ed., 2008. *Hotel Juárez: dramaturgia de feminicidios*. Durango, Mexico: Universidad Juárez del Estado de Durango/Union College/Editorial Espacio Vacío.

The Vagina Monologues by Eve Ensler, 1996. [Play].

Writing including poetry, literary and non-literary fiction

Adam, Peggy, 2006. *Luchadoras*. Geneva: Atrabile.

Agosín, Marjorie, 2006. *Secrets in the Sand: The Young Women of Juárez*. Buffalo: White Pine Press.

Arce, Evangelina, 2011. *Para mi hija, Silvia/For my daughter, Silvia*. London: Blank Slate Books.

Arona, Danila, 2007. *Finis terrae*. Milan: Mondadori.

Bard, Patrick, 2002. *La frontière: Thriller*. Paris: Seuil.

———, 2004. *La frontera*. Barcelona: Grijalbo.

Bartoli, Víctor, 2000. *Mujer alabastrina*. Ciudad Juárez: Arca de Saidah.

Baudoin-Troubs, Edmond, 2011. *Viva la vida: Los sueños de Ciudad Juárez*. Bilbao: Astiberri Ediciones.
Bellatin, Mario, and Liniers, 2017. *Bola negra*. Mexico: Sexto Pisto.
Benítez, Rohry, et al., 1999. *El silencio que la voz de todas quiebra*. Chihuahua: Ediciones del Azar.
Bolaño, Roberto, 2004. *2666*. Barcelona: Anagrama.
Bousquet, Charlotte, 2010. *Llorona on the rocks*. Saussay la Campagne: Argemmios.
D'Artali, Gino, 2003. *I Love You: 65 International Poets United Against Violence Against Women*. Fredericton, Canada, Ciudad Juárez, Mexico: Broken Jaw Press, Coalition of Artists United for Social Engagement.
Diez, Rolo, 2005. *Hurensohne* [Matamujeres]. Trans. by Horst Rosenberger. Heilbronn: Distel Literatureverlag.
Duque, Rocío. *El negocio de matar. Cuadernos feministas*. Available at: http://rociosart.blogspot.ie/p/el-negocio-de-matar-capitulo-1.html [Accessed 10 February 2018].
Escritores por Ciudad Juárez, 2017. [online]. Available at: http://escritoresporciudadjuarez.blogspot.ie/ [Accessed 9 February 2018].
Galán Benítez, Carmen, 2001. *Tierra Marchita*. Mexico: Fondo Editorial Tierra Adentro.
Gaspar de Alba, Alicia, 2005. *Desert Blood: The Juárez Murders*. Houston: Arte Público Press.
Gloeckner, Phoebe, 2008. *La tristeza*. In Mia Kirshner, et al., eds., I Live Here. New York: Pantheon Graphic Novels.
González Rodríguez, Sergio, 2002. *Huesos en el desierto*. Barcelona: Anagrama.
———, 2012. *The Femicide Machine*. Los Angeles: Semiotext(e).
González, Yeana, ed., 2016. *El silencio de los cuerpos: relatos sobre feminicidio*. Mexico: Ediciones B.
Gutier, Kama, 2007. *Ciudad final*. Barcelona: Montesinos.
Hawken, Sam, 2011. *The Dead Women of Juarez*. London: Serpent's Tail.
Huacuja del Toro, Malú, 2006. *La lágrima, la gota y el artificio*. Mexico: Plaza y Valdez.
Iturralde, Edna, 2013. *Las muchachas de la lluvia*. Madrid: Alfaguara Juvenil.
Killeen, Ger, 2014. *JuárOz: A Poetic Fiction*. Portland: Headlandia Press.
Kirshner, Mia, et al., 2008. *I Live Here*. New York: Pantheon Graphic Novels.
León, Gregorio, 2009. *Balada de perros muertos*. Madrid: Nowtilus.
Pendleton, Don, 2012. *Massacre à Ciudad Juárez*. Paris: Gerard de Villiers.
Pitarch Clark, Ricardo, 2007. *KRTM Snuff Movie*. Zaragoza: Maghenta.
Pope Duarte, Stella, 2008. *If I die in Juárez*. Tucson: University of Arizona Press.
Ronquillo, Víctor, 1999. *Las muertas de Juárez: crónica de una larga pesadilla*. Mexico: Planeta Mexicana.
Silva Márquez, César, 2014. *La balada de los arcos dorados*. Oaxaca: Almadía.
Solís, Micaela, 2004. *Elegía en el desierto*. Ciudad Juárez: Universidad Autónoma de Ciudad Juárez.
Stabile, Uberto, ed., 2015. *Ni una más: Poemas por Ciudad Juárez*. Madrid: Amargord.
Szolc, Izabela, 2007. *Ciotka matych dziewezynek*. Warsaw: Nowy Świat.
Tabachnik, Maud, 2005. *J'ai regarde le diable en face*. Paris: Albin Michel.
———, *He visto al diablo de frente: Los crímenes de Ciudad Juárez*. Spain: Artime Ediciones.
Villiers, Gérard de, 2011. *Ciudad Juárez*. Paris: Gérard de Villiers (S.A.S. 190).
Washington Valdez, Diana, 2005. *La cosecha de mujeres: Safari en el desierto mexicano*. Mexico: Océano.
———, 2006. *Harvest of Women: Safari in Mexico*. Burbank: Peace at the Border.
Whitechapel, Simon, 2000. *Crossing to Kill: The True Story of the Serial-Killer Playground*. London and New York: Virgin Books.
Wimmer, Stefan, 2008. *Der König von Mexiko*. Frankfurt am Main: Eichborn.

Index

activism 5–8, 12–13, 18, 20, 37–38, 50–52, 54–55, 58, 69–70, 72n6, 75, 79, 90, 99, 107, 113, 115, 124, 126–127, 129, 131–133, 139n5, 144–145, 147–148, 150, 154, 156, 165–166, 170, 184–185; feminist 6, 18; mother- 12, 52, 115, 148
Adorno, Theodor 5–6, 16n11, 16n12, 18–19, 53, 97, 111
Agamben, Giorgio 32–33, 44n31, 44n34, 44n35, 46–48, 68, 72, 77, 118, 126, 140n12, 143

Báez Ayala, Susana 50, 54–55, 77, 166, 177, 184, 187
Bataille, Georges 60, 64–66, 71, 76n38, 76n39, 77, 79, 183
Bejarano, Cynthia 3–4, 16n9, 19, 21, 23, 26, 28–29, 40, 45n43, 47, 49, 51–52, 78, 127, 144, 151, 178, 184
Bellatin, Mario 11, 18, 33, 43n24, 46, 141n21, 144, 151, 177, 189, 192
Benítez, Rohry 13, 144, 149, 151, 166–167, 174n1, 177, 186, 187, 192
Bolaño, Roberto 7, 11, 17n18, 26, 46, 53, 55–58, 60, 69, 71, 74n15, 74n17, 74n18, 75n33, 76n36, 77–82, 87, 110–111, 150–151, 176n26, 177, 183, 186–187, 191; 2666 i, vii–ix, 7, 11, 17n18, 26, 46, 53, 55–61, 63–65, 68–71, 74n14, 74n18, 74n20, 75n26, 75n33, 77–81, 87, 107n20, 110–111, 150–151, 176–177, 182–183, 186–187, 190–192
Bonilla, Rafael 12–13, 19, 111, 114, 128, 131, 133, 139n3, 142n27, 143n41, 146, 183, 186, 190
border 1–2, 4, 7, 11, 13–14, 25–27, 34, 38, 46–47, 49–53, 63, 68, 71, 80, 83–85, 89–90, 98, 101, 108n24, 108n26, 113, 118, 125, 129, 138n3, 141n20, 144, 146, 151, 153–158, 160, 162–166, 172, 174, 175n12, 179–180, 187, 189–190, 192; borderspace 97–98, 111; *Bordertown* 7, 9, 18, 114, 144, 189; city 1, 22, 84, 115, 134, 153; *frontera* 18–21, 46–47, 49–51, 78–81, 85, 107n14, 112–113, 133, 139, 144, 146–148, 153, 160, 177–180, 187–189, 191; land(s) 19, 23, 38, 47–48, 72, 78, 80, 145, 160, 162, 166, 168, 171, 174, 177–178, 186; region 2, 13, 30–33, 36, 69, 116–117, 122, 152; town 2, 7, 44n39, 54, 57, 69, 107n14, 181; US-Mexico 1–2, 11, 32, 36, 53–54, 73n12, 98, 101, 115, 141n20, 155, 181, 192
Bowden, Charles 9, 17n26, 43n24, 53, 72n1, 72n2, 77, 151, 175n9
Butler, Judith 12, 18, 90–92, 94–96, 98–104, 109n36, 109n37, 109n38, 110, 170, 174, 177, 183, 185, 187

community 5, 7, 12, 17n17, 18n30, 24, 26, 35, 53, 68, 85, 90, 92, 94, 101, 115, 126, 129, 132–135, 142n26, 154, 152, 164–166, 171–173; *comunalidad* 154, 173–174, 183, 187; *comunidad emocional* 17n17, 19, 171
Corona, Ignacio 29, 37–38, 41, 46, 49, 179

Desert Blood: The Juárez Murders 13, 49, 150, 153–166, 172, 175n18, 176n21, 176n22, 176n23, 176n26, 178–179, 183, 192
Domínguez-Ruvalcaba, Héctor 20, 29, 38, 45n43, 46n49, 46–47, 49, 177, 179, 183
Driver, Alice 5, 16n10, 17n20, 17n26, 19, 21, 33–35, 45n45, 47, 72n1, 74n15, 78,

194 Index

105n1, 111–112, 139n3, 139n4, 140, 145, 189

El silencio que la voz de todas quiebra 13, 139n8, 140n16, 144, 149–150, 154, 166, 173, 177, 183, 186–187, 192
ethics 8–9, 12, 18n32, 19, 46n50, 47, 53, 61, 78, 83, 87, 90–92, 109n36, 109n37, 110–111, 145–146, 171, 183–185; ethical 2, 5, 10, 61–62, 75n34, 83, 87, 91–92, 94, 97–98, 100–105, 109n37, 134, 152, 156, 166, 182–184

femicide 2–4, 15n4, 16n9, 17n23, 18–21, 23, 29, 34, 38, 42n16, 44n38, 46–52, 66–67, 78–79, 113, 139, 146–148, 159, 166, 178, 187, 190, 192
feminicide 3–5, 8–9, 12, 15, 16n7, 16n10, 19–21, 24, 26–29, 31–32, 36, 38, 40–41, 42n11, 44n29, 47, 49, 51–53, 55, 57, 65, 68, 72, 72n6, 76n41, 76n42, 78, 83–85, 89, 94, 103–104, 105n2, 106n5, 110n47, 111–112, 117, 119, 120, 122, 124, 135, 139n8, 139n9, 141n21, 145–146, 149–150, 153, 155, 161, 166–168, 170, 172, 174n3, 178, 182–185
feminism 6, 19, 40, 43n19, 43n21, 46, 48, 50, 176n31, 177; feminist 3–4, 6, 16n11, 18–19, 26–27, 38, 42n19, 46n49, 46, 49, 61, 64, 72n6, 81–82, 85, 100, 102, 111, 128, 130, 138, 144, 167, 177, 189
Flores, Paula 11–12, 28, 43n21, 115, 119, 126, 131, 137, 138, 140n15, 142n28, 143n41, 186
Fregoso, Rosa Linda 3–4, 16n9, 17n26, 19, 21, 23, 26, 28–29, 31–32, 36–38, 40, 45n43, 47, 49, 51–52, 66, 72n1, 76n41, 78, 115, 139n4, 140n12, 140n13, 142n24, 145, 151, 161, 176n25, 178, 183

Gaspar de Alba, Alicia 13, 17n20, 19, 21, 23, 26–27, 30, 42n12, 42n13, 42n18, 46–47, 49–51, 66–67, 76n43, 78, 106n6, 113, 147, 150, 153–156, 164, 166–167, 174, 176n21, 176n22, 176n23, 178–179, 183, 192
gender 3–4, 14, 16n10, 20–21, 28, 30, 33, 39, 42n7, 44n34, 48, 50, 51, 60, 75n26, 90, 113, 133, 147, 175, 178–179; roles 22, 29, 72, 116, 121, 161; violence 8, 12, 22–23, 27, 38, 40, 42n9, 42n17, 43n20, 44n34, 45n46, 46, 49, 51, 54, 75n34, 83–84, 93, 105n3, 107n14, 111, 118, 132, 140n10, 152–154, 161, 163, 174n4, 179, 182, 184
globalization 14, 22, 30–32, 36–37, 43n25, 48, 65, 71–72, 76n41, 116–117, 120, 122, 153, 161, 174, 178, 182
González Rodríguez, Sergio 5, 15n3, 17n18, 19, 26, 30, 34–35, 37–38, 42n16, 44n38, 45n44, 45n47, 48, 66, 73n8, 78–79, 151, 165, 175n8, 178, 183, 187, 192
Gutier, Kama 13, 150, 153–156, 158, 164, 174, 174n1, 178, 183, 192

Heidegger, Martin 121, 140n17, 141n22
human rights 2–3, 14, 15n2, 15n3, 15n5, 17n25, 21, 24, 26, 28–29, 37, 42n17, 43, 47, 58–59, 62, 69–70, 73n12, 84, 86, 89–90, 103–104, 105n1, 106n8, 107n18, 109n41, 113, 115, 144, 149, 152, 156, 178, 182

Jameson, Fredric 120–123, 140n17, 141n19, 141n22, 145, 183

La carta 12, 43n21, 111, 114–115, 120, 126, 128, 131, 135, 137, 142n27, 146
Lagarde y de los Ríos, Marcela 3–4, 18–19, 26, 28, 38, 42n19, 43n19, 43n20, 43n21, 48, 143n41, 165
Levinas, Emmanuel 12, 90–92, 94–99, 101–102, 105, 109n36, 109n37, 110, 112, 182–183
Lomas de Poleo (Ciudad Juárez neighborhood) 24, 129, 132, 142n28, 142n35, 143n38, 167

Maguire, Brian 12–13, 15n2, 17n21, 20, 84, 86–97, 99, 101–105, 107n13, 107n14, 107n19, 108n21, 108n23, 108n25, 108n26, 109n35, 109n39, 112, 182–183, 189
maquila 11–12, 20, 22, 25, 30–31, 40, 43n25, 44n26, 44n28, 48–49, 66, 68, 76, 115–119, 124–125, 141n20, 153, 155, 157, 160–161, 163, 165, 172, 176n24; *maquiladora* 2, 22, 25, 30, 40, 42n13, 46, 50–51, 55, 144, 148, 176, 180
masculinity 11, 22, 39, 46n49, 153, 182; masculinities 29, 46n49, 48
Mbembe, Achille 32–34, 44n33, 44n35, 49, 60, 68, 80, 140, 146

Index

McLoughlin, Mark 15n2, 17n21, 18, 84, 89, 102, 110, 139n3, 144, 189
memory 11, 55, 69–70, 75n27, 77n46, 86, 94, 111–112, 129, 132, 140, 144, 147, 153, 184
Monárrez Fragoso, Julia Estela 4, 16n9, 20, 23, 25, 29–30, 32, 34–35, 38, 42n11, 45n44, 49, 51, 183
mourning 8, 45n41, 53, 59, 72n5, 111, 126, 128, 132, 134–135, 142n27, 170, 173, 184

necropolitics 10–11, 18, 22, 32–34, 44n36, 46, 49, 52, 60, 80, 140n12, 144, 146, 177, 182; *necropolítica* 51; necropolitical 32–33, 68
North American Free Trade Agreement (NAFTA) 2, 30, 34, 116, 121

Oasis of Horror in a Desert of Boredom, An 9, 12, 17n21, 20, 86–87, 89, 189

Piñeda-Madrid, Nancy 23, 29, 36–37, 50
Pope Duarte, Stella 153, 179, 192
Portillo, Lourdes 7, 12–13, 17n18, 20, 76, 81, 90, 113–116, 118, 120, 123–124, 139, 142, 144, 145–147, 183

Rancière, Jacques 7, 17n16, 20, 41n3, 50, 183
rape 2–3, 11, 23, 25, 29, 32, 38, 40, 42n9, 45n46, 53–55, 59, 60, 62–63, 73n12, 74n24, 76n35, 96, 104, 120, 122, 124, 136, 139n9, 170, 172–173, 181
Ravelo Blancas, Patricia 3, 10, 16n8, 20, 29–30, 38, 42n18, 45n43, 47, 49, 51, 66, 80, 145, 177, 183
Rigola, Àlex 11, 13, 53, 55, 58, 60, 62–64, 68–71, 74n21, 74n23, 75n26, 75n28, 75n32, 77, 79–81, 182–183, 190
Rivera Garza, Cristina 13, 20, 45n47, 50, 149, 150, 152, 154, 171, 173–174, 176n35, 179, 183, 185–187
Rodríguez, Ileana 10, 18n32, 20, 35, 41, 50, 72n2, 140n16, 140n18, 147, 183

sacrifice 11, 29, 33, 53, 63, 66–68, 71–72, 76n38, 76n39, 77n45, 77, 80, 128, 182; sacrificial 11, 16n8, 20, 53–82; *sacrificio* 76n42, 76n44, 81; self- 127

Sandoval, Chela 72n6, 81, 121, 147, 183
Schlotterbeck, Marian E. 5, 21, 34, 86, 113, 181
Schmidt Camacho, Alicia 9, 17n25, 17n26, 20, 29, 32, 39, 44n30, 51, 61–64, 66, 72n1, 72n2, 81, 140, 183, 186–187
Segato, Rita Laura 30, 38–40, 46n49, 51, 76, 81, 183
Señorita Extraviada 7, 12, 17n18, 20, 76, 81, 90, 113–116, 120, 122–123, 125–126, 135–136, 139n4, 140n10, 144–147, 176, 183, 190
sexual violence 23, 62–63, 75n34, 176n31, 190
solidarity 7, 10–12, 20, 26, 42n17, 54, 61, 85, 98, 102–103, 126, 128, 131–134, 137–138, 142n26, 166–167, 183
Staudt, Kathleen 6, 20, 23–27, 29, 34–38, 42n18, 44n37, 45n41, 51, 90, 113, 140n18, 142n24, 147
structural violence 132
symbolic violence 54
systemic violence 4, 59, 76n36

Tabuenca Córdoba, María Socorro 16n7, 21, 30–31, 35–37, 44n39, 51, 138, 147, 183
Taylor, Diana 127–128, 142n33, 143n39, 147
testimony 15, 19, 28, 34, 36–37, 55, 60, 70–71, 76n40, 78–79, 89, 118, 120, 122, 124, 132, 136, 138, 142n24, 147, 149, 172, 176n34, 178, 187; *ecotestimonio* 34; *testimonio* 71, 77
trauma 10, 12, 17n17, 19, 94, 97–98, 103, 110, 112–113, 116–120, 124–125, 128, 132, 136–137, 146, 168, 176, 182, 184–185; traumatic 94, 117–118, 124–125, 176

Volk, Steven S. 5, 21, 34, 86, 113, 181

witness 12, 38, 55, 59, 71, 90, 99, 102, 120, 124, 128, 134, 142n24, 157, 177, 181, 184; witnessing 12, 21, 83, 91, 95, 97, 112–113, 180, 182–183
Wright, Melissa 17n24, 21, 26–27, 30–33, 36, 39, 51, 127, 141n20, 148, 176n24, 180

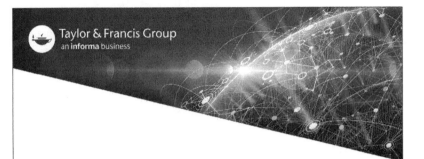